Leading Questions

Michigan Studies in International Political Economy

SERIES EDITORS: Edward Mansfield and Lisa Martin

Michael J. Gilligan
Empowering Exporters: Reciprocity, Delegation, and Collective Action in American Trade Policy

Barry Eichengreen and Jeffry Frieden, Editors
Forging an Integrated Europe

Thomas H. Oatley
Monetary Politics: Exchange Rate Cooperation in the European Union

Robert Pahre
Leading Questions: How Hegemony Affects the International Political Economy

Leading Questions

How Hegemony Affects
the International Political Economy

Robert Pahre

Ann Arbor

THE UNIVERSITY OF MICHIGAN PRESS

Copyright © by the University of Michigan 1999
All rights reserved
Published in the United States of America by
The University of Michigan Press
Manufactured in the United States of America
⊗ Printed on acid-free paper

2002   2001   2000   1999   4   3   2   1

A CIP catalog record for this book is available from the British Library.

Library of Congress Cataloging-in-Publication Data

Pahre, Robert.
    Leading questions : how hegemony affects the international
political economy / Robert Pahre.
        p.   cm. — (Michigan studies in international political
economy)
    Includes bibliographical references and index.
    ISBN 0-472-10970-7 (acid-free paper)
    1. Economic history 1990–   2. International economic relations.
I. Title.   II. Series.
HC59.15   .P33   1998
337—dc21   98-40162
                                                                    CIP

for Jennie

Contents

Figures

Tables

Preface

This book was shaped by three departments of political science—at the University of California at Los Angeles, the University of Rochester, and the University of Michigan. My first intellectual debts were incurred at UCLA, which I attended during a remarkable period in the department's history. As I arrived, the department hired a large cohort of young, intellectually vibrant assistant professors, many of whom were interested in political economy. Some were formal theorists, others were sympathetic to the approach, and a few were constructively critical. All shared an interest in history and a concern for applying political science to historical problems. Not only were they a great group under whom to study, but they also created a supportive community of graduate students who were critical through the genesis of this project.

Much of this book began as a dissertation under the supervision of David Lake. He has read the manuscript more often than anyone but me, and his comments and advice have been invaluable. Anyone familiar with his work will see his influence throughout this book.

There would be no formal theory in this book without Michael Wallerstein, who spent many hours one summer teaching me some of the tools of the trade. He also saved me from more than one slipshod result. Those that remain I thought up all by myself.

Jack Hirshleifer always managed to have my ideas five or ten years before me, and I benefited from his insights and from being able to build on his work. Richard Rosecrance, an open-minded skeptic of formal theory, always had the uncanny ability to drop damaging historical evidence in my lap. Arthur Stein was a shadow member of my dissertation committee whose theoretical playfulness inspired my development of variations on a single model. Jeffry Frieden put up with a year of the project in UCLA's workshop on international political economy and gave me devastating critiques of several early chapters. Cheryl

Schonhardt-Bailey, a fellow student at the time, also tore several chapters to shreds. All made this work much stronger.

The University of California's Institute for Global Conflict and Cooperation provided dissertation funding. The IGCC Fellows' Conference also forced me to think about how to make the project comprehensible—and perhaps even interesting—to historians, sociologists, and political scientists highly skeptical of positive theory, let alone rational-choice theory.

After UCLA, I landed at the University of Rochester, where I unwittingly began an immersion course in formal theory. I presented several chapters there and benefited from comments by David Austen-Smith, Jeff Banks, Bruce Bueno de Mesquita, Randall Calvert, John Mueller, William Riker, and Lawrence Rothenburg. I also inflicted my work on graduate students, especially Matthew Gabel, David Hayes, Fiona McGillivray, and Alistair Smith. I hope that their contributions to improving this manuscript show that they did not suffer in vain.

After a few years at Rochester, I moved on to the political science department at Michigan. In addition to providing a congenial place to get work done, that department's emphasis on empirical work has improved this book. The university's Rackham Graduate School financed invaluable research assistance from Jose-Raúl Perales Hernandez for chapter 8. I am also grateful for Jennifer Shulman's thorough research assistance in chapters 6 and 10. Gerald Schneider (of the University of Konstanz) and I jointly developed the research design behind the Trade Agreements Database described in appendix B.

Some of the ideas here were presented in the Junior Faculty Seminar at Michigan, where I benefited from comments by Chris Achen, Bear Braumoeller, Pradeep Chhibber, and Doug Dion. Several colleagues had the misfortune of running across me when I needed to thrash something out; though they may not remember the occasions, these conversations with Robert Axelrod, Pradeep Chhibber, John Huber, and Charles Myers were very helpful.

Parts of this book have also been presented at the University of California at San Diego, the University of Chicago, the University of Iowa, and various meetings of American Political Science Association and the International Studies Association. At the risk of leaving out people whose faces I did not recognize at the time, I would like to express thanks for comments from John Conybeare, Peter Cowhey, Gary Cox, James Fearon, Gary Jacobson, James Lindsay, Charles Lipson, and James Morrow. I would especially like to thank the intrepid souls who read the penultimate draft of this book in its entirety and gave thorough and insightful comments: Robert Axelrod, Svetla Dalbokova, Doug Dion, Don Herzog, Paul Huth, and two careful readers for the University of

Michigan Press. Charles Myers, editor at the University of Michigan Press, also provided many helpful suggestions throughout.

Finally, there are a lot of vagaries in the world of a graduate student and assistant professor. Jennie has not only borne these uncertainties but encouraged me throughout the writing of this book. It is for her.

Part I
Introduction

CHAPTER 1

Leadership and Hegemony

Journalists, historians, policymakers, political scientists, and other observers of international affairs use the term *international leadership* frequently and in many different contexts. Historians refer to British leadership in the days of empire, political scientists talk about John F. Kennedy's and George Bush's leadership of the international community, journalists and policymakers ask whether Germany and Japan are ready to take their position as global leaders or whether the United States is still willing and able to lead the international system.[1] A dominant nation's leadership of the international order may also be a recurrent feature of world politics (Carr 1939; Gilpin 1981; Keohane 1984; Modelski 1987; Organski 1968).

Moreover, leadership is apparently required to resolve many international problems. It long seemed that ending the wars of the Yugoslav succession, for instance, would require American leadership (if you were European) or European leadership (if you were American); either or both leaders would also require the assistance of Russian leadership (if you were Russian). The success of the World Trade Organization (WTO) or of international monetary coordination in the G-7 allegedly requires American leadership, perhaps with Japanese or European assistance. Further integration of the European Union is said to hinge on German leadership, on Franco-German leadership, or on an absence of German leadership—on just about anything except British leadership.

Political scientists often substitute the term *hegemony* for leadership.[2]

---

1. For introductions to these literatures, see Calleo 1987; Kennedy 1987: 438–535; Krauthammer 1992; Nau 1990; Romberg 1992; Rosecrance 1986; Rosecrance and Taw 1990; Scalera and Kahn 1976.

2. One might distinguish hegemony as a structural variable from leadership as a behavioral variable. This leads some theorists to ask how structural power is made manifest as leadership, through "force activation" (Keohane 1984). Such an approach risks tautology because we only know that force has been activated when we observe leadership behavior. I prefer to get the structural story right first. For this reason, I use the terms *hegemony* and *leadership* interchangeably.

Most define a hegemon as a state with predominant power in the international system, measured in terms of that state's share of world gross domestic product (GDP) or other material resources. Theorists use hegemony to explain developments in the international economy since World War II, arguing that American leadership of the Pax Americana resembles the Pax Britannica of the nineteenth century. According to the conventional wisdom, a hegemonic United States established the General Agreement on Tariffs and Trade (GATT, now WTO), the International Monetary Fund (IMF), the International Bank for Reconstruction and Development (IBRD, World Bank), the United Nations (UN), the Organization of Economic Cooperation and Development (OECD, née CEEC and then OEEC), and a host of other international regimes. These regimes in turn supported the system of freer trade enjoyed in the developed world since the late 1940s (see inter alia Keohane 1984; Krasner 1976; Ruggie 1983, 1992).

Reasonable as this argument sounds, the evidence for it is not strong. Several qualitative studies find evidence supporting the theory (e.g., Aggarwal 1985; Brawley 1993; Lake 1988), while others reach more ambiguous conclusions (Cowhey and Long 1983; Keohane 1980, 1984; Laitin 1982; Lawson 1983; Odell 1982). Quantitative tests also obtain ambiguous results if not outright falsifications of the theory (Conybeare 1983; Krasner 1977; Mansfield 1992, 1994; Martin 1992: 86–90; McKeown 1983, 1989, 1991). One major developer of the theory admits that the empirical evidence is "weak, and even its chief adherents have doubts about it" (Keohane 1984: 38).

Despite the scanty evidence, how hegemony matters remains a leading question in the field of international relations. The subject of hegemony is important across a wide range of theoretical perspectives, from Realism to Marxism (see Keohane 1984, 1986b; Organski 1968: 355–76; Sylvan 1981). Realists argue that a hegemon persuades other states to create an open international economy, even in a world of power-seeking states that find themselves in an anarchic international system (Gilpin 1981; Keohane 1984; Krasner 1976; Lake 1983, 1984, 1988; Rapkin and Avery 1982; Stein 1984). Marxists see hegemony as a recurring feature of the world-system by which the capitalist class in the core of the world economy exploits both its own workers and the peoples of other countries through its control of international finance, money, trade, and ideological production (Braudel 1979; Chase-Dunn 1981, 1982; Wallerstein 1974, 1979, 1989). Liberals see the hegemon as a guarantor of international cooperation and as a state that can help other states overcome problems of collective action (Keohane 1984; Kindleberger 1973, 1976, 1981).[3] Despite these differences, the central propositions across all perspectives are that hegemony leads to international order and that continued hegemony is sufficient for that order to continue.[4]

These perspectives differ on whether this hegemonic order is good or bad for the international community;[5] of course, some scholars admit shades of gray between the extremes of a purely malevolent or a purely benevolent leader. In hegemony as in kindergarten, goodness and badness are defined in terms of the leader's effects on others. A benevolent hegemon does things that are good for the rest of the world, while a malevolent hegemon hurts everyone else.[6] In other words, what matters is the counterfactual question: would everyone be better or worse off if the leader were just like the nonleaders in the system?

This is the central question of this book. The short answer is that leaders are both malevolent and benevolent but at different times and under different conditions.[7] Leadership has been benevolent in some periods (1815–54) and malevolent in others (1919–33, 1944–46). In other cases, such as 1870–1914 and 1946–67, I must move beyond the simple distinction between malevolence and benevolence to understand leadership.

Answering this leading question presents many problems. It is difficult to imagine a persuasive empirical demonstration that a leader's actions were good (or bad) for others because the appropriate baseline for comparison is not clear. Either claim rests on a historical counterfactual, raising problems of its own (James Fearon 1992). While I will often make counterfactual arguments in this book, I use other indirect tests of malevolence as well. For example, this question of malevolence or benevolence leads me to examine how states react

---

3. For definitions of these three theoretical perspectives and an overview of their strengths and weaknesses, the locus classicus is Gilpin 1975. Citing Keohane's work as both Realist and Liberal was not accidental; see Keohane 1986b.

4. There is also a consensus among non-Marxists that hegemony is not necessary to maintain an international order if a small group of large states cooperates (Keohane 1984; Snidal 1985b).

5. Snidal (1985b) argued forcefully that this is the central division in the literature. He called bad leaders "coercive," but I prefer the verbal parallelism of "malevolent."

6. One might also ask whether leadership is good for the leader, though almost everyone assumes that it is. For example, the literature on dominant nations and challengers (i.e., Organski 1968: chap. 14; Gilpin 1981; Brawley 1993) assumes that leadership of an international order is a prize worth winning. Still, a leader might have an interest in not leading, perhaps due to "relative gains" (Stein 1984) or particular features of the monetary system (see Eichengreen 1985, 1987).

7. This study is limited to the period from 1815 to 1967. For some different approaches to hegemonic theory that include earlier periods, see Brawley 1993; Gilpin 1981; Wallerstein 1974, 1979.

to each other's decisions. If states react in kind, returning trade concession for trade concession, leadership is probably good. Each makes some concessions and obtains some concessions in return. As a result, a leader can move toward openness, expecting others to follow suit. However, one state might also react to another by doing the opposite. For example, a state might contribute less to international cooperation because it knows that others will contribute more, picking up the slack. In such cases, a leader may act malevolently, doing less for the international political economy because it knows that others will respond by doing more. By using a strong theory that relates these patterns to system-level outcomes, these reactions are useful indicators of whether hegemony is benevolent or malevolent.

By emphasizing the interdependence of states' choices, this book downplays differences between states. One implication of this system-level focus is that I will not analyze the possibility that a hegemon's preferences determine whether it acts malevolently or benevolently. In contrast, some scholars have argued that certain types of states (capitalist liberal democracies) act benevolently, while others (communists, fascists, and traditional monarchies) act malevolently (see esp. Brawley 1993; Modelski 1987). Whatever the merits of such claims, the reaction of one state to another will still affect system-level outcomes. For this reason, I focus on how states' choices affect one another, holding preferences constant, to find out whether a leader is acting malevolently. Where different preferences may affect this analysis, as they do in chapter 3, I will discuss the implications even though I leave the origin of these preferences outside the theory.

By studying benevolence and malevolence, I look indirectly at the health of the international political economy. Setting other variables aside, the international economy will be healthier when a hegemon is doing things that improve global welfare than when the hegemon is malevolent. For example, the malevolent hegemony of the 1920s ended in the Great Depression though other factors also contributed to the crisis.

Both leadership and its effects on global welfare lead naturally to the policy question of how we might make bad leaders nicer. I will not say a lot on this subject because most causes of malevolence are beyond the control of most policymakers. However, international cooperation is more important during periods of malevolent hegemony. Existing theories already address some of the conditions that make cooperation more likely (Axelrod 1984; Keohane 1984; Oye 1986a), so the theory here does point out when we should be especially worried about influencing these conditions.

The Limits of Hegemony Theory

Hegemony theory began by observing a correlation: periods characterized by high levels of international trade seemed to be associated with the existence of a single dominant state, or hegemon. This hegemon provided many services for the international economy, such as guaranteeing freedom of the seas, encouraging trade, and managing the world's money.

After this theory gained wide acceptance in the 1970s, problems with it became increasingly clear. First, high trade levels continued even after the hegemon's dominance had declined. According to many measures, both the United States and Germany were more powerful than Great Britain in the decades leading up to World War I. Similarly, it appeared that West Germany and Japan, if not the Soviet Union, would surpass the United States along some dimensions in the 1980s. However, both the pre–1914 period and the 1980s saw continued openness despite the decline of the hegemon's power.

One reason for the persistent openness seemed to be that the international regimes created during hegemonic dominance could persist with the support of nonhegemonic states. As a result, the mainstream literature began to look more closely at international cooperation in general and at international economic regimes in particular (e.g., Krasner 1983).[8] Indeed, Keohane (1984: 15) argues that hegemony and regimes may substitute for each other since "both serve to make agreements possible and to facilitate compliance with rules."

Second, research revealed that the correlation between hegemony and international openness was imperfect at best (see Krasner 1976). American relative power was as great in the 1920s as in the 1950s, but the United States did not encourage international openness in the former period. One possible explanation was that the hegemon sometimes acted malevolently, a line of research developed most fully by Marxists (e.g., Wallerstein 1974, 1979, 1989). A second possibility was that some domestic political coalitions might retard the "right" hegemonic policies, as seemed to be the case for isolationists in the interwar United States. This pointed researchers toward greater attention to domestic politics (Brawley 1993; James and Lake 1989) or to other processes of force activation by which the latent power of a hegemon could become manifest (Keohane 1984; Modelski 1987).

Third, and related to both of these points, mainstream theory had left out

---

8. The standard definition of cooperation is "active attempts to adjust policies to meet the demands of others" (Keohane 1984: 12; cf. Stein 1983).

the role of nonhegemonic states in the international system. A hegemon could not "cooperate" if no one else was willing to cooperate with it (Stein 1984). By the same token, a small group of large countries might cooperate even without a hegemon's help (Snidal 1985b; Keohane 1984). Lake's (1988) theory of the "international economic structure" represents the fullest statement of this approach, examining the interaction of six different kinds of states.

Finally, a newer line of research argues that alliances make it more likely that a hegemon will act benevolently (Gowa 1989a, 1989b; see also Gowa and Mansfield 1994; Gowa 1994). The NATO alliance, and the Cold War more generally, certainly gave economic cooperation an important stimulus in the postwar period. Security concerns also helped reduce the domestic opposition to internationalism.

In sum, mainstream hegemony literature has increasingly looked at the role of nonhegemonic states, international cooperation and regimes, and the effects of alliances. Once I develop a basic theory of leadership, these concerns provide the motive for several variants of the theory. Building on the same basic idea helps bring together several strands of mainstream theory, though not in the way that previous theory would expect.

In contrast, domestic politics will remain largely outside the main model. Capturing domestic political processes requires a different kind of approach, one not easily synthesized with system-level concerns such as nonhegemonic states, international cooperation, regimes, and alliances. In addition, there is value in pushing system-level theory to its limits before asking how domestic-level variables influence state behavior (see Waltz 1979). Instead, appendix A sketches out a way to develop a model of domestic politics that is consistent in many ways with the systemic theory in the main text.

Conflict, Cooperation, and Collective Action

Recasting hegemony theory in light of these concerns forces me to ask several fundamental questions. The first of these is obvious: what does a leader do when it leads?

To answer this question, one must consider the nature of international relations. Oversimplifying enormously, there are two central questions in international relations: the problem of conflict and the possibility of cooperation (Keohane 1984: 5–10). The intertwined nature of these problems is evident in the continued existence of competing research programs interested in only half of the problem. Realism, which studies conflict, finds it difficult to explain cooperation;[9] Idealism and Liberalism are predicated on common interests of the sort found in cooperation and find it difficult to explain conflict (Stein 1990: chap. 1).

Cooperation and conflict become more interesting when we see how they interact. Cooperation normally entails quite a bit of conflict. The members of the EU haggle over common policies and budgets, though the EU is probably the most remarkable example of cooperation among sovereign nations in world history. Such conflicts do not negate the cooperation—in fact, the conflict is a necessary by-product of the increased cooperation. The same is true of Japanese-American trade conflicts, which reflect the deep postwar cooperation between these nations (Campbell 1993). Trade, investment, and other economic cooperation between these two countries are so important that they can disagree about many details.

Perhaps more intriguingly, cooperation is possible in an essentially conflictual relationship. Examples from the security realm include the Nazi-Soviet Pact of 1939, Soviet-American cooperation against Hitler, Israeli support for Jordan against Syria and the PLO in 1970, and the tacit alliance between Israel and Saudi Arabia against Saddam Hussein's Iraq. In economics, competitors may agree to divide a market, as does the OPEC cartel. States that believe exchange-rate policy is highly conflictual may nevertheless cooperate to maintain the status quo through a fixed exchange-rate system.

If both conflict and cooperation are ubiquitous, then a study of international leadership should address both. Theories of collective action (Margolis 1955; Olson 1965/1971; Samuelson 1954, 1955, 1958; Sandler 1992; Stigler 1974) provide a good way to study this interweaving of conflict and cooperation. Collective action may occur when people wish to provide some public good—that is, a good from which everyone benefits whether they pay for it or not.[10]

Collective-goods provision illustrates cooperation and conflict well because everyone likes to achieve group goals without having to pay for them: who would not want to have the neighbors pay for sewer lines, telephone poles, street lighting, snow plowing, and other services used in common? Nations, too, would like to enjoy credible collective security without providing the armed forces with which to defend others. Nations would also like to benefit

---

9. The exception to this proves the rule: Realists have studied alliances, a form of cooperation typically oriented toward military conflict.

10. Throughout this book, I will use the terms *public good* and *collective good* interchangeably.

from a system of trading rules, such as the GATT or WTO, that they alone are free to disobey.

These problems of collective action are at the core of much political behavior. At the international level of analysis, we see collective action in theories of international regimes (Ruggie 1972). Collective goods are also an important form of market failure, and these failures are an important reason for many regimes (see Keohane 1984: chap. 5).

Leadership affects whether and how people provide public goods. Kindleberger's (1973, 1981) leading study examined how the United States and United Kingdom failed to provide international collective goods such as free trade and monetary stability in the 1920s and 1930s. Mainstream theory argues that a hegemon will have an incentive to provide collective goods unilaterally if it is sufficiently large; a hegemon might also lead a small group of other large states in jointly providing such goods. As a result, an international system with hegemonic leadership will more easily provide international public goods than a system without one (Conybeare 1984, 1987; Keohane 1984; Ruggie 1972; Snidal 1979, 1985a, 1985b).

Charles Kindleberger (1981: 247; see also 1973, 1976) argues that the most important such good is the "maintenance of the world economy." To do this, a leader can provide a market for distress goods during recessions or depressions, can supply countercyclical flows of capital that minimize fluctuations in the business cycle, can manage international liquidity provision through its rediscount mechanisms, can stabilize foreign-exchange rates, and can encourage states to coordinate their monetary policies. Others analyze international public goods such as a stable exchange-rate system, the enforcement of trade agreements, the freedom of transit for trade, an international financial regime capable of facilitating capital flows across countries, global recognition of individual property rights, or the aggregate stimulus of the global economy (Gilpin 1972, 1975, 1981; Keohane 1979, 1980, 1982b, 1984; Kindleberger 1973, 1976, 1981; Krasner 1976, 1979b, 1982; Lake 1984, 1988: 34–35; Stein 1984; Yarbrough and Yarbrough 1985, 1987).[11]

At the same time, there are many forceful objections to the assumption

---

11. However, some theories of hegemony make no mention of collective goods (e.g., Krasner 1976), while others relegate them to a secondary role (e.g., Gilpin 1981). The collective-goods approach also excludes pure coordination games where countries share a common interest. A good example is the World Maritime Organization's rules on right-of-way on the high seas: nations and their merchant marines do not care whether ships yield to their right or left but may still need a regime to determine such rules (Stein 1983; see also Keohane 1984; Martin 1993; Stein 1990).

that collective goods are important in the international system. For example, free trade is not a public good, though some early theorists asserted that it was. Other alleged collective goods, such as "international infrastructure" (Lake 1988) or the enforcement of international agreements (Axelrod and Keohane 1985: 234–38), may not really be public (see Conybeare 1984, 1987; Gowa 1989b, 1994: 21–22; Snidal 1979, 1985a, 1985b: 581–82, 590–92; Pahre 1994: appendix). Some of the defining characteristics of a public good are lacking for many issues in international political economy (see chap. 2). For example, discriminatory economic policies can often keep other countries from enjoying a would-be public good such as free trade.

While very few of these are pure public goods, assuming publicness is, like any assumption, a simplification. It brings some parts of reality into sharper focus while pushing other aspects of the world out of the picture's frame. The real question is whether this assumption illuminates some interesting and important parts of international relations.

In this light, assuming publicness is a decent approximation for the problem of externalities. Trading, stabilizing currencies, contributing to international organizations, and giving foreign aid affect others—that is, they have positive or negative externalities. Trade agreements between two countries affect not only the participants but typically have trade-diversion effects on third parties, creating a collective-action problem (Aggarwal 1985). Even agreements that apparently concern private goods have externalities and some public characteristics. For example, a trade agreement between the United States and the European Union reducing agricultural export subsidies provides essentially public benefits to the world in the form of a less distorted market for agricultural products.[12] The presumed income gains for both the United States and EU also have public effects in that the increased demand for all goods would benefit producers in general. Such externalities are ubiquitous in much of what a nation does.

Critics who object to the publicness assumption are making the best the enemy of the good. The appropriate question is whether the collective-goods assumption is better or worse than some other assumption for some particular problem. The reigning alternative to a public-goods assumption is the Prisoners' Dilemma, or occasionally a more sophisticated menu of two-by-two games (e.g., Conybeare 1987; Gowa 1994; Keohane 1984; Lake 1988). Two-by-two

---

12. Countries would enjoy this "public good" differentially, since it would benefit high-income agricultural exporters such as Canada and Australia as well as Third World agricultural exporters.

games assume that states interact only in pairs and that they face dichotomous choices (cooperate or defect) with only four possible outcomes. These assumptions yield less robust results than does the publicness assumption because the ability to choose from a continuous degree of cooperation makes a big difference (see chaps. 3 and 7). In contrast, the public-goods model yields many results that are unchanged even by drastic changes in the assumptions, as I show in appendix A.

Assuming collective goods gives me a theory that captures this interplay between conflict and cooperation. The actors share an interest in cooperation because everyone wants at least some of the collective good to be provided. At the same time, the players are in conflict because each wants everyone else to foot the bill for the collective good. Left to themselves, the actors in a collective-goods model produce a suboptimal level of the good, so they must cooperate to improve their welfare. Yet there is conflict over how to share the costs of cooperation, and the countries might not cooperate at all. For this reason, such problems of collaboration when states share both common and divergent interests are central to many studies of international politics (e.g., Axelrod 1984; Keohane 1984; Oye 1986a; Stein 1983).

Of course, not all of international politics makes sense in terms of collective goods. International rivalries, territorial conflicts, and war itself are hardly collective goods. Without seeking a theory of war in this book, I will also analyze how conflict over security issues affects collective-goods provision and international cooperation.[13] Military spending is important in two respects. First, it takes resources away from economic cooperation. Second, each state's military spending affects the choices of other states. While states welcome the military spending of their friends and allies, the guns of rivals and enemies have important negative externalities (to say the least). Military rivalries may inhibit collective-goods provision.

In short, then, I will use a theory of collective-goods provision to study hegemonic leadership. My primary focus will be whether hegemony is benevolent or malevolent, which means in this context whether a hegemon makes welfare-improving collective-goods provision more or less likely. Because international cooperation furnishes nations with a way to achieve greater public-goods provision, I also look in detail at how leadership affects cooperation. I will flesh out the collective-goods theory by incorporating the externalities of security relationships.

---

13. For hegemonic theories of war, see Gilpin 1981; Modelski 1978, 1982, 1987; Organski 1968: chap. 14; Rasler and Thompson 1989.

Formalizing Hegemony

Collective-goods theories of hegemony are hardly new. Indeed, they date at least to Ruggie's (1972) article on public goods and Kindleberger's (1973) book on the Great Depression. The effect of security relations on economic cooperation has also received significant attention in the more recent literature on relative gains (Gowa 1994; Gowa and Mansfield 1993; Grieco 1988, 1990; Powell 1991, 1993; Snidal 1991a, 1991b; Stein 1984; Waltz 1979).

Surprisingly, it is possible to push this extensive literature further with the addition of one tool, formal theory. A formal model simply converts the core of a verbal argument into mathematical terms and then uses mathematics instead of verbal reasoning to derive additional propositions. It may seem unlikely at first that a formal model can yield much additional insight, since the nonformal literature has long been built on Mancur Olson's (1965/1971) formal model of collective-goods provision. Given this fact, it is particularly surprising that the first result from the model in chapter 2 directly contradicts Olson's most influential claim in political economy—the proposition that a concentrated, or privileged, group will more easily provide collective goods. In this, chapters 2 and 3 follow several more recent models of public goods (Bergstrom, Blume, and Varian 1986; Cornes and Sandler 1986: 84–87; Warr 1983) that flatly contradict Olson. Additional chapters build on this well-established core to model the security considerations and repeated-play concerns that are central to world politics.

The counter-Olsonian result stems from several assumptions that seem reasonable in the context of international politics. First, I assume that states act in an environment characterized by strategic behavior. States anticipate the reactions of other states when they make their own choices, so they face game-theoretic problems rather than decision-theoretic ones. Olson, whose model of collective action is decision theoretic, is therefore a poor guide for applications in international relations (cf. Snidal 1985b: 600). Olson's model also assumes single play, but analysis of a repeated-play game in part 3 yields further insights.

Second, actors do not merely face the question of whether to contribute to a collective good but also encounter the more important question of how much to contribute. In other words, contribution is a continuous variable and not a dichotomous one. The outcome is also continuous and not dichotomous—we should ask not whether the collective good is supplied but instead how much of the good is supplied. This too differs from Olson and much of the nonformal literature following him in which the language of dichotomization is commonplace. It is a particularly stark departure from the widespread use of the Prisoners' Dilemma, where states face a dichotomous choice between cooperation and defection.[14]

Third, formalization of existing collective-action arguments forces me to distinguish two kinds of privileged groups—those with a small number of actors and those with many actors in which resources are nonetheless concentrated in a few hands. Once I make this distinction, it follows that small groups may or may not make the provision of collective goods easier (see chaps. 2 and 5). The concentration of resources is irrelevant to the problem in single play but plays a more subtle role in repeated play.

Fourth, formalization lets me capture the problem of international cooperation and the role of leadership in making cooperation more or less likely. Again, I will assume that states cooperate to provide increased levels of public goods, though the publicness assumption is more easily relaxed in the cooperation model. While the model builds on a sizable literature using the Prisoners' Dilemma to theorize about international cooperation (e.g., Axelrod 1984; Gowa 1989a, 1994; Gowa and Mansfield 1993; Keohane 1984; Oye 1984; Stein 1983, 1990), it is possible to go further by relaxing some of the assumptions of the standard game. For instance, looking at degrees of more or less cooperation yields hypotheses about which kinds of states favor deep or shallow cooperation. Continuous strategies also affect the outcome of mutual defection, which affects in turn how the cooperation game is played.

Formalization also requires an explicit definition of hegemony. The non-Marxist literature makes two different assumptions about what makes a hegemon a hegemon.[15] One possible assumption is that hegemony is a dichotomous variable: a state is either a hegemon or not, and an international system either has a hegemon or not. The second group assumes that hegemony is a continuous variable: the bigger the state, the more powerful and therefore the more hegemonic it is. This assumption admits of multiple leadership, weak leadership, and other complexities that seem reasonable enough ways to think

14. The metastrategies underlying cooperation need not be dichotomous (see Axelrod 1984; Hirshleifer and Martinez Coll 1988). Indeed, by the Folk Theorem, there are an infinite number of such metastrategies, which may be indefinitely complex.

15. A third group, relying on Gramsci and other Marxists, defines hegemony as a set of relationships grounded in a capitalist mode of production (Cox 1977, 1986; Gill 1986; see Keohane 1984: 41–46 for review). For example, Robert Cox (1981: 153n) defines hegemony as a unity of structure (material forces) and superstructure (political ideas) in which ideology helps legitimize domination. The kind of leadership on which I focus is purely structural, but this does not preclude adding a superstructural analysis in future research. The superstructural question of whether states view hegemonic domination as legitimate may also be found in some non-Marxist theory (e.g., Keohane 1984; Maier 1977; Ruggie 1982).

about the world. By focusing on power, this approach also points attention towards the measurement of those material resources that give a state power (see Conybeare 1984; Keohane 1977, 1984; Krasner 1976; Lake 1983, 1984, 1988; Mansfield 1992, 1994; McKeown 1983; Nau 1990).

It turns out that I must assume that hegemony is a dichotomous variable to develop a theory in which hegemony plays a meaningful role in single play. This is because global public-goods provision depends on global resources rather than on the distribution of those resources among the various states in the system. Then, when I model hegemony as dichotomous, as something qualitatively different from nonhegemony, I find that it is bad for others.

Assuming hegemony is a dichotomous variable raises empirical difficulties. These problems stem not from any inadequacy of the theory but from an inadequacy of historical events. Because I argue that there has always been a hegemon during the modern period (1815 to the present), there is no variation in the independent variable for the key hypotheses of the theory.

Even if history were more generous in providing variation in the independent variable, there are problems of operationalization that make any theory's definition look tautological. For instance, a few authors (e.g., Lake 1988) argue that some periods lacked a hegemon, but any such statement must necessarily appear to be ad hoc, designed to bring theory and evidence closer together than they otherwise would be.[16] Various periods between 1494 and 1763 have been claimed for Portuguese, Spanish, Dutch, and English hegemony, with France a regular challenger to all. No matter which operationalization I might choose, the choices will appear to be ad hoc.

I am left, then, with a theory that explores the effects of hegemony in a period in which a hegemon always exists. A formal theory lets me do so by constructing a model that encompasses both observed and unobserved outcomes. Of course, I can test the theory only against observed outcomes that may not exhibit all the variation I desire. Even so, if the second-order predictions from the model are not falsified, then I infer that the observable parts of the model are not false. Since the observables are logically linked to the unobservables within the structure of the model, I may safely infer that untestable predictions of the model are also not false (see Lakatos 1970 for the epistemology behind this approach).

Furthermore, observables play an important role in formal theory because of the method's internal logic. If a number of empirically supported results fol-

---

16. Lake's definition of hegemony is not ad hoc, but it necessarily appears to be ad hoc since other scholars can argue that he chose one measure of power over some other measure to get the results he wanted.

low from a given set of assumptions, even if these results are obvious, then nonobvious results deduced from the same set of assumptions are much more plausible. This is useful whenever a particular result is difficult to test (perhaps it relies on variables that are difficult to operationalize) or impossible to test (because it makes predictions about things that have not happened). It may also make us more tolerant of statistical tests that yield rightly signed estimates of variables that fail to cross some threshold of statistical significance, since the hypothesis being tested is logically linked to other hypotheses that have stronger statistical evidence behind them. In this way, the logical rigor of a formal theory can subtly change how we approach empirical research.

Crescendoing Complexity

In addition to analytical clarity, formal theory helps me handle theories with a lot of "moving parts." Many theorists of international relations try to build sophisticated and nuanced theories that can capture the intricacies of a complex world. Alas, it is hard to do this well. First, a complex theory may be internally inconsistent in nonobvious ways. Second, a theorist may put the parts of a complex theory together in several different ways, changing the results. A book such as Kenneth Waltz's *Theory of International Politics* (1979) can engender two decades of scholarly debate not only about whether it is correct but about what the text actually means.

Formal theory avoids this kind of complexity by simplifying the world. Critics argue, not surprisingly, that it simplifies too much, leaving out much that matters. The right way to address this criticism, it seems to me, is not to turn our backs on the logic of formal theory but to make any theory gradually more complicated. For this reason, I have built this book around a series of increasingly complex, interconnected models. By starting simply, I make the assumptions explicit and the core logic of the model more accessible. Then, by making the model in each chapter more complicated, I better capture different parts of a complex world.[17]

Each theoretical chapter is then paired with an empirical chapter covering some period from 1815 to 1967. This period spans much of British hegemony—there is disagreement in the literature over when this hegemony began—through American leadership in the interwar and postwar periods. I end in 1967 because the theory does not address the internal developments of existing regimes, all of which are in place by 1967. These internal developments

---

17. For a related argument, in which formal theory provides a "rigorous flexibility" that lets us develop conjectures across entirely different models, see Pahre and Papayoanou 1997.

dominate change in the international political economy in the 1970s and 1980s and dominate the existing literature on hegemony (for some leading studies, see Aggarwal 1985; Keohane 1980, 1984; Odell 1982).

The empirical chapter in each pair provides a test to see whether the theory warrants being made more complex. The strength of the chapter's model and its success against these tests naturally vary. By pairing each theoretical chapter with an empirical chapter, the model is compartmentalized, allowing future research to build on some chapters but not others.

Part 2 begins this dialogue between theory and history with a theory of public-goods provision. Chapter 2 presents a simple model of collective goods and then considers two different conceptualizations of hegemony within it. The model shows that if I use a quantitative (or continuous) definition of hegemony, then hegemony has no effect on aggregate collective-goods provision. Chapter 3 uses a different, dichotomous definition of hegemony to study collective-goods provision. It shows, in contrast to chapter 2, that hegemony is unambiguously malevolent. Chapter 4 applies this latter version of the model to the 1920s, showing how American leadership was bad for the international political economy.

With this basic model in hand, chapter 5 introduces security affairs to the model. While the literature divides over whether hegemony is malevolent or benevolent, this chapter develops the more reasonable argument that hegemony is benevolent under certain well-defined conditions and malevolent at other times. Surprisingly, hegemons lacking allies are benevolent, while those with many allies are malevolent. Chapter 6 tests these propositions against the first half of British hegemony, from 1815 to 1854. This provides variation in the independent variable because Britain had many allies between 1815 and 1821 but almost no allies from 1821 until the Crimean War.

Part 2 considers only a single-play equilibrium, so there is no cooperation in the models of chapters 2, 3, and 5. By assuming repeated play, part 3 explicitly considers the problem of international cooperation. Formalization helps me distinguish between what happens when nations cooperate and what happens when they do not, a distinction not found in the existing literature. Because cooperation may occur whether the single-play equilibrium is malevolent or benevolent, it is important not to conflate cooperation with benevolence. These distinctions are not only analytically useful but substantively important because the outcome without cooperation affects whether states are likely to cooperate.

The first half of chapter 7 drops the security variables of chapter 5 and returns to the simpler framework of chapter 2 to develop a model of cooperation and hegemony. This model shows that a hegemon is less likely to cooperate than are other states. However, a malevolent hegemon induces cooperation among followers, who seek to reduce its ill effects. A benevolent leader creates a smaller incentive for others to cooperate. The second half of the chapter introduces security affairs to the repeated-play model. This leads to some surprises, such as a nonrelationship between alliances and the likelihood of cooperation.

Chapter 8 tests these results against the nineteenth century, providing an opportunity to synthesize some of the theoretical results from chapters 5 and 7 and to test them against an entire century. Later in the 1800s, malevolent hegemony caused other countries to create a beneficial network of international cooperation. By keeping cooperation distinct from hegemonic benevolence (or malevolence) in this way, I can consider more logical possibilities than the conventional assumption that cooperation is benevolent.

Chapter 9 turns to the problem of multilateral regimes, which have been a major focus of the existing hegemonic literature (e.g., Keohane 1984; Krasner 1983; Ruggie 1993). Hegemons, and in particular malevolent hegemons, are more likely to favor multilateral cooperation than are other states. Regional cooperation by follower states may also induce more multilateralism.

Chapter 10 provides an account of American leadership between 1944 and 1967, drawing on the findings from all the theoretical chapters but giving particular attention to chapter 9's model of multilateral cooperation. American malevolence, the rewards of cooperation among allies, and regional cooperation in Europe all help lead to greater multilateralism in both trade and monetary affairs. I give the Marshall Plan particular attention because George Marshall made multilateralism a precondition for the European Recovery Program.

The empirical analyses rest on several different kinds of evidence. Where data are available and relevant to the hypotheses at hand, I can use quantitative tests. These tests provide a useful contrast to most quantitative work, which disconfirms previous theories of hegemonic leadership (see esp. Krasner 1976; Mansfield 1992, 1994; Martin 1992: 86–90; McKeown 1983, 1989, 1991; see also Cowhey and Long 1983; Laitin 1982; Lawson 1983). My empirical claims for the theory depend on tight links to an internally coherent formal theory. Existing quantitative studies have done their best to test the hegemonic theories available to them, but I wish to get the theory right, not to save a faulty theory through a different statistical test or data set. To keep the logical links between theory and test tight, I avoid using statistical methods that impose assumptions on the hypotheses not found in the formal model. Instead, as I will discuss in part 2, I try to derive hypotheses in a functional form that is less subject to statistical problems in the data.

Sometimes the theory tells us that the world is indeterminate, so that a wide range of outcomes in the dependent variable are consistent with the theory. Trying to fit a line that predicts a single outcome is clearly the wrong test for such a model, and I will often rely on qualitative evidence to evaluate the theory. This is especially true for my analysis of American postwar leadership, which grapples with significant indeterminacy. These case studies also help trace the causal processes that the model captures. These processes are important for counterfactual claims about what the world would be like without the leader.

Finally, the empirical chapters help me evaluate the plausibility of a model's assumptions. This does not mean the assumptions must be "true"—in an indefinitely complex world, no assumption, concept, hypothesis, theory, or description can be "true."[18] However, these assumptions, concepts, and hypotheses must be useful approximations to reality.

By proceeding in this manner, each variation on the central model helps explain one or more historical periods. The empirical exercise is useful not only as theory testing but also as a way to develop novel interpretations of familiar periods. Moreover, each substantive chapter provides empirical support for an added layer of complexity before moving to the next.

Summary

To understand the role of international leadership in the interlocking problems of international cooperation and conflict, this book uses a theory of international collective action. By formalizing the argument, I develop a deductive theory that makes possible both surprising and intuitive results that I test against the historical record both quantitatively and qualitatively. This process is useful for hegemonic theory, since existing tests suffer from the fact that they test vague or unclear theories or that they must misspecify the theory to generate hypotheses about variables for which data are available (Lake 1993). By presenting both theory and tests together, in a structure of "crescendoing complexity," this book seeks to avoid these problems.

The main lesson of the book is that leadership is typically bad for the international political economy. However, there are several exceptions to this gen-

---

18. Besides, by Gödel's Theorem, any formal theory must be either incomplete or internally inconsistent.

eral rule. A leader with more rivals than friends will be benevolent. This directly contradicts the conventional wisdom, which expects a leader with many friends to be malevolent.

Second, a benevolent hegemon is less likely to cooperate with others. This means that benevolent hegemony is usually tacit, lacking much international cooperation. While such cases are anomalous for mainstream theory, this pattern characterizes British leadership between 1821 and 1854.

One interesting twist in the theory is that followers are more likely to cooperate whenever the hegemon acts malevolently. Chapter 8 shows that this pattern best describes British leadership in the second half of the nineteenth century. In this period, the followers' cooperation was the dominant characteristic of the international political economy. However, a hegemon may also act malevolently without it leading to significant international cooperation, as did the United States in the interwar period.

Though addressing a similar set of concerns, these findings represent a significant departure from existing theories of hegemony. The theory proposes relationships among hegemony, malevolence, and cooperation that contradict existing theory and yet have substantial support in the historical record.

Part 2
Hegemony and Collective Goods

CHAPTER 2

A Collective-Goods Model of International Interdependence

Scholars have used the theory of collective action to study international politics and hegemony for more than twenty-five years, at least since John Ruggie's classic article "Collective Goods and Future International Collaboration" (1972). Following Olson (1965/1971), previous theories have proposed that collective goods will be supplied at higher levels if a group is "privileged"—that is, if it is small in size, with one large member or a few large members who make disproportionally large contributions to the supply of the good. This hypothesis is the foundation of hegemonic-stability theory, which maintains that an open international economy is more easily created if there exists a single dominant state willing and able to support it.

This chapter will show that this central hypothesis does not follow from a reasonable model of public goods. This negative result sets the stage for developing variations on this basic model in subsequent chapters. The basic model in this chapter also generates some hypotheses that remain important across the models in later chapters.

This model differs from others, such as Mancur Olson's, in that I assume that the actors' choices are interdependent.[1] In the formulation here, i's choice will be critically affected by his evaluation of j's choices, just as each j's choice will be affected by her expectations concerning i and all other j. Olson, in contrast, assumes that choices are independent.

The difference between these assumptions is clear in the example of supplying the collective good of public television in response to pledge appeals.

---

1. Though it is not often noticed, Olson (1965/1971: 29n) admits that he "assumes independent behavior, and thus neglects the strategic interaction or bargaining that is possible in small groups."

Olson's assumption captures the reasonable supposition that no viewer considers the response of her neighbors to whatever her contributions may be. In contrast, a large corporation such as Mobil is likely to consider how Exxon will respond to its support for public television, and vice versa, so their choices are interdependent.

Both kinds of decision making clearly occur. In the study of international relations, however, the assumption of interdependent choice is more appropriate for most problems, since states clearly expend much effort anticipating one another's actions. Formalizing the public-goods problem is a good way to examine these incentives.

Public Goods and the International Political Economy

Though the public-goods model in this chapter provides a logical critique of existing hegemonic theory, mere criticism does not provide a theory of leadership. Using the public-goods assumption is problematic if public and quasi-public goods do not play an important role in the international political economy. For this reason, this section furnishes an overview of international public goods and goods with important externalities.

Unlike private goods, a public good can be consumed by people other than the purchaser. When the government purchases national defense, for example, everyone in the country consumes this good whether or not they pay taxes. In the international political economy, according to Charles Kindleberger (1981: 247; see also Kindleberger 1973), public goods include "maintenance of the world economy," which entails the provision of markets for distress goods, countercyclical flows of capital, rediscount mechanisms for liquidity provision, managing foreign-exchange rates, and helping to coordinate monetary policies. Others have added international public goods such as a stable exchange-rate system, the enforcement of trade agreements, or aggregate stimulus of the global economy via its sheer size (e.g., Gilpin 1972, 1975, 1981; Kindleberger 1973, 1976, 1981; Krasner 1976, 1979b, 1982; Keohane 1979, 1980, 1982b, 1984; Lake 1984, 1988; Stein 1984; Yarbrough and Yarbrough 1985, 1987). Using a different terminology, George Modelski (1987) makes similar claims: global leaders perform certain functions in the international system, including what he calls "macrodecision" and "implementation."

One good example of a near-public good is international exchange-rate stability. Providing this good requires that a country forgo national policy autonomy, which governments value, to achieve international stability. In addition, monetary adjustment under a stable exchange-rate regime is politically costly if achieved through deflation. Alternatively, a country might adjust by devaluing its currency or imposing tariffs (see Simmons 1994). These actions impose many adjustment costs onto other states by reducing their exports. Exchange-rate stability is public because third parties can benefit by conducting trade in stabilized currencies. For example, Cuba can sell sugar to Iraq in exchange for stable dollars even if both countries are subject to U.S. boycotts.

Externalities are closely related to public goods. If I plant a flower garden along a sidewalk in front of my house, this is a private good to me, though passers-by may also enjoy the flowers. Their enjoyment of my garden is an externality and may be thought of as a public good. In such a way, it is common for analytical purposes to decompose a private good with externalities into two jointly produced goods, one private and the other public (for a textbook treatment, see Cornes and Sandler 1986).

Some good international examples are fiscal and macroeconomic policies, both of which have important externalities for others. Governments may coordinate their macroeconomic policies to better supply the externalities that each enjoy from the economic expansion of the others. For instance, the locomotive theory of fiscal policy coordination holds that a large economy's fiscal stimulus might serve as the engine for global economic recovery (see Putnam and Bayne 1987 for political discussion; Oudiz and Sachs 1984 for theoretical and empirical welfare analysis).

A similar logic underlay many of the problems of European recovery after World War II. Capital investment in one country had externalities for others and thus multiplier effects in Europe as a whole. Aid from the United States allowed European countries to avoid deflation or trade controls, thereby continuing high levels of investment and imports (Milward 1984: 98–99). These too had multiplier effects, making aid a vehicle for expansion on both the production and demand sides.

We may think of these policies are part of the international infrastructure underlying global interdependence (e.g., Lake 1988). However, some international infrastructure is produced as a side effect of private economic activity (Keohane 1984: 155–57). For example, supplying finance to the world means that other states can benefit from the resulting financial infrastructure of banking networks, insurance arrangements, and legal precedents establishing property rights overseas. Similarly, opening one's market to imports leads private actors to create international infrastructure such as shipping lines, railroads, ports, and utilities. A single state's efforts to guarantee freedom of the seas also means that third parties can avoid piracy without paying the price of eliminating pirates. As David Lake (1988: 35) notes, "although the infrastructure of international trade is not a 'pure' public good, countries do possess an incentive to free ride on the efforts of others, and a collective action dilemma emerges."

Public goods (and externalities) vary on several dimensions. Some are subject to crowding. A public swimming pool may be enjoyed by all, but its consumption becomes more difficult as the number of users grows. Other goods are not subject to crowding, since my enjoyment of national defense does not diminish yours at all.

Though I will not model it in this book, crowding is important for some international public goods, such as Kindleberger's (1973) "market for international distress goods." The international economy will enjoy greater stability if, in times of recession or depression, a large country such as the United States commits to accepting the imports of other states. This "good" is indeed public if the United States chooses to keep its market open without discrimination. However, it is subject to crowding effects, since purchases of French distress goods reduce the market for distress goods from Germany or the United Kingdom.

In contrast, international liquidity provision is not subject to crowding. By its very nature, providing one state liquidity indirectly gives third parties liquidity as the first state engages in further transactions. Liquidity provision to overcome widespread dollar shortages presented one of the major problems of economic management after World War II, and it was also a major concern of both the IMF and the World Bank (see Hogan 1987; Milward 1994; cf. Kindleberger 1973). Public and private lending as well as grants-in-aid are ways a country can provide liquidity. Capital exporters might also provide international liquidity through tax subsidies, insurance schemes, the Export-Import Bank, and exchange guarantees as incentives for foreign investment (Block 1977: 114). Moreover, liquidity provision is closely related to trade policy, since capital exporters who liberalize trade enough to run an offsetting import surplus will ease pressure on their current account balance.[2] In this way, maintaining an open import market is a way to provide international finance (Kindleberger 1973: 292–94).

Capital importers contribute to international liquidity by loosening controls on foreign exchange that inhibit incoming foreign investment. After World War II, Europeans hesitated to remove quantitative controls on trade and on payments because, even if desirable in the long run, this liberalization

---

2. Discussions about these issues were commonplace during postwar reconstructions (see inter alia Block 1977) and in the interwar period (see Kindleberger 1973).

would lead to a rapid depletion of scarce dollar reserves in the short run. Such liberalization typically leads first to politically difficult increases in imports and only later to more palatable increases in exports. In this way, European contributions to an open international system came at a real political cost.

Finally, many of the goods I have discussed in this section might be supplied in either a discriminatory or a nondiscriminatory way. An open market for international distress goods is a good example, since a country might maintain high tariffs against some countries' imports and not against others. However, any such discrimination is costly. First, it involves monitoring costs because private actors will transship goods through countries that receive favorable tariff treatment (see Aggarwal 1985). Second, discrimination will entail deadweight losses because any meaningful discrimination will target countries that would otherwise be low-cost suppliers of the goods in question (for estimates under British hegemony, see McCloskey 1980). These deadweight losses affect the welfare of other countries because global resources are used less efficiently than they might otherwise be. These concerns make discrimination costly to the discriminator and third parties and thus a public bad; conversely, nondiscrimination shares some features of a public good. In this light it is not surprising that 1959 GATT negotiating guidelines stated, "Participating governments will be expected to take into consideration the indirect benefits which they will receive from the negotiations between other governments" (cited in Curzon and Curzon 1976: 172). Such exhortation would not be necessary if these benefits were purely private.

In sum, several economic policies have some features of a public good. Many other policies have important externalities that can be broken analytically into their public and private components. Of course, future research should differentiate these goods instead of lumping them together as I do throughout this book. I provide one example of such differentiation in appendix A, in a model that captures the political costs of tariff concessions and the political externalities of one country's tariffs on the government of other countries. This model yields many results similar to the public-goods model in the text, which suggests that the simplifications of a pure public-goods model are not too misleading.

Pending more such models, it is often helpful to have a simple proxy measure for contributions to international public goods when testing the model.[3] As I will argue in more detail in subsequent chapters, imports are a decent proxy for many of these goods even though free trade is not a pure public good.

---

3. Readers who balk at this operationalization should consult appendix A, which shows that many results from the public-goods model also follow from a model of international trade.

Providing a market for international distress goods leads to increased imports. Import surpluses may lead to capital exports, and both are an indirect measure of international infrastructure provision by private actors. In the 1920s and in the postwar period, imports were often seen as a way to provide liquidity to the international economy, with many public aspects. While it is hard to measure contributions to international monetary and financial stability, they will be closely associated with imports, which are measurable. Though not without problems, imports may be the best operationalization of contributions to public goods.

Concentration and Collective Action

Having discussed the assumption of public goods, I now turn to the model itself. In its most basic form, the theory of hegemonic stability maintains that international public goods are more easily provided if there is a single dominant country—a hegemon—to provide them. Mainstream theory argues further that there is a relationship between a disproportional distribution of resources—most notably, concentrated in a single country—and comparatively beneficial international outcomes.[4] Some authors explicitly cite Olson's privileged-group argument in support (e.g., Gilpin 1981: 168–69; Lake 1988: 7; Snidal 1985b; Stein 1984).

To evaluate this argument, consider a simple model in which actors make trade-offs between the consumption of public and private goods. I assume that the amount of the public good provided, Q, is equal to the sum of the contributions of each actor, q_i, so that $Q = \Sigma q_i$. Because resources are finite, each actor i operates under a budget constraint, B_i, that is the sum of its contributions to the public good, q_i, and its spending on private goods, m_i, such that for all i, $B_i = q_i + m_i$. Utility is a function of both private and public goods, yielding the following general model:[5]

$$U_i = U(m_i; Q) \qquad Q = \Sigma q_i \qquad B_i = m_i + q_i \qquad \text{for all } i \qquad (2.1)$$

---

4. They also argue that a hegemonic-led international system will be a more cooperative one in the sense that regimes will be more common there than in other systems. Chapter 7 addresses this issue.

5. For readers unfamiliar with such notation, equation 2.1 states that U_i is a function of m_i and Q—that is, utility depends on private goods and public goods in some unspecified way. By not specifying the exact nature of the relationship, such a utility function yields results that are as general as possible.

Substituting,

$$U_i = U(m_i; B_i - m_i + \Sigma B_j - \Sigma m_j) \qquad \text{for all } j \neq i \qquad (2.2)$$

This setup assumes that the government somehow allocates the country's resources among spending on public and private goods. Regulations, taxes, subsidies, and monetary policy are some tools that governments use to allocate a nation's resources, but the model says nothing about the choice of instruments.

This model lets me divide the privileged-group argument into two claims. The first is that the disproportionality of contributions increases as the disproportionality of income distribution increases. As I will show in the next section, this is theoretically robust. However, the second claim is not as sound. According to Olson and others, the total contributions to a public good increase as the disproportionality of resource distribution increases—as resources become more concentrated, a group may become privileged. The model here produces instead a nonconcentration hypothesis (or neutrality theorem), which states that the level of provision of the public good is independent of the concentration of resources among the actors.

To see this in equation 2.2, suppose the existence of a Cournot-Nash equilibrium with equilibrium choices m_i', m_j', q_i', q_j', and Q'.[6] Each state's choices in this equilibrium will be a function of the parameters, which are simply the resource constraints B_i and B_j (or "distribution of capabilities" in the terms of Waltz 1979). Now suppose that the distribution of resources changes without changing the sum $(B_i + \Sigma B_j)$. When the resource distribution changes, a positive change dB_i and negative $-\Sigma dB_j = dB_i$ indicates increasing concentration within the group (for $B_i > B_j$). While the parameters for each state's choice have changed, some of the choices have not. To see this, consider i's choice under the supposition that all m_j' remain unchanged: then there would exist a new Cournot-Nash equilibrium for i, m_i'', in which $m_i' = m_i''$. All of the parameters appear in the second term of i's utility function, in the term $B_i + \Sigma B_j$, which has not changed despite the change in the distribution of resources.

---

6. A Cournot-Nash equilibrium is defined as a set of strategies such that no actor may increase her utility by choosing a different strategy, holding all others constant. I use the term *Cournot-Nash* in place of the more familiar *Nash* because chapter 3 uses a Stackelberg equilibrium that is also Nash but not a Cournot equilibrium. These different types of equilibria are most common in the economics of industrial organization. See Kreps 1990; Tirole 1988 for full formal definitions.

Thus, i's choice of m_i does not change as long as j's choice of m_j does not change. A similar analysis of m_j shows that m_j does not change as long as m_i does not change. These two suppositions are consistent with each other, so there is a post-redistribution Cournot-Nash equilibrium in which all m_i'' equal the original m_i'. Because $Q = \Sigma B_i - \Sigma m_i$, the level of public goods also remains unchanged (cf. Blume, Bergstrom, and Varian 1986; Cornes and Sandler 1986: 84–87; Warr 1983).

The intuition behind this result is simple. Both the aggregate demand for and supply of public goods depends on the total resources available to that public. Redistributing the resources among individuals affects each individual's contributions but not the aggregate contributions.

Looking at the effects of redistribution on individual choices may also strengthen the intuition about the aggregate problem. Any reduction in some j's resources will cause j to decrease her contributions to the public good by some amount that is a fraction of that reduction. Similarly, a redistribution of that same amount to i will induce him to increase his contributions by some fraction of that increase. These responses are income effects. At the same time, j's decreased contributions will reduce i's utility, and i will compensate by making additional contributions to Q; i's additional contributions will, because of perfect substitutability, enable j to reduce her contributions still further. These are substitution effects. Formalizing the problem above shows that the end result of this process is for j to reduce her contributions by the entire amount of its resource loss. Given this, i can only regain the utility lost by allotting his entire increase in resources to the public good. This leaves each state's marginal valuation of its private good unchanged and equal to its marginal valuation of an additional contribution to the public good.

This model's explicit reliance on game-theoretic logic probably accounts for the difference between this claim and many scholars' intuition about the public-goods problem, just as it accounts for the difference from Olson's decision-theoretic model. While everyone recognizes that a leader's provision of collective goods allows others to free ride, many have not appreciated that this free riding induces the leader to increase its contributions even further, leading to still more free riding, and so on. This process leads to the surprising result that resource concentration does not affect aggregate provision.[7]

Because this result differs from many scholars' arguments, it is important to highlight the assumptions on which it rests. The result depends critically on

---

7. As I will discuss below, concentration does affect the distribution of costs.

the public-goods production function, where I assumed that the public good is a function of the sum of each state's contributions. If $Q = f(q_i) + g(q_j)$, and $f(q)$ ≠ $g(q)$, the result will not normally hold, because any $dq_i = -dq_j$ cannot be expected to result in an unchanged Q. However, the result does hold if $Q = f(q_i + q_j)$, because perfect substitutability is maintained—any $dq_i = -dq_j$ will not change $Q = f(q_i, q_j)$.

Nonsubstitutability is unlikely to present any substantive problem except in the case of either increasing or decreasing returns to scale. Changing returns to scale present no problem if they apply to both contributions jointly, for example, $Q = g(q_i + q_j)$. However, if there are changing returns to scale on each actor's contributions independent of the effects on the other actor's contributions, then substitutability breaks down; an example would be $Q = g[(q_i)^\alpha + (q_j)^\beta]$ if $\alpha + \beta > 1$, indicating increasing returns to scale. In such a case, it is difficult to obtain meaningful results in a general model. It is most unlikely that nonconstant returns can save the concentration hypothesis, for increasing returns to scale should have results opposite to those of decreasing returns, and one or the other cases should raise the specter of an anticoncentration hypothesis.

The result will also not necessarily hold in corner solutions, where some (smaller) states spend nothing on collective goods (for full analysis of this issue, see Bergstrom, Blume, and Varian 1986).[8] Here, the distribution of resources can matter, because the leader's contributions can go up with its resources while the followers' can go down no further than zero. Still, this problem is less severe than might be supposed in international relations. Even small states such as the Benelux and the Nordic countries contribute to collective goods such as NATO or collective exchange-rate policy. If Andorra free rides, the effect on the aggregate outcome is inconsequential.[9]

---

8. By a similar logic, the result is also not general if collective goods are lumpy (see Chamberlin 1974, 1978; Frohlich and Oppenheimer 1970), where no public goods are provided unless contributions exceed some threshold. Where lumpy goods are important, some variation of the concentration hypothesis may hold by forcing some states into corner solutions. If most states are at interior solutions, lumpiness will tend to have a greater effect on the distribution of costs than on the aggregate level of supply. Two-by-two games and k-group arguments generally assume some lumpiness (e.g., Snidal 1985b). By analyzing dichotomous choices between contribution and noncontribution, they imply that partial contribution would be ineffective.

9. Once again, this differs from domestic-level public-goods problems such as public television. In such cases, the number of noncontributors who enjoy the good number in the millions, and the aggregate outcome does change when resources move from the noncontributor group to the contributor group. Since it may happen in practice that resources move from one group to the other, we may observe changes in public-goods provision dependent on the distribution of income in a society.

I should also note that the analysis rests on a different way of thinking about public goods than in some mainstream literature. Some versions of hegemony theory argue that a leader can compel others to contribute through explicit use of power such as bribes or threats (e.g., Gilpin 1981; Snidal 1985b). There is no explicit use of power in the model here, such as a leader making costly threats to punish others for failing to contribute. However, states still use resources to achieve their interests in public- and private-goods provision. In this way, the model more nearly resembles hegemony theory based on latent power.

In sum, then, none of these issues present significant problems for the nonconcentration result applied to international political economy. Other assumptions may be better for some specific purposes but should be justified on a case-by-case basis. In the default case, the concentration of resources does not affect public-goods provision.

Cost Sharing

In addition to facilitating the examination of the aggregate supply of public goods, the model lets me address the question of cost sharing—that is, whether anyone pays more or less than her fair share. Here, the model is consistent with an important result also found in the theory of hegemonic stability, the disproportionality result. This hypothesis states that the share of each actor's contributions to a public good increases more rapidly than each actor's share of group resources. As a result, large actors pay more than their fair shares, and small actors pay less.

In the model here, even though a redistribution of income will not change the total supply of the public good, it will change the distribution of costs among the two parties. Because $m_i' = m_i''$ for any given resources transferred to i as dB_i, i's new contributions are $q_i'' = (B_i + dB_i) - m_i' = q_i' + dB_i$. Thus, q_i increases by the entire amount dB_i, and q_j decreases by the same amount (that is, for any $-dB_j = dB_i$, then $dB_i = -dB_j = dq_i = -dq_j$).

Since q_i and q_j are always less than B_i and B_j, respectively (spending on goods cannot be greater than the resources available), the ratio of contributions, $(q_i + dq_i)/(q_j + dq_j)$, will change at a higher rate than will the ratio of resources, $(B_i + dB_i)/(B_j + dB_j)$. Again thinking in terms of redistribution as a proxy for increasing concentration, big states will pay increasingly bigger shares of the costs of the collective good as they get bigger.

This result is consistent with the assertions of hegemony theorists, who, following Olson, argue that larger states pay a disproportionate amount of the costs of public goods.[10] Arthur Stein (1984) identifies the disproportionality result as the core of the "hegemon's dilemma." A large state finds that it maximizes its utility by making disproportionally large contributions to international public goods. However, this absolute gain implies relative loss, since other states will have more resources available to invest for private purposes. As a result, the disproportionality result may explain a hegemon's relative decline over time (Gilpin 1981; Keohane 1984; Stein 1984).

Because the disproportionality result follows where the concentration hypothesis does not, it suggests that traditional hegemonic theory may have logical problems that become evident only through formalization. Since hegemons pay a disproportionate share of the costs of public goods, it seems intuitively reasonable that their contributions would increase the aggregate supply of public goods. However, a game-theoretic model shows that this does not follow. As large states' contributions increase, other states decrease theirs, exactly canceling out the increases.

Translated to a concrete historical problem, an assertion that the United States played the leading role in establishing beneficial international institutions after World War II does not logically suffice to demonstrate the counterfactual claim that American actions made the world better off than it would have been without such leadership. The nonconcentration result forces us to consider the possibility that similar levels of international institutions would have been possible without American leadership, though the roles played by France or the United Kingdom would naturally have differed. Contrary to intuition, then, only one claim in the hegemonic literature actually follows from the claimed model.

Further Hypotheses

This simple collective-goods model is capable of yielding several other results that apply to the international political economy. For many of these results a more specific utility function and a reduction of the number of players to two

---

10. The disproportionality hypothesis is supported by evidence from member contributions to NATO, whether viewed in public-goods or club-goods terms (see, e.g., Murdoch and Sandler 1984; Olson and Zeckhauser 1966; Palmer 1990; Sandler 1977; Sandler and Forbes 1980).

or three will prove convenient. While the specific model is not necessary in this chapter, I introduce it here for ease of presentation.[11]

One simple type of specific utility function is a Cobb-Douglas function, which assumes that each actor attaches some relative importance to two goods, giving one good the weight α and the other good the weight $(1 - \alpha)$, where α is a fraction greater than zero and less than one. A second actor may weight the two goods differently than the first, so I will use β and $(1 - \beta)$ for it (where necessary, additional actors will use weight γ, δ, and so on through the Greek alphabet).

A Cobb-Douglas model uses exponents for the weights assigned to the two goods. Using exponents means that the first derivatives of these functions are algebraically simple linear equations. This yields the following model for the two-actor case:

$$
\begin{aligned}
U_i &= m_i^\alpha Q^{1-\alpha} \quad &\text{subject to } B_i = m_i + q_i \\
U_j &= m_j^\beta Q^{1-\beta} \quad &\text{subject to } B_j = m_j + q_j \\
Q &= q_i + q_j
\end{aligned}
\tag{2.3}
$$

These coefficients α and β also furnish a convenient way to talk about a state's preferences for public or private goods. The values of these parameters are external to the model, presumably as a result of some domestic political processes. Thus, while I do not theorize about domestic politics here, at least some domestic politics can be plugged into the system-level theory here.[12] Sometimes this has interesting effects, as I will note in chapter 3.

Since the actors' choices depend in part on the choices of the others, the first derivation from this model takes the form of reaction curves.[13] These show how each actor will allocate its resources given the parameters of the equation. Maximizing and solving for the four decision variables gives the following reaction functions:

---

11. For proof of these results in a general model, see Pahre 1995. I use the Cobb-Douglas form here to maintain direct comparability with later chapters, where the simplicity of the Cobb-Douglas form is very useful.

12. Appendix A shows further that much of the model here can be recast in terms of the domestic politics surrounding trade policy.

13. To find the reaction functions, set the first derivatives equal to zero to find out where U_i and U_j are at a maximum or minimum with respect to each variable. Then solve for the choice variables as a function of the parameters and the other country's choice variables. All the variables in this book yield global maxima only, so I do not bother to show the conditions for a negative second derivative.

$$m_i^* = \alpha(B_i + q_j) \qquad q_i^* = (1-\alpha)B_i - \alpha q_j$$
$$m_j^* = \beta(B_j + q_i) \qquad q_j^* = (1-\beta)B_j - \beta q_i \tag{2.4}$$

These reaction curves present little surprise. To see what these reaction curves describe, consider a few derivatives—equations that show how one variable will change if another variable changes. The derivatives dm_i^*/dB_i and dq_i^*/dB_i are α and $(1-\alpha)$, respectively. Both of these terms are positive, because α is defined to be greater than zero and less than one. Since both derivatives are positive, an increase in a state's resources (B_i) will cause that state to increase the amount it spends on both m_i and q_i; in economic terms, both are normal goods. The derivative $dq_i^*/dq_j = -\alpha$; this means that if j increases its spending on the public good by one unit for some exogenous reason such as an increase in resources, i will decrease its spending on the public good by α units, where α is less than one.[14] Because q_i and q_j are perfect substitutes, it makes sense for i to reduce q_i in response to any increase in q_j.

Here we see an important difference between this model and the Prisoners' Dilemma often used to model collective action. In the Prisoners' Dilemma, substitution is all or nothing. If neither actor is cooperating, mutual defection will persist. If they are at CC (mutual cooperation), and if j's contributions go down for some exogenous reason, then i must decide either to punish this defection or ignore this reduction as being outside j's control. Partial substitution does not occur in the Prisoners' Dilemma, but such substitution is presumably important in the real world and does occur in the model here.

Having found the reaction curves, I next find the equilibrium outcome. The reaction curves show how the second state reacts to the choices of the first, which reacts in turn to its choices, and so on. All this action and reaction ultimately converge around a Cournot-Nash equilibrium; if one state deviates from this equilibrium, the other state's reaction to this deviation drives both states back to the equilibrium. Finding the Cournot-Nash equilibrium requires solving the above equations for q_i^* and q_j^* simultaneously. In equation 2.4, q_i^* is a function of q_j, and q_j^* is a function of q_i in turn. This means that by substituting the reaction function q_j^* in for q_j in the reaction function q_i^*, I can eliminate the term q_j entirely. This solves for q_i^* as a function solely of the parameters of equation 2.4. Solving for the other variables in turn produces:

---

14. If j were changing its allocations because of a redistribution of resources between i and j, then i would be changing its allocations as well, and both would be responding to one another. For this reason, the equilibrium results are different than the reaction functions.

$$q_i^C = \frac{(1-\alpha)B_i - \alpha(1-\beta)B_j}{1-\alpha\beta}$$

$$Q^C = \frac{(1-\alpha)(1-\beta)(B_i + B_j)}{1-\alpha\beta}$$

$$q_j^C = \frac{(1-\beta)B_j - \beta(1-\alpha)B_i}{1-\alpha\beta} \qquad (2.5)$$

$$m_i^C = \frac{\alpha(1-\beta)(B_i + B_j)}{1-\alpha\beta}$$

$$m_j^C = \frac{\beta(1-\alpha)(B_i + B_j)}{1-\alpha\beta}$$

As must be true, the results on concentration and cost sharing from the general model continue to hold in a more specific model. Q^C is a function of ($B_i + B_j$), the sum of the two states' resource budgets, so a redistribution of income among these states will not change this sum.

Not surprisingly, preferences affect the outcome. In particular, aggregate public goods depend negatively on each state's weighting of private goods (α and β), and this weighting presumably reflects domestic politics. This feature of the model provides a partial response to claims that hegemony theory cannot explain how different domestic systems exhibit different forms of leadership (e.g., Keohane 1984: 25–29; Ruggie 1983, 1993). Because Stalinist countries have different preferences than do capitalist democracies, a hypothetical Soviet hegemony after World War II would have been different than American hegemony has been. The reasons for these differences lie outside the model, but they can be synthesized with the model through the weighting parameters α and β.

This simple model also yields several comparative statics results that are useful for quantitative tests in future chapters. First, Q is an increasing function of ΣB_i. Applied to international relations, this suggests the reasonable hypothesis that the level of public goods increases as the sum of global resources increases.

As I discussed earlier, it is often useful to take a country's imports as a proxy for contributions to international infrastructure and openness. With Q

an increasing function of global resources, this operationalization of contributions yields the sensible hypothesis that aggregate economic growth should produce commensurate increases in aggregate trade. At the most superficial level, this is the history of the global political economy over the past two centuries. Moreover, rapid contractions in GDPs, such as the Great Depression of 1929, have led to rapid reductions in aggregate trade (see Kindleberger 1973 inter alia).

Each state's contributions, q_i and q_j, are also functions of both B_i and B_j. However, the signs differ: i's contribution to the public good depends positively on its own resources but negatively on j's resources. As j's resources increase, i can better free ride on j's provision of public goods, so i's contributions decrease. This negative correlation between one state's contributions and other states' resources is easy to test quantitatively. As I will discuss in chapter 4, it also helps distinguish the public-goods model here from other predictions of import levels.

Those tests face some statistical difficulties that I discuss in later chapters. Instead of finding a statistical solution to these difficulties, I prefer to derive hypotheses from the formal model that are not subject to these problems.[15] For example, continuous and unbounded increases in a time series cause some statistical problems such as serial correlation. A good solution is to derive hypotheses that have a bounded dependent variable.

The variables q_i, q_j, and Q are not bounded on the upward side, since they can take any positive value. In contrast, contributions to public goods as a fraction of resources are bounded by zero and one. Finding this fraction, which I label "openness," requires only simple algebra:

$$O_i^C = \frac{q_i^C}{B_i} = \frac{1-\alpha}{1-\alpha\beta} - \left(\frac{\alpha(1-\beta)}{1-\alpha\beta}\right)\left(\frac{B_j}{B_i}\right) \tag{2.6}$$

Openness depends positively on a constant term and negatively on the ratio of foreign GNP to home GNP. As we would expect, small countries (small B_j/B_i) have a small negative effect on another's openness, while large countries have a large negative effect.

Equation 2.6 also captures the disproportionality result indirectly, showing how a country's burden relative to GNP depends on the ratio of foreign

<hr />

15. Statistical solutions typically entail assumptions about error terms that do not follow from the formal model. Including such operationalizing propositions weakens the logical connection between model and hypotheses (see Pahre 1996b).

GNP to its own. This makes possible an intertemporal test of the disproportionality hypothesis—that is, an examination of how a single state's contributions change over time as its relative size changes (cf. Lake 1988). This is less common than cross-national tests of the disproportionality result that look at different nations at the same point in time (e.g., Murdoch and Sandler 1982; Olson and Zeckhauser 1966; Pahre 1995; Sandler and Forbes 1980). Because of its versatility, equation 2.6 is my preferred test of the disproportionality hypothesis when the necessary data are available.

Summary

Because many theories of hegemonic stability have been interested in public goods, this chapter developed a simple game-theoretic model of public-goods provision. The results challenge the logic of the received theory. In particular, this model does not generate the prediction that lies at the heart of the theory of hegemonic stability: that the concentration of resources in a hegemon will increase the level of collective-goods provision. For this reason, it is not surprising that a significant empirical literature generally finds evidence contradicting the theory (e.g., Conybeare 1983; Martin 1992; McKeown 1983, 1989, 1991; for somewhat more supportive results, see Mansfield 1992, 1994).

Since mainstream theory is based on the provision of collective goods by a hegemon, this problem is serious indeed. As Duncan Snidal (1985a) rightly argues, "What is novel in the theory [of hegemonic stability] is not the claim that strong actors can impose regimes in international politics (which goes back at least as far as Thucydides) but the use of the collective action formulation and the implication that hegemony is more widely beneficial." More bluntly, John A. C. Conybeare (1987: 71) agrees: "Without public goods, hegemonic stability theory has no content."

This chapter's model also generates a number of hypotheses amenable to quantitative testing—some intuitive and some counterintuitive. Public-goods provision depends positively on aggregate resources in the system. A state's contributions increase with its own resources and with decreases in other states' resources. A state's openness depends negatively on the ratio of foreign resources to its own. These hypotheses persist across the variations of the basic model that I develop in future chapters.

The analysis in this chapter treats a leader in quantitative terms, as a state with a large share of total resources. One might also suppose that a leader might be a qualitatively different state. I develop such a model of qualitative leadership in the next chapter. While it does not save the original hegemony theory, it has several other important implications for a revised hegemonic theory.

CHAPTER 3

Stackelberg Leadership and Public Goods

The model in chapter 2 addressed questions of resource concentration and burden sharing among states. The analysis treated all states as qualitatively similar, using a symmetric equilibrium concept, the Cournot-Nash. Many scholars of international affairs (and diplomats) would quite rightly question these assumptions, believing that great powers are qualitatively different from lesser powers. Moreover, international equilibria are often hierarchical, with great-power diplomacy establishing the essential patterns of international politics and lesser powers maneuvering within these limits.

These qualitative kinds of leadership play a different role than does resource concentration. For example, hegemony might be important because it helps other states coordinate around the behavior of a single leader. Such coordination might be easier than adjusting to constantly changing relationships among several other states. The stabilizing function of a reserve currency in the nineteenth century is a good example of this phenomenon, as may be seen in Derek Aldcroft's (1977: 166) account:

> Sterling . . . could function without a large reserve backing. Had there been competitors of equal or near equal rank (say the franc or dollar) then . . . [a]ny temporary strains on sterling would have been magnified since speculators and financiers would have had alternative currencies to switch into, while London's ability to attract funds and resist departures would have been impaired. Under these circumstances sterling's reserve backing would probably have been inadequate and it is debatable whether the gold standard could have functioned as well as it did.

In short, having only one key currency is good for the international economy, while having two or three such currencies would undercut the gold standard.

The previous chapter showed that a quantitative definition of hegemony based on resource concentration is inconsistent with the main argument of benevolent hegemony theory. Still, this says nothing about the usefulness of qualitative definitions. Formalizing hegemony thus requires some way to capture the qualitative uniqueness of a hegemon. I use the concept of a Stackelberg equilibrium, taken from oligopoly theory, to capture asymmetry.[1] A hegemon, like the dominant firm in a market, moves first in an analytical sense. The Stackelberg solution relies on the premise that a follower is a rational actor who, because it is rational, is also predictable. Since the follower's response to anything the leader does is predictable if the leader knows the follower's reaction function, the leader can optimize anywhere along that function.

In oligopoly theory, the leader may or may not be better off for going first. In the classic duopoly case, the leader is better off in a Stackelberg equilibrium than in a Cournot equilibrium if the relevant decision variable is the total quantity produced; the leader can preempt much of the follower's production for a given level of demand. However, the leader is worse off if it must choose a price, since the follower will undercut the leader's price just enough to gain as large a share of the market as possible.

Traditional benevolent hegemony theory would suggest that the hegemon is worse off for its leadership, though it makes everyone else better off. The hegemon will have to supply public goods by itself because it knows that the followers will free ride no matter what it does. Once the hegemon's contributions are known, the marginal contribution of any smaller state will not provide sufficient utility to that state to outweigh the costs. As a result, "Hegemons do not impose openness, they bear its costs" (Stein 1984: 386).

This is not true of the model here. The leader can shift the costs of public-goods provision onto other states, thereby making the rest of the world worse

---

1. Other asymmetric models are possible. A good example is Frohlich, Oppenheimer, and Young's (1971; Frohlich and Oppenheimer 1970, 1974; see also Breton and Breton 1969; Salisbury 1969) model of leadership, the assumptions of which are geared toward explaining leaders of domestic entities such as political parties or interest groups. The political entrepreneurs in these models elicit contributions to a public good by providing selective incentives to contributors. However, it is not clear that these models help solve the problem of collective action, since the entrepreneur must somehow produce these selective incentives. There will be a surplus that might be applied to public goods only if the entrepreneur can earn above-market rates of profit or if public-goods contributors are willing to pay a higher price for selective incentives from a political entrepreneur than they are willing to pay on the open market. It is also not clear why entrepreneurs would want to spend their profits on public goods (see Freeman 1977; Laver 1980). Approaches to hegemonic leadership in this tradition therefore leave many questions unanswered.

off. Like chapter 2, then, the core result of this chapter challenges the received wisdom of the literature on hegemony.

Hegemony as Stackelberg Leadership

Though novel for hegemonic theory, a number of scholars have found Stackelberg leadership a useful way to model qualitatively different actors in political economy. Barry Eichengreen (1985) uses Stackelberg leadership to model an asymmetric game between central banks seeking price stability and the accumulation of foreign reserves. Neil Bruce (1990) explores the difference between Nash and Stackelberg equilibria in an arms-race model.[2] Finally, Alt, Calvert, and Humes's (1988) model of hegemonic leadership uses an extensive form that is essentially Stackelberg.

The Stackelberg assumption models a world in which states make choices after seeing the hegemon's choices because of its unique salience in the system. This assumption relies on actors' conjectures about one another's reactions. A hegemon makes choices dependent in part on the conjecture that other actors respond to its choices. In the nineteenth century, for example, Britain's market was so important for other countries' exports that foreigners waited for Britain to choose its economic policy before changing their own (James and Lake 1989). J. David Richardson (1988: 180) describes postwar American behavior in similar terms:

> Governments of relatively weak countries . . . tended to take U.S. trade policies as given and to adopt whatever trade policies seemed best for themselves without perceiving much scope for influencing the United States thereby. U.S. incentives were to act strategically, but in a unique way. The United States tended to choose trade initiatives mindful of collective foreign response . . . similar to what one might expect from a large firm in an industry with a fringe of small perfect competitors [i.e., a Stackelberg leader].

These conjectures may reflect a real power advantage. In banking, for example, "by the operation of her Bank Rate [Britain could] almost immediately adjust her reserve position. Other countries had, therefore, in the main to adjust con-

---

2. All Stackelberg equilibria are Nash equilibria because they are defined as a set of strategies such that everyone lacks a unilateral incentive to change their strategy. For convenience, I use the term *Stackelberg equilibria* for "Nash equilibria of a game form in which one player is the Stackelberg leader."

ditions to hers" (Macmillan Committee 1931: 125; cf. Eichengreen 1987).

Perhaps surprisingly, the Stackelberg assumption does not require that the hegemon actually moves first or that other states allow the leader to move first. The assumption implies only that the leader and followers share a common conjecture that all will make choices as if the leader moved first. Such conjectures, like preferences, originate outside any rational-choice model, although they have an important effect on the outcome. A theory from a different tradition, such as a Gramscian focus on hegemony's ideological domination, might help explicate these conjectures in future research.

In addition to the first-mover conjecture, we might require that the first-moving hegemon precommit to its strategy, perhaps by sinking substantial costs in that choice. This requirement is common in oligopoly applications. In its original form (Stackelberg 1934, 1952: 190–204), one firm could precommit to a given level of production and thereby inhibit production by the other; the canonical modern version precommits capital investment instead of production (Dixit 1979, 1980; Kreps 1990: 325–30, 443–49; Spence 1977, 1979; Tirole 1988). Choices such as military budgets, economic or military doctrines, and legislative reform are all ways for a state to commit to a given strategy. In Britain, for instance, the Corn Law of 1814 was accompanied by a repeal of the wartime income tax, committing the government to a peacetime economy of grain autarchy to the extent possible and a military to be financed mostly out of customs revenue (see Hilton 1977). Indeed, the government burned the income-tax records to show its commitment not to reintroduce that tax (cf. Schelling 1960).

The ability to precommit rests on power, which I do not consider here in any detail. In many cases, commitment involves not any literal physical commitment but changes in the conjectures that other states hold about the actor.

Unfortunately, exactly how a state becomes a Stackelberg leader is outside the theory. Much of mainstream theory argues that hegemony is forged in war: "Victory and defeat reestablish an unambiguous hierarchy of prestige congruent with the new distribution of power in the system" (Gilpin 1981: 198; see also Brawley 1993; Modelski 1987; Wallerstein 1980: chap. 3). If hegemony rests on a hierarchy of prestige, then Stackelberg leadership rests on conjectures rather than precommitment.

At the same time, there is a growing literature on the role of credible commitments in domestic political economy (e.g., North and Weingast 1989). It would not be hard in principle to extend this commitment argument to international political economy.

As these speculations suggest, the origins of hegemony remain an interesting problem for the literature. Still, the theory here need not choose between precommitment and conjectural foundations for Stackelberg leadership.[3] Either suffices to make the assumption a useful way to think about hegemony.

Hegemony and Public Goods

The utility functions and constraints developed in chapter 2 are unchanged in the Stackelberg equilibrium. However, instead of solving the two reaction functions in equation 2.4 simultaneously, I substitute the follower's reaction function, q_i^*, directly into the leader's utility function. This means that when the leader maximizes its utility, it does so with the follower's reactions taken into account. If i is the Stackelberg leader, it will maximize utility according to the following function:

$$U_i = m_i^\alpha Q^{1-\alpha} \quad \text{subject to } B_i = m_i + q_i$$
$$\text{where } Q = q_i + q_j^*(q_i) = (1 - \beta)(B_j + q_i) \tag{3.1}$$

Now set the first derivative of U_i with respect to q_i equal to zero and solve for q_i. Once q_i is known, then plug this value back into the follower's reaction function $q_j^*(q_i)$ to find the equilibrium levels of q_j and $Q = q_i + q_j$:

$$q_i^S = (1 - \alpha)B_i - \alpha B_j$$
$$q_j^S = (1 + \alpha\beta - \beta)B_j - \beta(1 - \alpha)B_i$$
$$Q^S = (1 - \alpha)(1 - \beta)(B_i - B_j) \tag{3.2}$$
$$m_i^S = \alpha(B_i + B_j) \quad m_j^S = \beta(1 - \alpha)(B_i - B_j)$$

These solutions provide enough information to make several comparisons. First, the supply of public goods Q is less when there is a Stackelberg leader. To see this, note that $1 - \alpha\beta = Q^S/Q^C$. Because α and β both lie between zero and one, $0 < (1 - \alpha\beta) < 1$. This implies that $Q^C > Q^S$. In other words, the supply of public goods in the Cournot-Nash equilibrium is greater than the supply in a Stackelberg equilibrium.

Exactly how much Stackelberg leadership reduces public-goods provision depends on both states' preferences because it hinges on the term $(1 - \alpha\beta)$. When states value private goods much more than public goods, α and β

---

3. Readers interested in classifying theories by level of analysis (e.g., Singer 1961; Waltz 1954, 1979) will note that this account treats shared conjectures as a systemic-level variable and precommitment as a unit-level variable. While I am agnostic here, this distinction might be useful for future theory building.

approach 1, so $(1 - \alpha\beta)$ approaches zero, and Q^C is very much larger than Q^S. When states value public goods much more than private goods, α and β approach zero, so $(1 - \alpha\beta)$ approaches one, and Q^S approaches Q^C. Because the domestic politics of most states lead them to value national consumption (private goods) much more than consumption of international private goods, it is a fair presumption that $(1 - \alpha\beta)$ is usually small. As a result, hegemony probably has a fairly large negative effect on public-goods provision.

Readers accustomed to the "levels of analysis" debate in political science (e.g., Singer 1961; Waltz 1954, 1979) will see here an interesting combination of system-level and domestic-level variables. The difference between the Cournot-Nash and Stackelberg equilibria is a system-level difference in how the actors relate to each other.[4] This system-level feature affects system-level outcomes: having a leader is bad for aggregate public-goods provision. However, each state's relative weights for public and private goods affects how bad the leader is. These weights presumably reflect differences in domestic politics that are outside the theory and are thus a domestic-level variable. In short, system-level variables determine that hegemony is malevolent, while domestic variables determine how malevolent it is.

I can also examine the distributional effects of hegemony by breaking Q into its two components, q_i and q_j, and comparing each with its Cournot levels (compare the equations in 3.2 with 2.5). With a little algebra, it is easy to verify that $q_i^S < q_i^C$, while $q_j^S > q_j^C$. In other words, the leader reduces its contributions to the public good to as low a level as possible, knowing that the follower will increase its contributions to make up some of the difference. By so doing, the leader can increase its consumption of the private good and thus its utility ($U_i^S > U_i^C$). The leader forces others to bear a disproportionate share of the costs of the public good, but this passing the buck has social deadweight losses.[5]

The Stackelberg result stands in marked contradiction to the hypotheses of most hegemony theory. "Benevolent" theorists argue that the presence of a hegemon will make the total supply of public goods increase, not decrease. For instance, Charles Kindleberger (1973: 305; see also 1981) argues both that international stability is a public good and that "for the world economy to be

---

4. Following Waltz 1979, the presence or absence of a leader is a system-level variable because we may classify systems in terms of whether Stackelberg conjectures are one of their ordering principles.

5. The optimal level does not change across the two equilibria. Because both actors are better off if they jointly increase their contributions to the public good, the Stackelberg equilibrium will be less optimal for the follower than the Cournot-Nash. Of course, since the Stackelberg equilibrium makes the leader better off, neither equilibrium is Pareto superior to the other.

stabilized, there has to be a stabilizer, one stabilizer." The model here counsels considerable skepticism. However, the result resembles the Realist claim that hegemons try to coerce smaller states into paying more than their fair share of public goods.

While modeled differently, several bodies of literature show the process by which the presence of a large state leads to undesirable outcomes. In monetary stability, the provider of the reserve currency has access to short-run credits, can issue IOUs in the form of currency, and may gain seigneurage. Some analysts argue that exploiting these advantages makes the international monetary system less stable and worse off and cite as an example American monetary policy in the 1960s and beyond.[6] In trade policy, the undesirability of Stackelberg leadership in my model parallels findings from international trade theory that, even after retaliation, a large country can benefit from an optimal tariff, resulting in an outcome that is globally suboptimal (Dixit and Norman 1980: 149–55). Indeed, appendix A shows that analogous results follow from a simple model of the politics of trade policy in which a Stackelberg leader chooses higher tariffs and forces the follower to liberalize, to the benefit of the leader's exporters.

It remains true in equation 3.2 that Q is a function of $(B_i + B_j)$, the total of the two states' budgets. Any concentration of income will still have no effect on the total supply of public goods, even if there is a Stackelberg leader. As in the Cournot equilibrium, aggregate provision is a function of aggregate resources.

Finally, the Stackelberg model of hegemony lets me distinguish two different effects of leadership on burden sharing. The leader benefits from a first-moving effect, shifting the costs of public-goods provision onto others. The second, disproportionality effect, stems from the concentration of resources in the hegemon's hands. This redistribution continues to affect the ratio of contributions, as in chapter 2. (Again, for any $dB_i = -dB_j$, then $dB_i = -dB_j = dq_i = -dq_j$.) As in the Cournot solution, the change in the ratio of contributions, $(q_i + dq_i)/(q_j + dq_j)$, will change at a higher rate than the ratio of resources, $(B_i + dB_i)/(B_j + dB_j)$. In other words, the disproportionality result still holds for follower states or for a hegemon over time.

However, the disproportionality result might not hold when we compare

---

6. For example, most one-hundred-dollar bills now circulate outside the United States as local currency in Russia and elsewhere. Holders of these bills effectively give the U.S. Treasury an interest-free loan before ultimately exchanging them for American goods and services; if these bills never return to the United States, exporting them is pure profit for the country (less the cost of printing).

the hegemon to nonhegemonic states, since it might be true that $q_i^S < q_j^S$ even if the leader is larger, $B_i > B_j$.[7] In such cases, the cost-shifting effect is larger than the disproportionality effect, so the hegemon contributes less than does some smaller state.

The existence of both effects may help explain the persistence of the debate over whether or not hegemons benefit relatively from hegemony (e.g., Conybeare 1984; Gilpin 1981; Keohane 1984; Stein 1984; Wallerstein 1974, 1979, 1989). The model here suggests that a hegemon benefits from being able to move first, while all large countries pay a disproportionate share of the costs of public goods. Both claims rely on a counterfactual argument that large countries would pay less under a "fair shares" taxation institution, though a hegemon would pay more in a Cournot-Nash equilibrium. The net effect of the cost-shifting and disproportionality effects on the hegemon may be positive or negative.[8] The existence of two countervailing counterfactual claims certainly makes it easy to keep a debate going about cost sharing.

Hierarchies of Leadership

So far, I have used a two-country model to explore the effects of leadership. Adding players to the game not only provides a good test of the model's robustness but also lets me explore a variety of different kinds of leadership. I can also explore systems with two (or more) leaders, with the model forcing me to specify exactly how multiple leadership might work. This is especially helpful since some versions of hegemonic theory explicitly allow for two hegemons or two near-hegemons (e.g., Lake 1983, 1984, 1988; Snidal 1985b).

As a benchmark, suppose the existence of three players, with these now-familiar utility functions and constraints:

$$U_i = m_i^\alpha Q^{1-\alpha} \qquad Q = \Sigma q_i$$
$$B_i = q_i + m_i \qquad \alpha = \alpha, \beta, \gamma \qquad \text{for } i = i, j, k \tag{3.3}$$

7. This will be true whenever $(1-\alpha)(1+\beta)B_i < (1+\alpha)(1-\beta)B_j$. This condition will never hold when the states have similar preferences ($\alpha = \beta$), but it might hold if the leader's preferences for private goods (α) are large relative to the follower's (β). Kindleberger (1973) makes just this argument about American and British preferences in the 1920s and 1930s. He argues that these preferences stem from the difference between new and mature international lenders. A similar result in chapter 5 will play an important role in my analysis of British leadership in chapter 6.

8. As a further complication, chapter 4 uses a quantitative test of the disproportionality effect but a qualitative test of the cost-shifting effect. Readers who find one kind of test more persuasive than the other will draw a biased conclusion about the relative weight of these two effects even though both follow equally from the same model.

Some simple matrix algebra, which I will not reproduce here, is the easiest way to solve this. The Cournot-Nash solution to this three-player game, indexed Q^3, and so forth, is:

$$q_i^3 = \frac{(1-\alpha)(1-\beta)B_i - \alpha(1-\beta)(1-\gamma)(B_j + B_k)}{1 - \alpha\beta - \alpha\gamma - \beta\gamma - 2\alpha\beta\gamma}$$

$$Q^3 = \frac{(1-\alpha)(1-\beta)(1-\gamma)(B_i - B_j + B_k)}{1 - \alpha\beta - \alpha\gamma - \beta\gamma - 2\alpha\beta\gamma}$$

(3.4)

Instead of the simultaneous moves behind Q^3, these three players might move in some sequence. Consider first a hierarchical equilibrium in which *i* moves first, *j* second, and *k* third. In this "1–2–3" hierarchy, the equilibrium outcomes are:

$$q_i^{123} = B_i - \alpha(B_i + B_j + B_k)$$
$$q_j^{123} = B_j - \beta(1-\alpha)(B_i + B_j + B_k)$$
$$q_k^{123} = B_k - \gamma(1-\beta)(1-\alpha)(B_i + B_j + B_k)$$
$$Q^{123} = (1-\alpha)(1-\beta)(1-\gamma)(B_i + B_j + B_k)$$

(3.5)

This three-player sequential game provides less public goods than the three-player Cournot; for any α, β, and γ, $Q^{123} < Q^3$ because the denominator in Q^3 lies between zero and one. As we might expect, this hierarchy of buck-passing reduces public-goods provision.

The hierarchy also affects the contributions of individual states. Each state's contributions equal its own resources less a fraction of all states' resources. This fraction is largest for *i*, less for *j*, and still less for *k*. As a result, early movers contribute less as a fraction of global resources than later movers. The further down the line you are, the more you are exploited. Those who move earlier have more players available onto whom to shift the costs.

Now consider a different kind of hierarchy, with a single leader and two followers. Here, the followers play a Cournot game with each other—that is, they move simultaneously, not sequentially. However, the leader moves before the two followers. I label this Q^{2F}, for "two followers," and again I will show only the equilibrium levels:

$$q_i^{2F} = (1-\alpha)B_i - \alpha(B_j + B_k)$$

$$q_j^{2F} = \frac{[1 - \beta + \alpha\beta(1 - \gamma)]B_j - \beta(1 - \alpha)(1 - \gamma)(B_i + B_k)}{1 - \beta\gamma}$$

$$Q^{2F} = \frac{(1 - \alpha)(1 - \beta)(1 - \gamma)(B_i + B_j + B_k)}{1 - \beta\gamma}$$

(3.6)

The level of public goods in this game is less than in the three-player Cournot game but is more than in the sequential 1–2–3 game. Having only one leader limits the number of exploiters to one, improving on the earlier outcome. Yet again, a hegemon can shift some of the costs of public-goods provision onto others, but doing so makes the world as a whole worse off.

The final hierarchical equilibrium introduces an interesting twist. Consider a game with two leaders (i and j) and one follower (k), in which the leaders play simultaneously against each other but before the follower. The equilibrium of this two leader game, indexed $2L$, is:

$$q_i^{2L} = \frac{(1 - \alpha)B_i - \alpha(1 - \beta)(B_j + B_k)}{1 - \alpha\beta}$$

$$q_j^{2L} = \frac{(1 - \beta)B_j - \beta(1 - \alpha)(B_i + B_k)}{1 - \alpha\beta}$$

$$q_k^{2L} = B_k - \frac{\gamma(1 - \alpha)(1 - \beta)(B_i + B_j + B_k)}{1 - \alpha\beta}$$

$$Q^{2L} = \frac{(1 - \alpha)(1 - \beta)(1 - \gamma)(B_i + B_j + B_k)}{1 - \alpha\beta}$$

(3.7)

Like the two-follower case, the two-leader game provides public goods better than the sequential equilibrium but not as well as the Cournot equilibrium. The intuition here is that the leaders constrain one another's buck-passing, though they still jointly force some of the costs of public-goods provision onto the follower.

I cannot compare the two-leader and two-follower equilibria without knowing something about the states' preferences. If all three states have identical preferences ($\alpha = \beta = \gamma$), then $Q^{2F} = Q^{2L}$. Two leaders may provide public goods at a level indistinguishable from the case with one leader and multiple followers, though still inferior to the no-leader case. When $\alpha \neq \beta \neq \gamma$, no general comparison of the two-leader and two-follower cases is possible: in short, $Q^3 > \{Q^{2F}, Q^{2L}\} > Q^{123}$. Phrased differently, as long as there is at least a single leader, moving other states between the categories of leader and follower has unclear effects on aggregate supply of public goods. Having two leaders does not necessarily make the international system any worse off than having one leader. The exact effects depend on preferences and thus presumably on domestic politics.

These results are somewhat different from previous arguments about the effects of multiple leaders. In Charles Kindleberger's (1973) analysis of the Great Depression, neither would-be leader was both willing and able to provide monetary stability. David Lake (1988) argues that having two near-hegemons, or "opportunists," is bad for the system, while a single hegemon is good.[9] Opportunists seek to free ride on each other, so neither provides the public good of international infrastructure. However, extending Lake's two-country logic to a three-country model here shows how the leaders' anticipation of third-party reactions limits how far they can free ride on each other.

In all of the three-player equilibria, as in the two-player equilibria, each state's contributions to the public good are a positive function of its own resources and a nonpositive function of the rest of the world's resources (see q_i in equations 3.4–3.7). This is one of the most easily tested implications of the theory presented earlier, so it is useful that it holds in a model with more than two actors.

Summary

This chapter has introduced both Stackelberg leaders and hierarchies of leaders into the public-goods model of chapter 2. Introducing qualitative asymmetry yields results that are even more challenging for traditional hegemonic theory than the symmetrical model. Leadership reduces the supply of public goods, and a hierarchy of leaders reduces public goods further still. Only when there are two symmetrical leaders does leadership play any positive role—each leader limits the exploitativeness of the other.

While provocative, these results only constitute a persuasive indictment of hegemonic theory if they obtain empirical support. The model will be particularly useful if it can explain anomalies of received theory. I turn to this task in the next chapter.

---

9. Two opportunists may successfully cooperate, however.

CHAPTER 4

Predatory Hegemony: The 1920s

This chapter tests the model of chapter 3 with the case of American hegemony in the 1920s. I chose the 1920s because the interwar period is anomalous for most hegemonic theories.[1] Jeffry Frieden (1988: 60) sums up the problem well:

> The United States clearly had the military, industrial, and financial capacity to impose its will on Europe. . . . Yet . . . [it] did not play the part of international economic hegemon, arbiter and bankroller of the world economic order.

Because of its anomalous status, any theory of international leadership must address this period.

The 1920s are a poor test of the model to the extent that international cooperation is important, since I do not develop a model of cooperation until chapter 7. Fortunately for the test, international cooperation was sporadic and generally weak in this period (Simmons 1994; see also Pahre 1990: chap. 8).[2] Moreover, even when cooperation occurred, it was usually insufficient to overcome the malevolent effects of U.S. hegemony.

My central claim in this chapter is that American hegemony reduced the level of public-goods provision in the 1920s. I demonstrate this phenomenon by analyzing the effects of American leadership on the international monetary and trade regimes. A second claim is that the United States reduced its contri-

---

1. I also knew that I could ignore security concerns in the 1920s and early 1930s, because the period meets the condition for malevolent hegemony derived in chapter 5 (see Pahre 1990 for evidence).

2. This changed a bit in the late 1930s and beyond. By 1945 the United States had negotiated thirty-two treaties with twenty-seven countries under the Reciprocal Trade Agreements Act of 1934, granting tariff concessions on 64 percent of all dutiable imports and thereby reducing duties by an average of 44 percent (Nau 1990: 88).

butions to international public goods, expecting other states to make up the difference.

Both of these are counterfactual claims, resting on an analysis of what the international political economy would have looked like in the absence of American leadership. Because there is no change in the hegemonic variable, these hypotheses cannot be tested directly. Instead, the core of my test is a qualitative argument that the U.S. role after World War I reduced welfare for the world as a whole and that American cost shifting forced others to bear the costs of international public goods. Cost shifting also forced others to bear the costs of American adjustment policy.

Another way to test the model is to look at some of its secondary claims in which there is variation. For instance, the results in chapters 2 and 3 suggest that each country's contributions to public goods should vary inversely with other countries' resources. Using import volume as a proxy for contributions to interdependent production, this means that American imports will decrease as other countries' resources increase, and vice versa. Transforming contributions into openness, U.S. openness depends negatively on the ratio of foreign to U.S. GNP. While these GNP ratios indirectly capture disproportionality effects, I also test the disproportionality result directly.

Some of the tests in this chapter allow me to distinguish the theory here from mainstream hegemonic theory. For instance, I argue that system-level concentration will not affect system-level openness. This flatly contradicts the received theory. Other findings, such as the disproportionality hypothesis, are consistent with both mainstream theory and the theory here. Finally, the quantitative hypotheses have no parallel in the received theory, which has been largely unconcerned with developing hypotheses amenable to quantitative testing (Lake 1993).

These second-order hypotheses are important for allowing me to infer malevolence. The negative relationship between American imports and foreign resources rests on the leader's ability to free ride on others. If the United States were acting benevolently, it would open its market as foreign markets expand.

While the quantitative tests help me draw a contrast between the public-goods theory and mainstream hegemony theory, they cannot distinguish between the Stackelberg and Cournot-Nash equilibria of chapters 2 and 3. These equilibria share the comparative statics result that imports depend negatively on foreign resources. For this reason, the qualitative tests are essential for the Stackelberg model of chapter 3.

This period also lets me carefully examine the assumptions of the model. I will look at three such assumptions: that the United States was a Stackelberg leader in this period; that international openness approximated a public good; and that government preferences mirrored the utility functions of chapters 2 and 3.

The United States as Stackelberg Leader

In most of the other chapters, identifying a uniquely dominant country is an easy task. However, the existing literature has not reached consensus on whether there existed a leader in the 1920s. The main difficulty is the gap between U.S. capabilities and its willingness to use those capabilities abroad (see Carr 1939/1962: 234; Frieden 1988; Kindleberger 1973). This gap has pointed existing research toward theories of power activation, which examine whether and how latent resources are converted into actual power. Whatever their merit for other purposes, these theories furnish a poor way to operationalize leadership. A noncircular definition of leadership might explain successful or unsuccessful force activation instead of using observed force activation to explain leadership or its absence.

Using Stackelberg leadership means that the key question is whether the United States moved first. A good illustration of the first-mover position was the fact that most states waited to ratify the League of Nations Covenant until after the American decision. Monetary and financial decision makers also responded to developments in New York and Washington when considering policy choices. German borrowers were especially sensitive to developments in the United States (McNeil 1986). American- and British-led initiatives established the basic rules of the monetary order, such as the gold-exchange system used by many smaller European countries. As Jeffry Frieden (1988: 31) points out,

> During the 1920s, United States private bankers initiated, supervised, and funded most of the central developments in the world economy. They built international organizations, stabilized currencies, and oversaw government economic programs in Europe and Latin America. Decision making in the 1920s international economy centered on Wall Street; the United States was a crucial component of the decisions taken; and the world operated in large part on a dollar standard.

This salience across many fields is a good indicator of Stackelberg conjectures.
Resources have an indirect effect on these Stackelberg conjectures. The United States was the world's leading exporter in the interwar period and was

second in imports only to the United Kingdom. More strikingly, the United States accounted for 46 percent of world industrial production in 1925–29 and for about half of great-power GNP. U.S. capital markets were equally dominant: the $7.5 billion in foreign loans floated in the United States between 1919 and 1929 exceeded the total of similar issues floated in all other lending countries combined. American foreign direct investments also constituted an impressive share of the world total (Lary 1943: 29–31). When faced with such a dominant state, others will either wait to make their own choices or hold the conjecture that the follower states will act as if they had waited to move second.

American military potential doubtless helped establish its first-mover position. World War I had ended quickly once the doughboys arrived in significant numbers, and this demonstration of strength was not unnoticed. American naval dominance was so great that it brought others to limit shipbuilding in the 1922 Washington Treaty, since the alternative was to risk an arms race (Gathorne-Hardy 1950: 63): "the United States . . . enjoyed at the time so unassailable a financial superiority that no other Power was in a position to compete with them if unrestricted ship-building was allowed to continue." In short, as John A. C. Conybeare (1987: 234) argues, "By 1929, the United States clearly had substantial hegemonic power."

While the United States was clearly hegemonic, other nations may have held a secondary leadership position. The most important of these countries was the United Kingdom, which played a critical role in the financial and monetary system. Many of my comments about the role of New York financial markets would apply with equal force to London. For this reason, one might also agree with David Lake (1988) that there were two near-hegemons in the 1920s. However, the model in chapter 3 suggests that this might be a distinction without a difference. Whether the United States was a single leader or one of two, leadership still makes other states worse off; I cannot determine on theoretical grounds whether it is better to have one leader than two. Having a second leader does not affect the central claims of this chapter—that leadership hurts and that the United States shifted costs onto others.

Still, the sequential-leadership game suggests that having two leaders, one moving after the other, is worse than having one. Like the other hegemonic claims, this one rests on a counterfactual that is hard to test directly; moreover, there are no secondary results that might let me distinguish it quantitatively from the other Stackelberg equilibria in this model. Still, toward the end of this chapter I will examine the position of the United Kingdom and ask whether some of the difficulties of the period can be traced to the presence of two leaders. Having a second leader would only be anomalous for the theory if the

United Kingdom was able to counteract the ill effects of American leadership and make the international system better off than it would have been without any leaders. As I will show, this clearly was not the case.

International Interdependence and Public Goods

A second assumption of the model is that states contribute to international joint production in ways that approximate a public good. We can break these goods into three categories: trade, money, and finance.

Trade is not, of course, a public good. But a trading regime can be. The institutional framework for trade policy has some characteristics of a public good. For example, a country could adhere to the most-favored-nation regime (MFN) by signing treaties with other countries granting one another MFN. This means that a state benefits if its partners negotiate tariff reductions with third parties in the future, as Alfred Marshall (cited in Gowa 1994: 91) explains: "nearly everyone who is trying to get any taxes on imports lowered on behalf of his own country is likely to be working for England's good under this clause, unless he gives himself a great deal of trouble to avoid it." These future concessions are, then, public goods. Moreover, by failing to negotiate one's own reciprocal treaties with these third parties, a state could free ride on the MFN regime. This is exactly what the United States did before 1934 by following its peculiar conditional interpretation of MFN clauses (Conybeare 1987).

The monetary regime also had some characteristics of a public good. The gold standard had collapsed during World War I as countries suspended gold payments or left the gold standard entirely. Rebuilding this regime would require that states take politically costly actions from which others would benefit (Simmons 1994). In addition, exchange-rate stability has near-public benefits for all traders in the economy, providing greater certainty, which states value (Lake 1988: 163–66). States could contribute to exchange-rate stability through open-market operations or interest-rate management.

One state's monetary adjustment also had externalities for others, generally negative. A country might seek to adjust by deflating its own economy, or it might devalue its currency or impose tariffs (see Simmons 1994 for full discussion). The last two choices imposed many of the costs of adjustment onto other states: tariffs harmed others' exports, as did devaluation or deflation.

Important financial issues in the period included reconstruction finance, such as loans to German municipalities or newly independent states for infrastructure development. While not a public good, this commercial activity had externalities in the form of demand stimulus and multiplication effects.

Changing government regulations concerning the issuance or ownership of foreign securities and other assets were common ways to influence the supply of such finance.

In sum, international trade, monetary, and financial policies all had important externalities. They sometimes entailed contributions to public or near-public goods. Though the model exaggerates these effects by assuming public goods, it does capture an important feature of the international political economy.

National Preferences

The final assumption of the model that I will examine is that states make trade-offs at the margin across internationalist and domestic goals. States value both, though (as the model assumes) they may weigh these two goods differently. At the margin, then, each state weighs the benefit of contributions to international public goods against the consumption of private goods. Economics aside, these different kinds of goods also brought very different political gains, and contributions to each entailed different political costs.

For this period, these trade-offs were couched in terms of a ubiquitous choice between internationalism and isolationism. Internationalists advocated greater contributions to internationalist goals and greater openness to the international economy. Isolationists favored fewer such contributions and wanted to use American resources to achieve domestic goals. In this respect, the United States furnishes a good example of a widespread conflict between domestic and international interests in modern political economy (Frieden 1988: 89–90).

The model's assumption that politicians consider trade-offs among these goals is thus isomorphic to assuming that politicians make trade-offs across the political support they can obtain from members of these coalitions. (See appendix A for a formal illustration of this claim.) Contributions to international public goods come at the cost of alienating isolationists, while private goods are policies that lose political support from internationalists. Given the politics of the time, a government could not fully satisfy both coalitions but had to make trade-offs across them at the margin.

Once we see this similarity between the model and the traditional coalitional arguments, the modeling strategy here may even enrich coalitional and interest-group theories. To say that two powerful groups fought over some policy and often reached a stalemate or compromise does not necessarily explain the details of that policy outcome. Because many compromise outcomes can be imagined, the domestic-group explanation cannot explain why the outcome of the conflicts between nationalists and internationalists converged around a predatory strategy, shifting the costs of collective-goods provision onto others and using moderate protection to maintain a trade surplus. However, the model here does make sense of the logic of cost shifting under Stackelberg leadership. Conversely, Stackelberg leadership does not address the way that cost shifting played out in domestic political debates. I turn in the next sections to the specific policy areas in which this cost shifting occurred.

Monetary Policies

Having looked at the assumptions of the model, I am now in a position to consider the theory's predictions for American leadership. Unlike the post–1945 policy, the United States did not attempt to create a postwar international monetary system after World War I. Instead, a de facto gold exchange standard emerged, especially after 1924–25 (see Feis 1950; Hogan 1987). In such a system, key currencies such as the dollar or pound sterling are backed by gold. Secondary currencies use these gold-backed currencies as their own reserves, with the result that foreign exchange comprised 45 percent of the reserves of the Continental European states by 1928, for example (Oye 1986c: 177). This gave the United States and United Kingdom seigneurage, the ability to obtain real goods in exchange for dollars that foreigners want to hold in reserve.

Predation is also evident in the American response to the disturbances of the reconstruction period. Having become a net creditor only during the war, the United States rapidly became the leading financial power in the world (see Frieden 1988). The United States ran a huge export surplus as other countries recovered from the war. Instead of lending this surplus back to foreigners in the long term, the United States demanded payment in either short-term liquid claims or in gold (Macmillan Report 1931: para. 247). As a result, American gold reserves more than tripled between 1914 and 1924, growing from 23 to 46 percent of the world total; most of this increase came from 1921 to 1924. The total increase exceeded $4 billion, which is greater than the world production of gold over this period (League of Nations 1944: 88–90). As foreigners exported gold, their economies deflated.

In a gold-exchange standard, the primary source of growth in international liquidity is the payment deficits of key-currency countries. The United States, however, tended to run a payments surplus and therefore attract inward flows of gold and foreign currency. Instead of using this gold to expand the domestic money supply, the Fed sterilized it, converting it into currency in the form of gold certificates or using the gold to liquidate domestic credit (Clarke 1967: 37; Peter Fearon 1987: 76–77; League of Nations 1944).

Sterilizing gold inflows violated the prewar gold-standard rules in that American money and prices did not rise to make American goods less attractive and thereby reduce the payments imbalance. The United States neutralized the inflow rather than using it to finance expansion out of a fear that much of this gold would leave when the European economy stabilized, contracting the American economy (League of Nations 1944: 73–74). Neutralizing the gold would keep the American domestic economy free from these external disturbances.

Unfortunately, insulating the American economy tended to magnify the disturbances elsewhere. European and other countries adjusted through a deflation sufficient to restore international balance (Macmillan Report 1931: para. 43). The prices of most agricultural products and many other raw materials declined precipitously beginning in 1926–27, contributing both to the crash of 1929 and to the subsequent banking crisis, at least for banks involved in agriculture (Kindleberger 1973: 83–107; Temin 1976: 1–3, 145–50).[3] This reflects a Stackelberg process in which the United States first made the decision to insulate its own economy from external disturbances, forcing followers to adjust in more costly ways. In this way, the American response to its new position reduced the rest of the world's welfare.

It is still true that the United States made some contributions to international liquidity growth, which makes sense if we keep in mind both the disproportionality result and the Stackelberg results from the model. By the disproportionality result, the largest states bear proportionately greater shares of the costs of providing international liquidity. This predicts large contributions from the United States, the United Kingdom, and France, in that order. However, the United States was able to reduce its share of these costs and raise the share borne by others. This action also thrust Britain into the leadership of a subgroup of the international economy, the sterling area, which I examine in a later section.

The American contribution to liquidity growth usually took the form of market-rate private finance. Europeans needed credits because the United States insisted that its former allies repay the debts incurred before American

---

3. Falkus (1971) has taken issue with this aspect of the standard indictment of American policy. He argues that U.S. imports were generally price inelastic, so the higher prices brought about by tariffs should have had relatively little effect on import volume. Even if correct, however, some of the cost of each tariff would still have been borne by foreign exporters, depressing their income; in short, even if exaggerated, "the basic problem still remains" (Aldcroft 1977: 261).

entry into the war (see Feis 1950; Kindleberger 1973: 34–42). The result was a vicious triangle, in which Britain and France used German reparations to repay war debts they owed the United States, while the Germans financed these reparations in large part with American loans (Frieden 1988: 75–78; Kindleberger 1973: 34–42). While benefiting in the short term, the U.S. policy imposed large costs on the international economy as a whole. When the stock-market speculation of 1928–29 dried up American funds for overseas lending, the house of cards collapsed (Clarke 1967: 147–48; Kindleberger 1973: 113–23; Macmillan Report 1931; McNeil 1986: chap. 8; for critiques of this argument, see Meyer 1970; Temin 1976: 151–60).

In general, these developments correspond well with the predictions of the theory. The United States minimized its contributions to the international monetary regime, forcing its costs onto others. At the same time, the theory is at too high a level of abstraction to explain the processes of predation in detail. For example, the theory does not predict a given war-debts regime or even that war debts will be an important issue. It merely predicts that, whatever the issue and whatever the regime, a predatory hegemon's policy will be such that it benefits unilaterally, imposes costs on others, and creates social costs. The precise mix of monetary policies is difficult to predict from an abstract theory, but the relative burdens imposed by the chosen policy mix and its social effects accord well with the theory.

American Trade Policy in the 1920s

As in monetary policy, American leadership led to welfare-reducing outcomes in trade policy. The model suggests that the United States would keep its domestic market relatively closed, expecting others to open theirs in response. This is exactly Conybeare's (1987: 234) interpretation of American policy:

> Keeping its own tariffs high, refusing to negotiate, but claiming the benefits of the MFN norm, the United States provided a good example of both free-riding and hegemonic predation: raising its own tariffs while attempting to lower (or at least benefit from the lowering of) foreign tariffs.

American tariffs in this period ranged between 10 and 20 percent of the value of all imports and were typically in the 13–16 percent range (see Lake 1988: 155, 194; Magee, Brock, and Young 1989: 326–27 for data). The duties of the 1922 Fordney-McCumber tariff marked a retreat from the more liberal prewar tariffs of 1913. Under the new tariff, the average duty on all imports increased from 8.8 to 13.9 percent, the average duty on dutiable imports rose from 26.8 to 38.2 percent, and the number of items on the free list shrank slightly from 67.5 to 63.5 percent of all imports (Lake 1988: 167).

American protectionism also had its deleterious effects on monetary policy. By making it more difficult to export to the United States, these tariffs fostered a dollar gap, helping to keep prices depressed throughout the decade even during boom periods. After the crisis of 1929, the even higher Smoot-Hawley tariff further depressed world trade and set off a spiral of retaliation (Peter Fearon 1987: 129; Kindleberger 1973: 172). These tariffs also made it difficult for foreign borrowers to earn dollars with which to repay war debts and postwar loans. This problem was especially severe for borrowers who relied on primary-products exports to the United States, such as Argentina, Brazil, Canada, Colombia, and Cuba (Peter Fearon 1987: 132).

Trade policy is also a good place to test the secondary implications of the model, since data are generally available. In each variation of the model in chapters 2 and 3, a country's contribution to the public good is a positive function of its own resources and a negative function of all other countries' resources. The measure of contributions that I will use here is import volume. As I discussed in chapter 2, import volume should be associated with a country's contributions to international openness.

With this measure, the hypothesis from the model is very counterintuitive, since it states that i's imports depend negatively on the GNP of foreign countries. This hypothesis runs directly counter to the intuition that large foreign GNPs should present greater trading opportunities, leading to greater exports and indirectly to imports. It also contradicts gravity models of international trade, in which bilateral trade between any two countries is positively related to the product of their GNPs and inversely related to the square of the distance between them, by analogy to Newton's law of gravity (Linnemann 1966; Pöyhönen 1963; Tinbergen 1962). Though these gravity models are poorly linked to economic theory, they are the best predictors of bilateral trade volume (Deardorff 1984).

Tables 1 and 2 show tests of the negative-reaction hypothesis for major trading countries—the United States, the United Kingdom, France, Germany, Canada, and Japan.[4] These are the major economic powers of the period aside from the isolationist Soviet Union, for which even the limited data available are suspect. While Japan and Canada were significantly smaller than the other

---

4. I show two significant digits for the estimated coefficients because most of the underlying data have two or three significant digits.

powers at this time, I include them because they were important trading partners for the United States. Data are only available for Germany from 1926 to
1938, so I report tests both with Germany over this shorter period and without
Germany from 1921 to 1938.

There is a steady decline in imports during this period because of the Great
Depression, so I include a control variable, *Year*. *Year* has a consistently negative effect, though it is never statistically significant at conventional levels. I
retain it because it has a consistent effect across specifications and because
including it improves the efficiency of the other estimates in the model.

Because there is serial correlation in the untransformed regressions, not
reported here, I use first differences of all variables except *Year*. While I could
choose several different ways to address this serial correlation, I prefer to use
first differences throughout this book. In the data here, using first differences

TABLE 1.   Imports as a Function of Foreign and Home Resources

	Dependent Variables				
	U.S. Imports	U.K. Imports	France Imports	Canada Imports	Japan Imports
Constant	54.	14.	23.	71.	49.
(in thousands)	(44.)	(13.)	(46.)	(46.)	(57.)
U.S. GNP	.099****	.014†††	.47††	−.041***	.045††
	(.012)	(.0037)	(.13)	(.013)	(.016)
U.K. GNP	.40	.44***	6.8	.57	−.046
	(.37)	(.11)	(3.9)	(.38)	(.48)
France GNP	−.0040*	.00024	.18****	.008†††	−.007**
	(.0026)	(.00078)	(.027)	(.003)	(.003)
Canada GNP	−.97***	−.22***	−7.0**	.75***	−.53*
	(.25)	(.076)	(.26)	(.26)	(.33)
Japan GNP	.15†	.011	−.350	−.26***	.26***
	(.07)	(.022)	(.77)	(.075)	(.096)
Year	−28.	−7.5	−120.	−36.	−25.
	(23.)	(6.9)	(240.)	(23.)	(30.)
N	18	18	18	18	18
(Years)	(1921–38)	(1921–38)	(1921–38)	(1921–38)	(1921–38)
F	23.3	15.2	27.8	5.2	3.2
Adjusted R^2	.89	.83	.91	.60	.64

Note: GNP data are in billions of national currency. All variables are first differences. Standard errors are
in parentheses. Data sources in appendix B.
    †$p < .10$, two-tailed; ††$p < .05$, two-tailed; †††$p < .01$, two-tailed; ††††$p < .001$, two-tailed.
    *$p < .10$, one-tailed; **$p < .05$, one-tailed; ***$p < .01$, one-tailed; ****$p < .001$, one-tailed.

not only solves the serial correlation problem but generally also eliminates the heteroskedacity found in most of the untransformed regressions using GNP data. First differences also transform nonstationary data series such as GNP or import volume into a series that is usually stationary measured by standard tests such as Dickey-Fuller or Augmented Dickey-Fuller. (First differences are also algebraically equivalent to a one-period lag model, a popular alternative.)

Finally, first differences have a natural substantive interpretation in that they capture the change in a variable from year to year in response to changes in other variables in the same year. This captures well the essence of the comparative statics method with which I derived the hypotheses in chapters 2 and 3. A comparative statics result shows how changing the parameters of a model

TABLE 2.   Imports as a Function of Foreign and Home Resources, with Germany

	Dependent Variables					
	U.S. Imports	U.K. Imports	France Imports	Canada Imports	Japan Imports	Germany Imports
Constant	120.	8.9	1100.	200.†	82.	650.
(in thousands)	(67.)	(14.)	(880.)	(97.)	(120.)	(270.)
U.S. GNP	.086***	.0090††	.58††	−.032	.048	.017
	(.016)	(.0034)	(.21)	(.023)	(.030)	(.065)
U.K. GNP	−1.0	.12	3.8	2.8	−1.4	7.4
	(1.2)	(.25)	(15.)	(1.7)	(2.1)	(4.7)
France GNP	−.0070**	−.0051	.16***	.0086†	−.011**	−.0056
	(.0024)	(.0052)	(.032)	(.0035)	(.004)	(.0098)
Canada GNP	−.37	−.0058	−8.8	.34	.20	−1.7
	(.60)	(.13)	(7.9)	(.87)	(1.1)	(2.4)
Japan GNP	.30	.031	.66	−.21*	.46**	.24
	(.081)	(.017)	(1.1)	(.12)	(.15)	(.33)
Germany GNP	−.0039	−.0035	.014	−.043*	−.038	.14**
	(.017)	(.0035)	(.22)	(.024)	(.030)	(.07)
Year	−63.	−4.6	−580.	−100.†	−42.	−340.†
	(35.9)	(7.4)	(450.)	(50.)	(64.)	(140.)
N	13	13	13	13	13	13
(Years)	(1926–38)	(1926–38)	(1926–38)	(1926–38)	(1926–38)	(1926–38)
F	14.9	8.9	16.2	5.0	2.7	8.3
Adjusted R^2	.89	.82	.90	.70	.49	.81

Note: GNP data are in billions of national currency. All variables are first differences. Standard errors are in parentheses. Data sources in appendix B.

†$p < .10$, two-tailed; ††$p < .05$, two-tailed; †††$p < .01$, two-tailed; ††††$p < .001$, two-tailed.

*$p < .10$, one-tailed; **$p < .05$, one-tailed; ***$p < .01$, one-tailed; ****$p < .001$, one-tailed.

produces a new equilibrium, without regard to the process involved. This is analogous to comparing snapshots of equilibria. Taking the first differences of a time series also compares annual snapshots of the data; unlike more complicated methods of time-series analysis, it does not attempt to model the process of change.[5]

The tables use a one-tailed test whenever the theory predicts a coefficient's sign, a two-tailed test otherwise. When the estimated coefficient has the wrong sign, I use a two-tailed test because a wrong sign is obviously not predicted by the theory; however, only one estimate crosses a significance threshold level by using this instead of a one-tailed test. If these tables represented a full-blown test of chapter 3's theory against a rival hypothesis such as gravity models,[6] the rival hypothesis obviously would be fully specified and I would use a one-tailed test for its predictions.

Not surprisingly, the proposition that a country's imports depend positively on its own resources receives strong confirmation: the estimates are always rightly signed and statistically significant at the $p < .001$ level over 1921–38. While the estimates are also rightly signed between 1926 and 1938, the t-ratios fall in this shorter and more turbulent period.

The second proposition, that a country's imports depend negatively on other countries' resources, receives less strong support. Among the estimates significant at the $p < .10$ level, eight are rightly signed and five wrongly signed in 1921–38; four are rightly signed and three wrongly signed in 1926–38. These results are mixed at best.

Looked at differently, however, the model's strongly counterintuitive hypothesis that one country's imports depend negatively on the resources of foreign countries still performs better than the strongly intuitive claim, consistent with gravity models of trade, that imports depend positively on the size of foreign markets. It is not surprising that the counterintuitive hypothesis receives mixed support: it is a wonder that it receives any support at all. After all, the model claims that American imports will decrease as the world's GNP increases and that American imports will increase as the world's GNP decreases. This seemingly ludicrous claim receives at least as much support as

5. Underlying the discussion in this paragraph is a concern for the operationalizing assumptions of a formal model and the way that these assumptions might weaken the link between model and empirical test. For a fuller discussion, applied to mathematical discourse between disciplines, see Pahre 1996b.

6. The theories are not precisely comparable. Gravity models estimate bilateral trade as a function of the product of GNPs divided by the square of distance, so it is conventional to use a logarithmic transformation of the gravity equation to obtain a linear model. This means that a test would use the logarithm of the GNPs instead of simply using GNPs as the model here.

the more intuitive rival hypothesis.[7] Moreover, the rival hypothesis tends to predict only the estimates on U.S. GNP. If we set aside the United States, the model's hypothesis outperforms the rival hypothesis among significant coefficients seven to two in 1921–38 and four to one in 1926–38. This success is striking.

Oddly enough, the U.S. anomaly disappears if we transform imports into openness, or imports divided by GNP. When we divide both sides of this equation by U.S. GNP, as I did in chapter 2, American openness depends negatively on the ratio of foreign GNP to U.S. GNP (see equation 2.6). Equation 2.6 also predicts a positive constant term, which comes from dividing U.S. GNP by itself.

Table 3 presents a test of these hypotheses, using the untransformed values of all variables because there do not seem to be any of the problems with serial correlation and heteroskedacity found in most of the other data in this book.[8] I show the tests with and without the control variable *Year;* curiously, including *Year* in 1926–38 creates a problem with serial correlation that is absent when *Year* is excluded. Of the statistically significant estimates, eight are rightly signed and only two wrongly signed. The results are especially good for the most important relationship, the ratio of U.K. GNP to U.S. GNP. The equation estimated for 1921–38 with the control variable *Year* yields good results for the United Kingdom, France, and Canada. However, the estimates for Japan are always wrongly signed.

The openness test is especially interesting because the formal model predicts a precise functional relationship between American GNP and openness. Instead of controlling for GNP on the assumption that wealthier countries are more likely to be open, American GNP enters the denominator of a series of ratios with other countries' GNPs. The formal model also predicts a positive constant term, which is indeed statistically significant in all four specifications.[9]

7. Two caveats are necessary, one for each theory. First, gravity models use other control variables such as population (Linnemann 1963) and, as noted in the previous footnote, are best tested with logarithmic transformations of the variables. Second, the negative relationship between one country's imports and foreigners' resources may or may not follow from the more elaborate models developed in chapters 5 and 7, in which a positive relationship is also possible. Because I include these other variables in these later chapters, they obtain stronger statistical results.

8. There is apparently a straightforward reason why these problems are not present here. GNP time series are usually nonstationary and serially correlated, contributing to both serial correlation and heteroskedacity. Using a ratio of two GNPs generally makes the time series stationary.

9. The estimated constant is different in the second and fourth equations than in the first and third because of the *Year* term, which takes only values from 1921 to 1938. I performed an F-test to see if the start value of *Year* accounted for the difference in constants, checking to see if $1921 \times Year$ −7.56 = constant for the second column, $1926 \times Year$ −9.23 = constant for the fourth column. These tests yielded F-values of 22.13 and 18.55, respectively, both of which are significant at $p <$ .001.

This significant constant is even more interesting when placed against the constant terms in tables 1 and 2, which are significant at exactly the frequency we would expect by chance. In those earlier regressions, the theory made no prediction about the sign of the constant term.

This evidence also presents an indirect test of the disproportionality hypothesis. U.S. openness increases as American GNP increases relative to foreign GNP. The theory here is even more persuasive when compared to traditional hegemonic theory. While hegemonic theorists agree with the model on the disproportionality hypothesis, most go further, arguing that the concentration of resources in a hegemon leads to a more open international economy. I argue that resource concentration per se should have no effect at all, by the nonconcentration result, and that hegemony should reduce openness.

TABLE 3.   GNP Ratios and U.S. Openness

	Predict	Dependent Variables			
		U.S. Openness	U.S. Openness	U.S. Openness	U.S. Openness
Constant	+	7.6****	210.****	9.2**	310.***
		(1.2)	(44.)	(3.2)	(73.)
U.K./U.S.	−	−64.****	−52.****	−59.**	−56.***
		(16.)	(11.)	(24.)	(13.)
France/U.S.	−	−0.50***	−0.27***	−0.21	−0.56*
		(0.13)	(0.10)	(0.56)	(0.32)
Canada/U.S.	−	17.	−30.*	−26.	0.32
		(21.)	(17.)	(99.)	(54.)
Japan/U.S.	−	2.6	7.3†††	1.0	14.†
		(3.3)	(2.3)	(16.)	(9.3)
Germany/U.S.	−			−0.18	−0.43
				(4.7)	(2.6)
Year	N/A		−0.10††††		−0.16†††
			(.023)		(0.038)
N		18	18	13	13
(Years)		(1921–38)	(1921–38)	(1926–38)	(1926–38)
Adjusted R^2		.80	.92	.69	.91
F		18.2	40.5	6.3	20.5
Durbin-Watson		1.37	1.99	1.49	2.65

Note: GNP data are in billions of national currency, so GNP ratios depend both on size and on currency values. Standard errors are in parentheses. Data sources in appendix B.

†$p < .10$, two-tailed; ††$p < .05$, two-tailed; †††$p < .01$, two-tailed; ††††$p < .001$, two-tailed.
*$p < .10$, one-tailed; **$p < .05$, one-tailed; ***$p < .01$, one-tailed; ****$p < .001$, one-tailed.

Table 4 shows a test of these contending claims, relating global trade to the American share of world GNP and the concentration of GNP among five large trading nations: the United States, United Kingdom, France, Canada, and Japan. The test does not support traditional theory. Neither of the two explanatory variables is statistically significant, and the key variable, U.S. relative size, is wrongly signed.

Table 4 also tests whether the hegemon's own policy is affected by how hegemonic it is, a common mainstream claim. According to the conventional wisdom, American imports should depend on the U.S. share of world GNP and on the degree of resource concentration in the system. Neither of these propositions receives any support when we look at hegemony among either five or six nations.

For reasons shared with mainstream theory, the disproportionality result tested in table 3 also implies relative decline of the leader. The United States did decline throughout this period, as shown in the simple regression in table 5. However, as figure 1 shows, most of this decline came during the Great Depression. Because the decline is so limited in time, we should not rely too much on the regressions in the table. Yet it is interesting that during the 1930s there was some American decline, which was temporarily reversed in the 1940s because the United States was spared most of the destruction of World War II. In con-

TABLE 4.   Hegemony and Global Trade: Tests of the Conventional Theory

	World Trade	U.S. Imports (in billion dollars)	
Constant	−0.72	−1.6	−1.9
	(6.2)	(3.1)	(2.7)
U.S. share of five-power GNP	−14.	11.	
	(30.)	(15.)	
Concentration among five	46.	−4.2	
	(50.)	(25.)	
U.S. share of six-power GNP			7.9
			(16.)
Concentration among six			2.5
			(28.)
N	19	19	14
Adjusted R^2	.16	.09	.14
F	1.5	1.9	2.1

Note: The five powers are the United States, United Kingdom, France, Canada, and Japan. The sixth is Germany, for which no data are available before 1926.

Data are first differences. Standard errors in parentheses. Data sources in appendix B.

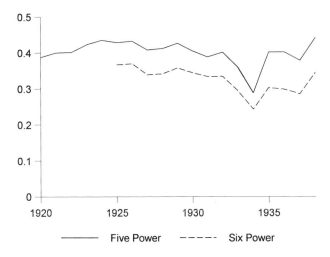

1. Hegemonic decline: U.S. share of great-power GNP

trast, the conventional wisdom dates American decline only to the 1960s and 1970s (see Gilpin 1981; Keohane 1980 inter alia).

Taken together, these tests provide significant support for the model and show that the theory performs substantially better than plausible alternatives. The data suggest that there was a negative relationship between American and foreign policies. Because the counterintuitive negative reaction functions are

TABLE 5.   Hegemonic Decline?

	Predict	U.S. Share of Five-Power GNP 1920–38	U.S. Share of Six-Power GNP 1926–38
Constant		9.7††	24.†††
		(4.5)	(6.2)
Year	—	−.0047**	−.012***
		(.0023)	(.0032)
N		19	13
Adjusted R^2		.16	.52
F		4.2	14.0

Note: The five powers are the United States, United Kingdom, France, Canada, and Japan. The sixth is Germany, for which no data are available before 1926. Standard errors in parentheses. Data sources in appendix B.

†$p < .10$, two-tailed; ††$p < .05$, two-tailed; †††$p < .01$, two-tailed; ††††$p < .001$, two-tailed.
*$p < .10$, one-tailed; **$p < .05$, one-tailed; ***$p < .01$, one-tailed; ****$p < .001$, one-tailed.

found in all the Cournot and Stackelberg models, the quantitative tests in this section do not provide a test of my claim that Stackelberg leadership reduces public-goods provision. However, because this claim depends on negative reaction functions, finding these negative reaction functions makes the main claim more plausible because of the logical tightness of a formal theory.

Furthermore, the theoretical argument that these policies produce Pareto-inferior results for the world economy certainly accords well with the conventional wisdom among historians, if not with many hegemony theorists.

The Role of the United Kingdom

One of the puzzles of the interwar period for the existing hegemony literature has been the presence of two large states. Lake (1988) argues that the 1920s had two near-leaders, neither powerful enough to lead the international system alone. Kindleberger's (1973) classic formulation was that the United Kingdom was willing to lead the international economy but lacked the ability to do so, while the United States was able but unwilling to lead. Such cases might suggest that we need a force-activation theory of hegemony (Keohane 1984) that relates a state's latent power to its mobilization of that power toward some end.

Chapter 3 calls some of these arguments into question. The theory suggests that having a hierarchy of leaders is very bad for the international economy, while having two leaders move simultaneously may not be any better or worse than having a single leader. Any of the leaders or near-leaders can shift costs onto the followers, though two identical leaders might constrain one another's cost shifting. In either case, the problem is not a surfeit of leaders but the existence of them.

There are no statistical tests that will let me distinguish which pattern of leadership best characterizes the period, since all the models make the same comparative statics prediction. However, qualitative evidence can help illuminate the causal mechanisms underlying these results. In particular, looking at Great Britain in the 1920s helps show how other potential leaders are unable to counteract the ill effects of American leadership and how they may also shift costs onto others. American policy thrust Britain into the leadership of a subgroup of the international economy, the sterling area (Kindleberger 1973: 63–64, 220; Shonfield 1976: 49–50). The members of the sterling area consisted of the Commonwealth and countries with which Britain had strong economic ties, such as Argentina, or traditional economic and security relationships (i.e., Greece, Iraq, Portugal, Scandinavia, and Thailand).

The United Kingdom ran a large and increasing trade deficit with the sterling area, providing liquidity for this subsystem (Oye 1986c: 176, 186–91;

Kindleberger 1973: 63–64). Since its position made Britain responsible for set-tling the balances of all sterling-area countries with all nonmember countries, Britain needed to hold gold reserves for contingencies in which it was not directly involved: a sudden change in the trade balance between Argentina and Brazil, for example, would be settled with reserves in London. More to the point, when primary-products producers in the sterling area suffered from a general fall in prices in the late 1920s, Britain had to pay some of the adjust-ment costs, though it was not a primary-goods producer.

Despite some costs, this leadership role had advantages for the United Kingdom. By forcing the British to play a large role, American policy helped maintain London as an important financial center (Clarke 1976: 72) . At the same time, having two financial centers had some social costs. Since there were two reserve centers, the system was more volatile (Aldcroft 1977: 166; League of Nations 1944). With two centers, small discount-rate differentials could eas-ily induce the movement of reserves from one center to the other, making each subject to disturbances from these movements. Each reserve center had to hold gold reserves against such eventualities, making this gold unavailable for back-ing other countries' currencies and restricting the degree of liquidity expansion possible from a given amount of gold, with deflationary effects on the system.

In these ways, British leadership interacted with American leadership to produce undesirable outcomes in monetary policy. The asymmetry between the United States and the United Kingdom suggests two leaders moving one after the other, where the American ability to shift costs constrains Britain's ability to shift costs onto the sterling area. Had British policy mimicked Amer-ican policy, it would have reduced trade with many of its most important trad-ing partners. Instead, Britain began giving them trade preferences, reducing access to its market for nonsterling countries.

We can identify both the costs and benefits of leadership to the United Kingdom. The evidence also suggests that having two leaders is detrimental for the international economy, though not necessarily any worse than having a single leader. Britain's efforts certainly could not counteract the ill effects of American leadership, which would be the only way two leaders would be better than one. These results are consistent with the theory, though its predictions are not sufficiently precise to test them more rigorously.

Alternative Explanations

Besides testing the theory against mainstream hegemonic theory, it is worth-while to compare the explanation of the 1920s here against other possible inter-pretations. This kind of comparison cannot falsify the theory here, but it does speak to the usefulness of the theory for understanding leadership of the international economy.

The mainstream interpretation of American policy among historians points out the contradictions between the policies desired by isolationists and internationalists. Building on these arguments, Jeffry Frieden (1988) argues that internationalist groups had rapidly grown in influence but were highly concentrated in banking and a few industries: most of the American economy remained relatively isolated from external events. A political deadlock (or compromise) resulted, with internationalists playing a greater role in banking policy and isolationists most influential in trade policy. J. P. Morgan and other American bankers cooperated with their British counterparts to manage international monetary relations with tacit support from the Federal Reserve and the state and treasury departments. Isolationists dominated Congress and thus tariff policy.

Reasonable as this sounds, we should question how internationalist American banking policy really was, since it tended to impose the costs of gold-exchange adjustment onto others. At the same time, such monetary cooperation as occurred in 1925–29 and again in 1936–39 falls outside the model in chapters 2 and 3 (but see chap. 7).

The standard account also faces a theoretical problem in that any argument about the power of domestic groups in different issue areas is essentially tautological—we know only that isolationists were more powerful over trade policy because trade policy was protectionist. Frieden (1988) attempts to solve this problem by studying trends in power relationships. Nonetheless, the facts that nationalists had more power before 1914 than they did later and that internationalists had more power after 1940 than they did earlier do not logically imply stalemate between the two groups from 1914 to 1940. This assertion still relies on circular reasoning.

Other explanations suggest that features of domestic political or economic institutions explain the American failure to lead. For instance, Kindleberger (1973) argues that imperfections in the American financial system played an important role in American policy. He argues that foreign lending to a new creditor tends to be procyclical, driven by domestic savings that are distributed among domestic and foreign investments in constant proportion. Foreign lending to a mature creditor is countercyclical, going abroad when faced with domestic depression and therefore aiding foreign recovery.

Going beyond the purely economic, Paul Kennedy (1987: 282) instead highlights a number of political imperfections:

the quite different structure of the American economy—less dependent upon foreign commerce and much less integrated into the world economy, protectionist-inclined (especially in agriculture) rather than free-trading, lacking a full equivalent to the Bank of England, fluctuating much more wildly in its booms and busts, with politicians much more directly influenced by domestic lobbies—meant that the international financial and commercial system revolved around a volatile and flawed central point.

Whatever their historiographic plausibility for the 1920s, the arguments about economic and political imperfections raise theoretical questions. Kennedy's description of the United States would hold as easily for the 1940s and 1950s as for the 1920s and 1930s, and parts of it still apply today. The same is true for Kindleberger's thesis. By relying on a relatively constant domestic structure, neither can explain variation in American foreign economic policies over a longer period of time. In particular, they would find it hard to account both for the evidence in this chapter and for the case of post–1945 leadership that I will discuss in chapter 10.

These forms of American exceptionalism might be useful in a cross-national study. Because differences in national preferences affect how bad leadership is for public-goods provision, any imperfections in the American political economy may have made American leadership worse than some other country's leadership. Unfortunately, this counterfactual is very difficult to test. In any case, the Stackelberg theory shows that any country's leadership would be bad for the rest of the world—as American policy was.

Conclusion

The interwar period has been anomalous for most previous theories of hegemonic leadership. In this chapter, I have argued that a theory of public-goods provision can explain much of the period. My alternative also makes a series of counterintuitive predictions about the world that are amenable to quantitative test.

While no longer anomalous, the period does raise a series of interesting questions and suggests areas where the theory would benefit from being fleshed out to provide more detailed predictions. For example, the theory works at a relatively high level of abstraction. The detailed processes of American predation in the 1920s are quite different from the processes in other periods, although the outcomes are broadly similar. Capturing some of these differences requires additional variables. The first of these is security relationships, to which I turn in the next chapter.

CHAPTER 5

Security Concerns and Foreign Economic Policy

Chapters 2 and 3 presented a simple model of international leadership and collective-goods provision. They showed that the central propositions of traditional hegemonic theory can no longer be sustained, a position supported by the evidence of chapter 4. Still, existing studies of some other periods suggest that the traditional arguments sometimes seem to work (e.g., Krasner 1976; Keohane 1979; Lake 1988). To account for these, this chapter uses a more complex model in which the predictions of benevolent hegemonic theory sometimes hold. Adding these variables is essential to find any circumstances in which hegemony will have beneficial effects on the international economy.

The earlier model leaves out some things that many scholars believe are central to international politics. For instance, Realists argue that each member of the system must look to guarantee its own existence because the international system lacks central authority. A state can best do so by acquiring military power. This relentless pursuit of security and thus power, they argue, has important implications for economic policy (see Grieco 1988, 1990; Waltz 1979).

Although usually classified as Realist because of its focus on state action, the theory of hegemonic stability has generally downplayed the effects of security considerations on economic strategies. Robert Keohane (1984: 137), echoing many others, argues that "it is justifiable to focus principally on the political economy without continually taking into account the politics of international security." Reintroducing security considerations into a revamped theory of hegemony calls Keohane's claim into question (see also Gowa 1989).

This chapter will draw on both neo-Realism and collective-goods theory, assuming that states worry not only about collective goods but also about their security. In the first section, I present a model capturing the trade-off between guns and butter in the presence of (exogenous) alliances. This develops the intuitions that are important when I bring this model into the collective-goods model in the next section. The third section compares the Stackelberg and Cournot-Nash equilibria to derive the conditions under which hegemony is malevolent or benevolent. Like the rest of part 2, the results in this chapter predict only state behavior in the absence of explicit bargaining between states, a subject addressed in part 3.

Military Spending and Security Relationships

Because they are concerned about their internal and external security, states receive some utility from spending on weapons. States also receive utility from spending on a wide range of other goods that we may lump together into a basket of private goods. Obviously, the more a state spends on one good, the less it can spend on the other. In other words, states allocate resources between military spending (g_i) and some other goods (m_i) subject to the resource constraint $B_i = g_i + m_i$. This parallels the trite distinction that states choose between guns and butter or power and plenty (Viner 1948; see also Katzenstein 1978). With two states, these assumptions give us the following utility functions, again using the Cobb-Douglas form:

$$U_i = g_i^{\alpha} m_i^{1-\alpha} \qquad B_i = g_i + m_i$$

$$U_j = g_j^{\beta} m_j^{1-\beta} \qquad B_j = g_j + m_j \tag{5.1}$$

These two states could be either friends or foes.[1] Friends will each receive some benefit from the other's military spending, as it might be available against external foes or internal threats (both of which are unmodeled here). I capture these security ties with a parameter, p. When they are friends, $p > 0$; when rivals, $p < 0$. Let the term pg_j show the benefit or cost to i associated with j's military spending, which is positive for friends, negative for foes, and sensitive to the strength of the relationship. I add pg_j to i's own military spending and add pg_i to g_j. Presumably, no state gets more utility from the military spending of a strong ally than it would receive from owning the weapons itself, so p will

---

1. One version of relative-gains theory assumes that even close allies such as the United States and members of the European Union are potential foes, so that no true friends exist (e.g., Grieco 1990). However, this position is exceptional. Most Realists allow for true alliances as long as they are directed at a common foe (e.g., Morgenthau 1978/1985; Waltz 1979). For an n-player model with both friends and rivals, see later in this chapter.

always be less than one. Negative p ranges symmetrically between zero and negative one, since nothing can be worse than knowing that all of an opponent's armaments are pointed at you alone.[2] This results in the following utility functions and resource constraints:

$$U_i = (g_i + pg_j)^\alpha m_i^{1-\alpha} \qquad B_i = g_i + m_i$$
$$U_j = (g_j + pg_i)^\beta m_j^{1-\beta} \qquad B_j = g_j + m_j \tag{5.2}$$

While plausible enough, this formalization of alliance relationships may differ from how Realists conceive of power and alliances. Because power is a relative term, many Realists think of it as implying a ratio form (i.e., g_i/g_j or ($g_i + pg_j)/(g_i + g_j)$), not a difference form as in equation 5.2. Still, both forms are plausible representations of relative power, since each makes power depend on both home and foreign spending. The ratio form is overly sensitive to small differences when the number of weapons is small; the difference form is probably oversensitive to small differences between two large forces (see Hirshleifer 1989). The ratio form also raises some computational problems, best seen in arms-race models (Caspary 1967; see also Luterbacher 1975; Rattinger 1976). Since either form is plausible, the simpler difference form is the proper choice for an initial model.

A second feature of these utility functions also deserves comment. If p were taken as the primary decision variable, the utility-maximizing choice is for each state to be a perfect ally of all other states (i.e., $p = 1$). This enables military spending to be reduced to very low levels.[3] This outcome obviously does not occur, notwithstanding the arguments of idealists in its favor. That this does not occur suggests that p must be at least partly exogenous. For simplicity, I will treat this relationship as fully exogenous.[4]

This simple model yields intuitive results. An alliance permits each state to

---

2. Because I do not model the price and effectiveness of a military, this conceptualization of p rules out cases in which allies might yield more bang for the buck than spending on one's own military. For example, suppose that one American soldier costs as much as ten foreign soldiers but is only as effective in combat as five of them. If every four foreign soldiers produces as much American security as a single American soldier, the United States may still be better off transferring cash directly to foreign governments to hire their own soldiers. Obviously, there are a few countries that receive such cash transfers, so the model does not capture an important feature of these alliances.

3. Some low level of military spending may still be necessary for internal security purposes, as contributions to collective security, or as insurance against the rise of an irrational expansionary power.

4. In this respect, the model is only a reduced-form equation for a larger game over security (see Powell 1991, 1993). The best way to judge the usefulness of these different assumptions is not (only) to build still bigger and fuller models but to test the observable implications of each.

rely in part on the other's military spending for its own security, freeing up resources for other purposes. Formally, I derive the following reaction functions:

$$m_i^* = (1 - \alpha)(B_i + pB_j) - p(1 - \alpha)m_j \qquad g_i^* = \alpha B_i - p(1 - \alpha)g_j$$
$$m_j^* = (1 - \beta)(B_j + pB_i) - p(1 - \beta)m_i \qquad g_j^* = \beta B_j - p(1 - \beta)g_i \qquad (5.3)$$

Among allies, both dg_i^*/dg_j and dg_j^*/dg_i are negative. An ally's spending on weapons is a partial substitute for a state's own spending; military spending increasingly becomes a public good among allies and, like all collective goods, is undersupplied. Where p is negative, dg_i^*/dg_j and dg_j^*/dg_i are positive, meaning that any additional military spending by either side will result in an increase by the other. In other words, the model includes a very simple arms-race result among opponents.[5] The same is true in reverse: among opponents, one state's forbearance of military spending in favor of butter will enable the other also to forgo such spending.[6]

These reaction functions tell only part of the story. The Cournot equilibrium levels are as follows (m_i^C, m_j^C may be found from $B_i - q_i^C$, etc.):

$$g_i^C = \frac{\alpha B_i - \beta p(1 - \alpha)B_j}{1 - p^2(1 - \alpha)(1 - \beta)}$$

$$g_j^C = \frac{\beta B_j - \alpha p(1 - \beta)B_i}{1 - p^2(1 - \alpha)(1 - \beta)} \qquad (5.4)$$

$$\frac{\partial g_i^C}{\partial B_j} = \frac{-\beta p(1 - \alpha)}{1 - p^2(1 - \alpha)(1 - \beta)}$$

$$\frac{\partial g_i}{\partial p} = \frac{(1 - \alpha)[2p(1 - \beta)B_i - \beta(1 + p^2(1 - \alpha)(1 - \beta)B_j]}{[1 - p^2(1 - \alpha)(1 - \beta)]^2}$$

---

5. Strictly speaking, this result is not an arms race, which would require a dynamic model (see Zinnes and Gillespie 1973). However, it is an arms race–like result.

6. While perfectly intuitive, this model has the advantage of capturing both the negative relationship between two allies' military spending and the positive relationship between two rivals' spending. Arms-race (Lewis Fry Richardson 1960; Zinnes and Gillespie 1973) or alliance-spending models (Murdoch and Sandler 1984; Olson and Zeckhauser 1966; Palmer 1990; Sandler 1977; Sandler and Forbes 1980) derive only one or the other.

Of course, the equilibrium outcomes continue to capture the arms-race result. It is also not surprising that spending on both guns and butter is an increasing function of a state's resources (cf. Gilpin 1981: 18–25).

Other more interesting implications also follow from the first derivatives, which show how these values change as the parameters change. First, alliances affect how a state's military spending depends on the other state's resources. The derivative $\partial g_i^c / \partial B_j$ is greater than zero among rivals ($p < 0$), but $\partial g_i^c / \partial B_j$ is less than zero among friends ($p > 0$). In other words, if the second state is an ally, a state spends less on defense as the ally grows larger (increasing B_j), because the ally will pick up an increasing share of collective defense. Conversely, if the other state is a foe, a state spends more on defense as the rival grows larger, since it poses an increasing threat. While both results are reasonable, they lie behind some more surprising results in the next section.

Less intuitive perhaps are some implications of the derivative dg_i/dp. It is negative for all p from -1 to 0. In other words, among opponents, increasing animosity (decreasing p; i.e., increasing $|p|$ where $p < 0$) leads to increased military spending by each state. This is not surprising. Even so, the converse is not necessarily true. Where $p > 0$, the sign of the derivative depends on the parameters and the distribution of resources among the two states.[7] Increasing degrees of friendship (increasing p) will decrease the total military spending by the two friends, but this aggregate may hide an increase by one ally and a decrease by the other.

I can also find the Stackelberg equilibrium to see how leadership affects these choices:

$$m_i^S = (1 - \alpha) B_i + \frac{(1 - \alpha)\beta p}{1 - p^2(1 - \beta)} B_j$$

$$m_i^C = \frac{(1 - \alpha)[1 - p^2(1 - \beta)] B_i + \beta p(1 - \alpha) B_j}{1 - p^2(1 - \alpha)(1 - \beta)} \tag{5.5}$$

$$\frac{\partial m_i^S}{\partial p} = \frac{2\beta p^2(1 - \alpha)(1 - \beta)}{[1 - p^2(1 - \beta)]^2} B_j$$

---

7. Specifically, $\partial g_i / \partial p < 0$ for $p > 0$ iff $B_i/B_j < \beta[1 + p(1 - \alpha)(1 - \beta)]/2p(1 - \beta)$. This will not be satisfied if B_i is sufficiently large. In other words, it is possible for a sufficiently large state to increase its military spending as an alliance grows tighter. This dynamic may underlie American concern about burden sharing in NATO.

$$m_j^S = \alpha p(1-\beta)B_i + \frac{1-\beta p(1-\alpha)}{1-p^2(1-\beta)}\, B_j$$

The effect of Stackelberg leadership depends on the parameters of the model. Comparison of these values with the Cournot values shows that $m_i^S >$ m_i^C and $g_i^S < g_i^C$ if and only if $B_i/B_j > -\alpha\beta p/[1 - p^2(1-\beta)]$. This is always true among friends ($p > 0$), which means that a Stackelberg leader can always push the costs of defense onto its ally. As military spending becomes a partly public good, the Stackelberg leader can force others to pay more of the costs of collective defense. The logic is the same as in the public-goods model of chapter 2.

If $p < 0$, this condition may or may not hold, depending the ratio of resources (B_i/B_j), which makes up its left-hand side. The condition holds, and thus a leader can reduce its military spending, if B_i is sufficiently larger than B_j. A sufficiently large Stackelberg leader can reduce its military spending and increase spending on other goods, while a small leader cannot.[8] A large Stackelberg leader will pursue an economically based strategy at the expense of military expenditures, consistent with the theory of hegemonic stability. A similar result will follow when I consider public goods in the next section.

In short, the guns-and-butter model yields several generally intuitive results. Taken by itself it is not useful for explaining leadership of the international economy, but it provides the foundation for the next variation of the model. In addition, the intuitions behind the results are clearer in this simple model, making it easier to see how the results of the next section follow from a more elaborate model.

Distinguishing Economic Policies

Realists would argue that security considerations of the sort analyzed in the previous section must influence the problem of collective-goods provision. For example, the Realist literature on relative gains maintains that allies are more likely to trade than nonallies and that military rivals are less likely to trade (Gowa 1989, 1994; Gowa and Mansfield 1993; Grieco 1988, 1990; cf. Pollins 1989). To bring this into the model, I distinguish private and public goods within the basket of nonmilitary goods. Again, the public good may be thought of as a proxy for openness and free trade, the private good as production for

---

8. The follower may or may not reduce its military spending as well; the conditions for $m_j^S < m_j^C$ are too complex to say more than this.

domestic consumption. The budget constraint is analogous to a macroeconomic allocation problem.

Returning to the earlier notation for private and public goods and adding them to the security game yields the following utility function for i:

$$U_i = (g_i + pg_j)^\alpha m_i^{\alpha'} Q^{1-\alpha-\alpha'} \quad \text{subject to } B_i = g_i + m_i + q_i \quad (5.6)$$

To analyze the effects of security policy on openness, this is unnecessarily complex. The private goods in m_i are just a residual category, so I may exclude them for computational simplicity without any theoretically relevant effects. (See notes 10, 12, and 13 for how this affects the model's robustness.) Excluding m_i means that I must redefine the budget constraint, so define a new $B_i' = B_i - m_i = q_i + g_i$. Having eliminated m_i, there is no reason to weight Q by the exponent $(1 - \alpha - \alpha')$, so I monotonically transform the old α and $(1 - \alpha - \alpha')$ into a new α and $(1 - \alpha)$. These simplifications yield the following streamlined utility function:

$$U_i = (g_i + pg_j)^\alpha Q^{1-\alpha} \quad \text{with } m_i = \text{constant}$$
$$g_i + q_i = B_i' \ (= B_i - m_i) \quad (5.7)$$

For simpler notation, let $B_i' = B_i$ from this point on. This equation produces the following reaction functions:

$$q_i^* = (1 - \alpha)(B_i + pB_j) + (\alpha p - \alpha - p)q_j$$
$$q_j^* = (1 - \beta)(B_j + pB_i) + (\beta p - \beta - p)q_i$$
$$g_i^* = \alpha(B_i + B_j) + (\alpha p - \alpha - p)g_j \quad (5.8)$$
$$g_j^* = \beta(B_i + B_j) + (\beta p - \beta - p)g_i$$

These reaction functions yield some interesting results. Among friends or allies ($p > 0$), dq_i^*/dq_j and dq_j^*/dq_i are negative. This means that if one state increases its contributions to the public good, the other will decrease its contributions.[9] This is the same result as in the simple collective-goods model of chapters 2 and 3, tested in chapter 4. Since the Western powers and Japan analyzed in chapter 4 were generally on friendly terms with the United States in the 1920s or even longer, the hypotheses tested there would be largely unchanged if I had substituted this more complex model.

9. Or, with q as a proxy for openness in trade, one country's tariff reductions will prompt its friends to raise their tariffs. To see the same result in a theory of tariffs proper, see appendix A.

Among nonfriends, $dq_i/dq_j > 0$ when $p < -\alpha /(1 - \alpha)$.[10] Here, one state's openness leads others to respond in kind. The intuition behind this result stems from the intuition from the guns-and-butter game in the previous section. Because states allocate resources between g_i and q_i subject to a fixed constraint, whenever military spending in the two states is positively correlated, openness will also be positively correlated; whenever military spending is negatively correlated, openness will be, too. As in the guns-and-butter game, among allies ($p > 0$), it is true that $dg_i*/dg_j < 0$; that is, military spending becomes a collective good and the spending of one state is a partial substitute for the spending of the other. Among opponents, this derivative may be either positive or negative; again it is negative where $p < -\alpha/(1 - \alpha)$. A positive dg_i*/dg_j suggests an arms race, where one state's increases are at least partially met by the other.[11]

Since these parameters are unobservable, it may be difficult to operationalize this condition. Still, we may approach the problem indirectly. If α and β are approximately 0.05—suggesting preferences for defense spending near 5 percent of GDP before adding reactions to others' spending—then p need only be less than -0.053 for the derivative to be negative. Since this figure would suggest that i receives disutility from only 5 percent of j's military spending, a low figure for major powers, we may presume that for great powers $dq_i/dq_j < 0$.[12]

---

10. If I had not dropped m_i and m_j for simplicity, the cut point for p would depend on a much messier term, but the basic logic of the model is unchanged. The residual category m_i attracts resources from Q and g_i, depending on α and α', but the term $(g_i + pg_j)$ still drives the changing sign on $\partial g_i/\partial q_j*$.

11. Because $p \geq -1$ by assumption, it also follows that a necessary but not sufficient condition for arms races is that $\alpha < 0.5$. This condition is apparently always met, even in wartime, as $\alpha > 0.5$ would show a state preference for spending more than half of GDP on the military (before taking threats or alliances into account). Such cases are rare, but many states reached this level in World War II (Milward 1979). Still, in these cases external threats were very important, so spending half of GDP on the military does not necessarily imply a preference for spending that much without taking other states' spending into account.

12. Limiting the comparison of α and β to military spending relative to international trade imposes slightly more restrictive requirements. First, take the observed allocations as approximately equal to the underlying preferences. With observed military preferences at 3–7 percent of GNP, and typical levels of international trade at 20–50 percent of GNP, then α and β (allocations to military compared to open sector) will be between 0.06 and 0.33. Thus, the required level of p might be as high as -0.064 or as low as -0.5. The typical range would be -0.1 to -0.2, which are still low figures for great powers. In a world in which states have more nonfriends than friends, observed military spending will be higher than the underlying preferences (weighting parameters α, β). For $\alpha = .01$ and trade at 30 percent of GDP, for example, $p \approx -.035$ is sufficiently hostile for benevolent hegemony to occur. This makes even more useful the rule of thumb that all negative p are less than $-\alpha/(1 - \alpha)$.

Solving for the Cournot equilibrium value of Q^C and its derivative with respect to p yields:

$$q_i^C = \frac{[(1-\alpha) - \alpha p(1-\beta) - p^2(1-\alpha)(1-\beta)]B_i + [\beta p(1-\alpha) - \alpha(1-\beta)]B_j}{(1-p)[p(1-\alpha)(1-\beta) + (1-\alpha\beta)]}$$

$$g_i^C = \frac{[\alpha(1-\beta) - \beta p(1-\alpha)](B_i + B_j)}{(1-p)[p(1-\alpha)(1-\beta) + (1-\alpha\beta)]} \tag{5.9}$$

q_j^C and g_j^C are symmetrical (substitute α for β, B_i for B_j, and vice versa)

$$Q^C = (B_i + B_j) \frac{(1+p)(1-\alpha)(1-\beta)}{p(1-\alpha)(1-\beta) + (1-\alpha\beta)}$$

$$\frac{\partial Q^C}{\partial p} = (B_i + B_j) \frac{(1-\alpha)(1-\beta)(\alpha+\beta-2\alpha\beta)}{p(1-\alpha)(1-\beta) + (1-\alpha\beta)}$$

Yet again, and in contrast to hegemonic-stability theory, redistribution of the total $(B_i + B_j)$ does not change the aggregate supply of the public good. The intuition is unchanged in that aggregate supply depends on aggregate resources.

The new variable, p, does matter. Its role appears in the derivative, which is positive for all p between -1 and 1. Not surprisingly, increasing the strength of an alliance will increase the amount of a public good supplied. Similarly, increasing degrees of animosity (that is, decreasing p) will decrease the amount of the public good.

This result parallels the common claim that alliance politics affects economic strategy (e.g. Gowa 1989, 1994; Gowa and Mansfield 1993; Pollins 1989). It is reasonable to suppose that a state is more likely to contribute to a collective good from which its allies benefit. This would increase the allies' effective resources and therefore raise their military spending, increasing the first state's security. In this model, contributions to a public good do not directly increase the allies' resources, but the same effect occurs indirectly, by freeing up part of the other state's budget for military spending.[13]

---

13. This indirect effect parallels David Baldwin's (1985: 214–24) critique of the "strategic materials fallacy." One cannot separate trade in "strategic" materials from general trade because money is fungible.

The disproportionality result continues to hold. Notice that g_i^C is a function of the sum $(B_i + B_j)$, so that it remains constant for any redistribution of resources among the two countries. Since $g_i = B_i - q_i$, for any $dB_i = -dB_j$, constant g_i implies $dq_i = dB_i$. This may easily be verified in the solution for q_i in equation 5.8. Thus, $(q_i + dq_i)/(q_j - dq_i)$ will continue to change more rapidly than $(B_i + dB_i)/(B_j - dB_i)$. Because the disproportionality result continues to hold, we should observe hegemonic decline whether the hegemon faces friends or adversaries.

Is Hegemony Malevolent or Benevolent?

I can also explore hegemonic leadership in this model by comparing the Stackelberg and the Cournot equilibria. Solving for the Stackelberg value of Q and the derivative dQ^S/dp gives the following:

$$q_i^S = \frac{(1 - \alpha - \alpha p - p^2 + \beta p^2)B_i + (\beta p - \alpha - \alpha p)B_j}{(1 - p)(1 + p - \beta p)}$$

$$Q^S = \frac{(1 - \alpha)(1 - \beta)(1 + p)(B_i + B_j)}{(1 + p - \beta p)} \tag{5.10}$$

$$q_j^S = \frac{[\beta(1 - \alpha) + \alpha p^2(1 - \beta) + \alpha p]B_i + [(1 - p)(1 + \alpha\beta) + \alpha p - \beta]B_j}{(1 - p)(1 + p - \beta p)}$$

$$\frac{\partial Q^S}{\partial p} = \frac{\beta(1 - \alpha)(1 - \beta)(B_i + B_j)}{(1 + p - \beta p)^2}$$

Hegemony improves on the Cournot level of Q only when $p < -\beta/(1 - \beta)$. This condition parallels the break point for a negative or positive relationship between the two countries' openness (or military spending). Indeed, the condition implies that whenever the followers' allocations are positively related to the leader's allocations, hegemony is benevolent. If the follower's allocations are negatively related to the leader's, then the leader reduces spending on public goods, forcing the follower to increase its contributions.

The intuition in this model is that a hegemon will increase its own military spending within an alliance, forcing the costs of nonmilitary collective goods onto its allies. Among foes, conversely, high levels of military spending can always be topped by the rival, moving second; thus, a leader's attempts to force the costs of public goods onto an opponent backfire by stimulating an arms race. Knowing this, the hegemon exhibits military restraint, and collective goods are better supplied.

What drives the result is the fact that I model two (quasi-)public goods. The variable Q is a pure public good, while military spending is a mixed good in which some of an ally's spending contributes to a state's own defense. Chapter 3 showed that a leader can force the costs of collective-goods provision onto others. Here, the leader chooses whether to force the cost of pure public goods or military spending onto the ally. It is better off forcing the ally to pay for the more-public good than the less-public good.[14] The logic would hold even if I modeled both as mixed goods, as long as $Q = f_1(q_i, q_j)$ is more public than $G = f_2(g_i, g_j)$.

This is a reasonable assumption. Countries find it much easier to exclude countries from the group defense they provide than to exclude them from the benefits provided by international infrastructure and regimes. To take an extreme example, communist Cuba benefits from a stable dollar despite the American embargo because this money stability eases third-party purchase of Cuban exports. In contrast, during the Cold War an economically friendly Sweden could easily be excluded from NATO's collective defense in the event of a Soviet attack.

Because benevolent hegemony requires that $p < -\beta/(1 - \beta)$, domestic preferences as captured by β influence the outcome. The parameter β is likely to be small, since it measures the weighting given to military spending before considering reactions to others. Given historical military spending, a value of $\beta = .05$ is probably high (see notes 11–12 for full discussion). This implies that benevolent hegemony requires only low levels of hostility (small $|p|$ where $p < 0$). I conclude, then, that in a two-state model, hegemony leads to less openness than nonhegemony when the two states are allies and more openness when the two states are diplomatic rivals (except for a very low degree of rivalry near zero). I consider the case of more than two states, some of which are allies and others rivals of the hegemon, in a later section.

The result has welfare implications as well. For any p, the Pareto-optimal level of collective goods is independent of whether the equilibrium is Cournot or Stackelberg. Therefore, when Stackelberg leadership reduces Q, the result is

---

14. Reintroducing the excluded m_i does not change the basic intuition: the leader forces its allies to shoulder a greater burden of both goods, but this effect is greater for the pure public good than for the mixed good of joint security. However, including m_i does make the algebra substantially messier.

less optimal than that produced by the Cournot; when Stackelberg leadership increases Q, the result is more optimal. It is in this sense, then, that I may talk of benevolent or malevolent hegemonic leadership.

Equations 5.10 also show that $\partial Q^S/\partial p > 0$ for all p. In the Stackelberg equilibrium as in the Cournot, allies are more likely to contribute to a collective good as their alliance grows tighter. Opponents are less likely to contribute to a collective good as their animosity becomes deeper. Both results are intuitively reasonable and are consistent with other theories of security externalities (e.g., Gowa 1989, 1993). However, Gowa does not analyze the strategic implications of strategic externalities, which increase the incentive for allies to free ride on one another.[15] With the assumption of Stackelberg leadership, which Gowa does not analyze, the hegemon is in an excellent position to free ride on its allies, yielding the result found here.

One point may risk confusion, especially when this result is extended to the multiplayer games of the real world (see later in this chapter). The result that $\partial Q^S/\partial p$ is positive means that allies are more likely to trade than foes, whereas the comparison between Q^S and Q^C implies that trade between a hegemon and its allies will be less than it would be if the hegemon were not a Stackelberg leader. There is no contradiction between these results, the first of which is a matter of comparative statics while the second depends on a counterfactual. Since the theory of hegemonic stability has implicitly relied on counterfactuals, this comparison of Cournot-Nash and Stackelberg equilibria should be relevant for applications of hegemony theory. However, the comparative statics result is useful as a hypothesis amenable to quantitative testing.

Finally, the cost-shifting, disproportionality, and alliance effects interact to produce some interesting changes in the leader's contributions to public goods near the threshold between having friends and having rivals. Knowing that followers decrease the contributions to public goods as security relations worsen (that is, $\partial q_f/\partial p > 0$), a leader losing allies faces several cross-pressures. First, the follower will decrease contributions to public goods because of the worsening security relations; so will the leader, but the leader also anticipates the follower's lost contributions and increases its own accordingly. When the follower changes from an ally to a rival, the leader will also switch from anticipating the positive externality of an ally's military spending to anticipating the negative externality of a rival's military spending. This means that the leader must anticipate different reactions by the follower to its own military spending, a negative reaction by an ally and a positive reaction by a rival. Reducing its

---

15. However, Gowa's (1994: 17–20) discussion of limit pricing suggests that the hegemon has a first-mover advantage. I am grateful to an anonymous reader for pointing this out.

own military spending as a former ally becomes a rival may make sense, because it induces a smaller military in the other state as the follower switches from friend to foe. The leader's reductions in military spending entail increased contributions to public goods.

The net result of these considerations is that losing allies may cause the leader to increase its spending on public goods. Having a formal model makes it possible to see these complex effects at work and to derive the unexpected result. First, I find the derivative $\partial q_i^S / \partial p$:

$$\frac{\partial q_i^S}{\partial p} = \frac{[(\beta - \alpha)(1 + p^2(1 - \beta)) - \alpha\beta](B_i + B_j) - 2p(2p - \alpha)(1 - \beta)B_i}{(1 - p)^2(1 + p - \beta p)^2} \quad (5.11)$$

The sign of $\partial q_i^S / \partial p$ depends on the numerator of equation 5.11 because the denominator is always greater than zero. The conditions under which the counterintuitive result holds (that is, $\partial q_i^S / \partial p < 0$) are complex but depend critically on a term $Z = (\beta - \alpha)(1 + p^2(1 - \beta)) - \alpha\beta]$. It will be true that $\partial q_i^S / \partial p < 0$ when $Z < B_i/(B_i + B_j)$ for $p > \alpha/2$, when $Z > B_i/(B_i + B_j)$ for $0 < p < \alpha/2$, and when $Z < B_i/(B_i + B_j)$ for $p < 0$. The term Z may be greater or less than zero because its sign depends mostly on the term $(\beta - \alpha)$, so it will certainly be true that sometimes $Z < B_i/(B_i + B_j)$.

This algebra means that as p moves down from $\alpha/2$ to zero and beyond, the sign of the derivative $\partial q_i^S / \partial p$ is likely to change. Included in this change is some range where $\partial q_i^S / \partial p < 0$—that is, where worsening security ties (decreasing p) cause an increase in the leader's contributions to public goods. Unfortunately, the relevant range depends not only on difficult-to-measure security ties but on the unobservable preferences captured by α.

For this reason, the result is best envisioned as an existence proof. In other words, it is possible that a leader will increase its contributions to public goods as it loses allies. This directly contradicts the claim of relative-gains theory that worsening security relations lead to less economic cooperation among all states.

Existence results are often difficult to test. However, this result has a simple observable implication. When a leader that is losing allies raises its contributions to public goods, the followers will decrease theirs.[16] This difference between the leader and follower responses should stand out in the evidence.

In summary, as security relations between the two states move from alliance through zero to a rivalry, I predict a dramatic shift in the leader's pol-

---

16. It must be true that $\partial q_j / \partial p > 0$ when $\partial q_i / \partial p > 0$ because $\partial Q / \partial p > 0$ and $Q = q_i + q_j$.

icy. This shift will include a period of increased contributions to public goods even as security relations worsen. Whenever this occurs, I predict also that the follower will reduce its contributions.

While fairly complex, this result has an important referent. Indeed, it is central to chapter 6, which examines how Britain's loss of allies in 1819–21 brought on its switch to a policy of free trade. Before looking at that period, however, I must examine whether a model of more than two states makes a qualitative difference for the results found in this section.

Hegemony in an *n*-Player Model

If the international system consisted of only two actors, I could stop with the results of the previous section. However, the system obviously has many states. In addition, an *n*-player model is much better poised to answer questions left hanging in the two-player model. For instance, if the two states are allied, are they allied against anyone? If not, why are they allied? While I will not model these alliance choices, instead treating p as exogenous, it is still desirable to use a version of the model in which I could model p endogenously.

In a general model, I need a new variable p_{ij} to capture the security relationship between any two states i, j. I also need more general weighting parameters for the two goods; let each i give military spending the weight α_i and collective goods the weight $(1 - \alpha_i)$. This now means that each state has the following utility function and constraint:

$$U_i = (g_i + \Sigma p_{ij} g_j)^{\alpha_i} (q_i + \Sigma q_j)^{1-\alpha_i} \qquad (5.12)$$

$$B_i = g_i + q_i$$

Solving this is messy, since I would want to take into account a wide range of possible hierarchies of leadership, with multiple leaders, multiple followers, and/or a particular sequence of play for all states. However, I can prove some statements about how these equilibria will look. For states $i \neq j \neq k$, with i as Stackelberg leader, the reaction functions of i and any j are:

$$q_i^* = (1 - \alpha_i)(B_i + \sum_j^n p_{ij} B_j) + \sum_j^n (\alpha_i p_{ij} - \alpha_i - p_{ij}) q_j \qquad (5.13)$$

$$q_j^* = (1 - \alpha_j)(B_j + p_{ij} B_i + \sum_k^n p_{jk} B_k) + \sum_k^n (\alpha_j p_{jk} - \alpha_j - p_{jk}) q_k + (\alpha_j p_{ij} - \alpha_j - p_{ij}) q_i$$

In all of the models so far, whether hegemony is benevolent or malevolent depends on the follower's reaction function $\partial q_j/\partial q_i$.[17] Where $\partial q_j/\partial q_i > 0$, the followers increase their contributions to public goods after the leader increases its own; anticipating this, the hegemon contributes more than in the Cournot-Nash. Conversely, where $\partial q_j/\partial q_i < 0$, the hegemon can reduce its contributions and expect the followers to respond by making up the difference. Equation 5.13 shows that hegemony is malevolent if, for each j, $p_{ij} > \alpha_j/(1 - \alpha_j)$. This exactly parallels the two-player game.

When $\partial q_j/\partial q_i < 0$ for some j but $\partial q_j/\partial q_i > 0$ for the others, then whether hegemony is benevolent overall depends on the average effect of all j on the hegemon—that is, on $\Sigma(\partial q_j/\partial q_i)$. It is easy to derive the condition that $\Sigma(\partial q_i/\partial q_j) < 0$ if $\Sigma p_{ij} > -\Sigma \alpha_j/(1 - \Sigma \alpha_j)$. This is the same condition as in the two-country case, except that I now compare sums on the left and right sides of the inequality. This is equivalent to comparing averages: if the average follower is a friend, then hegemony is malevolent, while if the average follower is sufficiently hostile, hegemony is benevolent.[18]

While this captures the most natural single-play solution, the *n*-player game is potentially different from the two-player game in yet another way. In particular, the followers might combine to thwart the hegemon's attempts to shift costs onto them. To analyze this, suppose that all of the followers can fully coordinate their strategies—that is, choose as if they were a single state maximizing the sum of their utility functions.[19] It seems reasonable that if hegemony is malevolent against a unified coalition of nonhegemonic states, then it will be malevolent when the followers move separately. The reaction function for the follower coalition is:

---

17. This is true not only in chapters 2 and 3 but also in the conditions for $\partial q_j/\partial q_i > 0$ and $Q^S > Q^C$ in this chapter, which are exactly the same. It also characterizes the trade model in appendix A. For that matter, the relationship is also found in oligopoly applications. When the choice variable is production, the leader raises and the follower reduces production. The outcome of this game with a negative reaction function is bad for the follower. When the choice variable is price, the follower matches the leader's price reductions, and this positive reaction function leads to an outcome that is good for the follower.

18. Perhaps surprisingly, this is an unweighted average. The relevant coefficient captures the hegemon's anticipated reaction to the follower's choices, converted into a common unit—the hegemon's contributions to the public good. Moreover, the followers' reactions to each other are already factored into the leader's calculations and affect only the distribution of contributions among the followers. Because this result only holds in interior solutions, very small states that make no contributions to public goods are irrelevant to this averaged diplomatic relations variable.

19. For simplicity, I solve only for the unweighted sum of their utilities.

$$\sum_{j}^{n} q_j^* = \sum_{j}^{n} B_j + \frac{[\sum_{j}^{n}(1 - \alpha_j) p_{ij} B_i + \sum_{j}^{n}(\alpha_j p_{ij} - \alpha_j - p_{ij}) q_i]}{\sum_{j}^{n}[1 + \alpha_j + \sum_{k}^{n} p_{jk}(1 - \alpha_k)]} \tag{5.14}$$

Here, hegemony is malevolent ($\sum(\partial q_j / \partial q_i) < 0$) if

$$\frac{\sum_{j}^{n}(\alpha_j p_{ij} - \alpha_j - p_{ij})}{\sum_{j}^{n}[1 - \alpha_j - \sum_{k}^{n} p_{jk}(1 - \alpha_k)]} \tag{5.15}$$

The sign of the numerator hinges on whether $\sum(\alpha_j p_{ij} - \alpha_j - p_{ij}) < 0$, and once again rearranges to the condition $\sum p_{ij} > -\sum \alpha_j / (1 - \sum \alpha_j)$. Once again, this exactly parallels the condition for the two-country case, and what matters is whether the condition holds for the average follower as long as the denominator is greater than zero. By forming a coalition, the followers can increase public-goods provision, but they cannot make malevolent hegemony benevolent.[20]

The only difference from the noncoalition case is the term in the denominator of equation 5.15, which may be negative if the followers are sufficiently hostile to each other (that is, $\sum p_{jk}(1 - \alpha_k) > (1 + \alpha_j)$ for many follower j). This case is uninteresting if the numerator is also negative, since this will make the left-hand side greater than zero so that equation 5.15 will not hold. When this happens, benevolent hegemony remains benevolent because the condition for benevolent hegemony, which also appears in the numerator of equation 5.15, holds. However, it is possible that the numerator is positive and the denominator negative, in which case the follower coalition could make malevolent hegemony benevolent. This happens only if the followers are, on average, allied to the leader (making the numerator positive) and yet the followers are mostly hostile to each other (making the denominator negative). The negative denominator is the more stringent condition, because the sum $\sum p_{jk}(1 - \alpha_k)$ must not only be less than zero but less than zero by at least the amount $(1 + \alpha_j)$. In other words, it is theoretically possible that a follower coalition could make a malevolent hegemon benevolent, but only if the followers are the leader's friends but one another's rivals. Balance-of-power logic, in which the enemy of one's enemy is one's friend and the friend of one's enemy an enemy, makes this condition unlikely to hold.

Summarizing this line of argument, I can safely say that if a hegemon is surrounded mostly by allies and friends, then hegemony will be malevolent.

---

20. There is one caution necessary. These equations compare hegemony and a coalition of followers against the case of nonhegemony and a coalition of followers. They do not compare hegemony with a follower coalition against the nonhegemonic noncoalition case.

Even if all its friends were to move as one, the hegemon will be able to shift the costs of public goods onto them. Conversely, if a hegemon is surrounded by nonfriends and enemies, fears of an even worse arms race will constrain the hegemon's military spending.[21] This military restraint leads to benevolent hegemony.

This analysis implies that hegemonic leadership improves welfare for the international system in periods of a classic balance-of-power system. A state in a balance-of-power system has "no permanent friends, only permanent interests," in Lord Palmerston's classic phrase (cited in Bourne 1970: 293). This implies that the average foreign state will not be friendly, which is the condition for benevolent hegemony.

Conversely, when the hegemon is part of an overly large coalition, or when it lacks foes more generally, leadership is malevolent. This was the case in the 1920s, when the United States was implicitly (and sometimes explicitly) friendly to most other countries. In other words, the case study in chapter 4 would not be fundamentally changed by the theory in this chapter.

Summary

The foregoing has developed a number of hypotheses, and it is useful to summarize the most important. First, leadership increases public-goods provision when foreigners are not friendly but decreases public-goods provision when foreign states are mostly friends and allies. This is true even if the follower states fully coordinate their strategies.

Second, the disproportionality result continues to hold. The larger the state, the more it contributes to public goods across any pattern of alliance relationships. For this reason, I should still observe hegemonic decline.

Third, the model is consistent with the common intuition that any pair of states will contribute more to public goods as they become increasingly tightly allied. At the same time, the model yields a counterintuitive hypothesis about how two allies react to one another. When allied, their contributions will be negatively correlated, as in the basic model. When not allied, two states' contributions to public goods will be positively correlated.

Fourth, Stackelberg leadership, the alliance reactions, and the disproportionality result combine to furnish the counterintuitive result that a leader may increase its contributions to public goods as it loses allies. When this occurs,

---

21. Recall, however, that it is still true that $\partial g_i/\partial g_j > 0$, which is the arms race–like result. Leadership does not end arms races, but a leader that anticipates them makes these arms races occur at a lower level of military spending than they otherwise would.

the followers will decrease their contributions to public goods, so this difficult-to-operationalize result has observable implications.

Testing these results requires finding a period with a dramatic change in the hegemon's security relationship with most other countries. The next chapter examines such a case.

CHAPTER 6

The Rise of Free Trade in Britain, 1815–1853

The most novel claim in chapter 5 concerns the effect of security relationships on hegemony. A hegemon is malevolent when allied with everyone, benevolent when allied with no one. A good test of this claim requires variation in security relationships. An ideal test would have a hegemon that is allied against everyone in the system at one point and allied with everyone at another. This minimizes the measurement problems associated with calculating the average security relationship between the hegemon and all followers and eliminates ambiguity in predicting malevolent or benevolent hegemony.

Something close to this case exists. Before the collapse of the anti-Napoleonic coalition in 1821, Great Britain was allied with virtually everyone else except France (and the United States). After 1821, Britain faced a still-hostile France, conflicts with the neo–Holy Alliance, and regional opponents such as Belgium and Spain (though with regional allies Portugal and the Netherlands).[1] I predict, then, a switch from malevolent to benevolent hegemony in 1821.

Changing security relations around the friend/rival threshold also produce dramatic changes in the leader's direction of policy. These changes occur when security relations move through a particular range from weak allies to weak rivals (that is, as p moves from $\alpha/2$ through zero). These shifts produce policy changes that include a counterintuitive increase in a leader's contributions to

---

1. Both here and in chapters 8 and 10, I prefer to make qualitative judgments about diplomatic relationships rather than to use one of several possible databases. When making these judgments, I use the codings in the COW data set on alliances as a starting point, and I usually use these codings unchanged in the quantitative tests. Some additional judgment is necessary, since this alliance data set does not allow us to distinguish nonallied friends from nonallied rivals; moreover, some alliances formally remain in effect even when the parties are openly hostile.

public goods as it loses allies. When this happens, the follower states will decrease their contributions to public goods. This qualitative difference between the leader's increase and the followers' decrease when the leader loses allies provides a striking test of the theory. This test has the further advantage that it does not require detailed quantitative data, which are generally unavailable around 1821.

Given the existing literature, this is a remarkably hard test for the theory. Neither the historiography nor the political science literature has attributed any policy switch in 1821 to security concerns, and much of the literature seems unaware of a switch at all. Instead, most historians and economists trace free trade in Great Britain to the domestic politics surrounding the repeal of the Corn Laws in 1846 (see Schonhardt-Bailey 1996 inter alia). The argument here points away from the Corn Laws and toward William Huskisson's reforms at the Board of Trade in the 1820s.

The case also shows how deductive theory can lead to a search for overlooked facts and provide new interpretations of history. This is very different from chapter 4, which followed one common line of mainstream research. Moreover, the qualitative evidence from the 1920s and early 1930s was a motivating force in developing the model, while the case examined in this chapter played no role at all in developing the theory. It reflects instead a Popperian approach to falsification: make strong claims and then try to falsify them by looking for the hardest possible test.

Because the argument departs significantly from the historiography, it is a long chapter. I examine the assumptions of the model, look at the evidence at the coarsest correlative level, search for causal mechanisms, and seek further implications of the theory for policy, such as the Navigation Acts or votes on the Corn Laws. Because the quantitative data are poor for this period, much of the argument rests on historical narrative. Finally, I will distinguish the argument in this chapter from the existing literature and consider alternative explanations of the same events. By relying on a variety of types of evidence, the argument is more plausible and the test of chapter 5's theory more impressive.

Britain as Stackelberg Leader

This section, like the two following it, examines the assumptions of the theory for Britain in the nineteenth century. Three assumptions are especially important: first, that Britain was a Stackelberg leader; second, that British politicians made trade-offs across three types of "goods"—security policy, foreign economic policy, and private goods; and third, that the diplomatic situation changed in the early 1820s such that Britain went from having more friends than opponents to having more opponents than friends. Taken together, these assumptions lead me to predict first malevolent hegemony (1815–21) and then benevolent hegemony (1822–53). I end the chapter in 1854, at the onset of the Crimean War, which inaugurated two decades of rapid change in European security relations (but see chap. 8).

British dominance was evident in commercial, financial, industrial, naval, and colonial affairs. It had the largest overseas empire, the largest navy, the largest and most rapidly growing manufacturing sector, and the leading financial sector. In short, it was "the only real world power at that time" (Kennedy 1976: 150). One sign of its unique position was that the Treaty of Chaumont (1814) imposed the same troop obligations on all four powers but included an added financial obligation for Britain.

Among common indicators of power, Britain ranks first in every measure but the number of army personnel. At its peak, Britain produced half the world's manufactured goods, half its iron, half its coal and lignite. On the consumption side, it bought half the world's raw cotton. Britain also overshadowed world trade and was responsible for one-fifth of the world's commerce, two-fifths of its trade in manufactures, and one-third of its merchant marine (Kennedy 1987: 151). With a little hyperbole, Charles Villiers (in Schonhardt-Bailey 1996: 24) noted in 1838 that

At the close of the [Napoleonic] war [in 1815] we had exclusive possession of all the markets in the world. We had the means of maintaining that possession.

Villiers continued that Britain had wasted its power by reverting to protectionism.

Britain's dominance affected everyone's conjectures. Scott James and David Lake (1989) have argued that participants in American tariff debates waited to see the result of Robert Peel's reforms in the 1840s before choosing their own tariffs. Moreover, informed British opinion knew that the United States was waiting for Britain to move first (see also Villiers in Schonhardt-Bailey 1996: 26). While we lack comparably systematic studies of other countries, most histories describe countries that follow English politics closely (see inter alia Dunham 1930; Henderson 1939; Ratcliffe 1978). In short, Britain acted as a Stackelberg leader.

British Utility Functions

The model assumes that states face a three-way trade-off across security goals, private goals, and openness and that they make choices while considering the choices that other states make. This may seem far-fetched, but there is some evidence that public figures thought this way. Part 1 of George Browning's (1834) influential review of Britain's domestic and financial condition consisted of a survey of French, Russian, Austrian, and Prussian foreign policy, fiscal policy, and commerce; Britain's external position provided an essential backdrop for his proposed reforms of the Poor Laws, the Corn Laws, the customs, and British banking policy. Browning (1834: 2) argued:

> The political, domestic, and financial condition of Great Britain is so essentially influenced by that of other nations, that we have deemed it necessary, *in limine*, to give a brief outline of the resources and politics of the four continental powers which, in connexion with Great Britain, preside over the destinies of Europe.

Modern historians echo this contemporary analysis (a good example is Kennedy 1987: chap. 4).

A concern with these trade-offs is also evident in contemporary Radical thought. Military spending takes resources away from commerce and is thus inimicable to free trade; conversely, friendly nations are in a position to reduce military spending and encourage mutual trade.[2] In the late 1850s, Richard Cobden even believed that increased naval estimates would be inconsistent with any trade treaty (see Dunham 1930: 50–51).

We also see a concern for these trade-offs in policymakers' analysis of particular events. For example, when authorizing Cobden to negotiate a trade treaty with Michel Chevalier in the 1850s, William Gladstone wanted "to increase trade and reduce the enormous establishments military and naval" (cited in Dunham 1930: 87). While this points only to the simple trade-off between openness and military spending, others saw the three-way trade-off that the model captures. French Foreign Minister Jean Gilbert Victor Fialin, duc de Persigny believed that if Britain opposed France in Italy in 1859, France would lack the fiscal resources to compensate domestic interests for any losses from the coming liberalization of Anglo-French trade. This substitution

---

2. Radicals also believed that commerce between nations induced greater friendship and thus allowed lower military spending, an argument that treats p as endogenous.

among military spending, external liberalization, and other private goods of value to a state is exactly captured in this model.

British leaders analyzed the situation in the same way, as we can see in Lord John Russell's paraphrase of Persigny in a letter to Gladstone:

> de Persigny had "said that if England should determine to give no support to France in Italy, France might have an Austrian war on her hands, and then she could not afford to pay the compensations to the protected interests, which had been promised in case of the abolition of prohibitions and reductions of duty—But, if England and France should be united in the affairs of Italy, no war need be feared, and the Commercial Treaty might go on." (cited in Dunham, 1930: 77)

Gladstone's response shows that he too thought in terms of the three-way trade-off that Russell and de Persigny saw: "If France were to be involved in war with Austria, it would be difficult for her to pay compensation to the classes affected by the coming changes" (cited in Dunham 1930: 77). This compensation is one of the private goods captured in the model.

Moving beyond anecdotal evidence, we can also ask whether the available data reveal these trade-offs between military spending and openness. We should observe a negative correlation between openness and the share of military expenditures in British GNP. The results of such a test are presented in table 6, using first differences to correct for serial correlation. (There is no test of a trade-off between openness and private goods, since the only available measure would be GNP less openness.)

I find that there is indeed a statistically significant negative relationship between the percentage of U.K. GNP devoted to military spending and the share of imports in GNP. The effect is substantively smaller than the assumption of the model (16 percent versus 100 percent in the stripped-down model),

TABLE 6.   The Military-Openness Trade-off

	U.K. Openness
Constant	.330
U.K. military spending as percent of GNP	−0.16*
	(0.12)
R^2	.08

Note: Data are first differences. Data sources in appendix 2.
*$p < .10$, one-tailed test

but this difference is attributable to the simplifications discussed in chapter 5. For instance, the stripped-down model ignores trade-offs with nonmilitary private goods, exaggerating the extent of the trade-off between military spending and openness. The assumption that openness is a pure public good further exaggerates the trade-offs.

The modest substantive meaning of the empirical correlation reminds us that many contributions to international production are in fact goods with substantial externalities rather than pure public goods. Even so, it shows that there were trade-offs between military spending and free trade, as the model assumes. The qualitative evidence presented earlier in this section shows that decision makers were aware of these trade-offs.

Diplomatic Changes

The third major assumption of the model concerns security relations. First, the theory assumes that diplomatic relations (p) are exogenous while foreign economic policy is endogenous. Realists argue that security needs are more important to a state than are economic goals, so that changes in the first are more likely to affect economic policy than the other way around. Beyond this, diplomatic relationships are probably more changeable than commercial relationships because diplomacy is the result of policy choices while commerce depends in part on economic variables such as private investment and long-term commercial relationships outside the policymaker's control. French Foreign Minister de Persigny believed such to be the case during the prelude to the Cobden-Chevalier commercial treaty, when many diplomats anticipated an Anglo-French alliance in Italian affairs:

> si j'avais à choisir entre un traité secret d'alliance défensive et offensive et un traité de commerce, je préferérais le second, car les effets politiques du premier pourraient être annulés par un changement de Cabinet et non pas, ceux du second.[3] (cited in Dunham 1930: 77n)

This suggests that observing changeable security ties will provide more useful variation than changeable commerce.

To do so, of course, we should also understand the factors that determine security relationships. Some factors that also affect alignments in concrete

---

3. "If I must choose between a secret treaty of defensive and offensive alliance and a commercial treaty, I would prefer the latter, because the political effects of the former could be destroyed by a change of Cabinet, but not those of the second."

cases include geography (Morgenthau 1978/1985; Niou, Ordeshook, and Rose 1989), systemic polarity (Deutsch and Singer 1964; Kaplan 1957), systemic polarization (Rapkin and Thompson with Christopherson 1979), relative power (Waltz 1979), and responses to changes in some state's relations with some third power. Domestic politics also might affect alliances.

Realists argue that each state's primary goal is self-preservation and that each state will maximize its international power to achieve this end. In response, other states will combine to frustrate this expansion, both to maximize their own relative power and to prevent a dominant state from threatening the existence of all other states in the international system. With coalitions forming both for and against such aggrandizement, balances of power may occur (Niou, Ordeshook, and Rose 1989; Waltz 1979). However, the period after each global war has seen an imbalance, with a large victorious coalition and a vanquished would-be empire (Jervis 1986). The post-Napoleonic period is a good example. Having twice beaten back the French, the allies wanted to maintain a coalition against France, which they formalized in the Treaty of Chaumont (March 1814). As a result, Britain clearly had more friends than rivals at the end of the Napoleonic Wars.

Within this status quo alliance, however, there was ample room for great-power rivalry between Britain and Russia. Prussia and Austria were noticeably weaker than the two outside powers and looked to them for protection. Its geographic position gave Prussia little choice but to throw itself into the Russian camp. Austria was better able to oppose potential Russian expansion but found itself in a precarious geographic position. By giving Austria Italian territories such as Lombardy and Venetia, Robert Stewart, Viscount Castlereagh, the British foreign secretary, made Austria a bulwark against French expansion to the southeast. Austria also headed the new German confederation, where it could enlist Prussian help to contain France on the Rhine. However, these gains overstretched Austria, which would need continued support from allies such as Great Britain (see Bourne 1970; Bridge 1979; Kissinger 1957; Temperley 1925; Webster 1925).

As a result, there were two rival pairs within the Quadruple Alliance. Each side was willing to use French support against the other, and this double wooing sufficed to rehabilitate France as a great power by 1818, as part of the Concert of Europe (Bridge 1979). Though still excluded from the Quadruple Alliance, France participated in the concert, providing the last component of the five-power Vienna system.

At about the same time, the Italian revolutions of 1820 began to undermine the Austro-British alliance. Austria favored maintaining the status quo by whatever means, as when Prince Metternich suppressed the Italian revolts. Britain preferred to allow gradual change. The difference comes naturally from their power positions, because Austria was overextended, whereas Britain was rapidly growing in power. Thus, Britain was likely to gain from moderate change in the status quo, while the Austrians were not (Kissinger 1957: 5, 318). Looking elsewhere for friends, Metternich turned to Russian support for his intervention in Italy, beginning a relationship that grew closer over the next few years.

These two changes in the postwar coalition led to the Troppau Protocol of 1820, which created the Holy Alliance of the reactionary monarchies of Austria, Prussia, and Russia. Though neither would join the Holy Alliance, an alliance between England and France was still out of the question. In addition to French revisionism, the memory of Napoleon was too near and naval and colonial rivalries too strong for an alliance. For instance, Britain opposed the 1823 French invasion of Spain, which was carried out with Russian support. At the same time, Britain and France could work together in solving the crisis over Belgian independence in the early 1830s or over the Iberian peninsula (see Temperley 1925).

In part because of Troppau, Britain formally pulled out of the concert after the Verona Congress (December 1822). Still, this action did not lead to a polarized conflict between Britain and the Holy Alliance, and future coalitions shifted depending on the issue. Even after the July Revolution in France and the appointment of a reformist Whig government in England, Europe was hardly divided between eastern autocracies and a western liberal entente. Whig Prime Minister William Lamb, the second Viscount Melbourne (in office 1834, 1835–41), saw no reason to support liberals and progressives abroad, arguing that "All these chambers and free presses in other countries are very fine things, but depend upon it they are still as hostile to England as the old governments" (cited in Cecil 1954: 264). Even Lord Palmerston, the outspokenly liberal foreign secretary, was just as committed to the containment of France as his Tory predecessors had been. He believed that containment of liberal France and preservation of the continental balance were more important than the ties of liberalism across the English Channel (Bullen 1974).

In sum, the British diplomatic position had evolved from being the leader of a four-power alliance to being a nation concerned mostly with the balance of power on the Continent. It had no major allies in this endeavor, and it faced a loose opposing alliance in the East and an intermittent rivalry with France in the West. The system remained flexible, as attested by Palmerston's famous 1848 statement in the House of Commons, "We have no eternal allies, and we have no perpetual enemies. Our interests are eternal and perpetual, and those interests it is our duty to follow" (cited in Bourne 1970: 293).

This brief summary of diplomatic history lets me determine the relevant values of the diplomatic variables in the model. As long as the Quadruple Alliance was tolerably unified against France, Britain, the hegemon, had more allies than rivals. As the alliance broke up, and especially after Austria switched sides from Britain to the Holy Alliance, Britain had more rivals than foes. I expect malevolent leadership in the first period, benevolent leadership in the second. In the transition, chapter 5 showed that a leader losing allies may dramatically change its policy direction and increase its contributions to public goods even as it loses allies. When this happens, other states will respond by decreasing their own contributions.

Trends in Tariffs and Trade

To begin, let me review the pattern of British tariffs in the first half of the nineteenth century. The data are shown in figure 2; because of the obvious effects of tariffs on the level of trade, these figures are also shown, in figure 3. Tariffs reached a peak of 64 percent in 1822 (Imlah 1958). From 1826 onward, tariffs moved steadily downward, with the exception of a minor uptick in the early 1840s. The theory predicts exactly this change of policy direction in the early 1820s.

Trade follows a similar pattern. Since tariffs have a direct effect on imports, import volume moves with tariffs, decreasing into the early 1820s, increasing from 1826 (again with a minor downswing in the early 1840s). The effect of tariffs on exports is indirect, so there is a slight lag before they, too, move in line with tariffs and with imports (see fig. 3).

No period stands out as making the most rapid liberalization. Figure 2 shows that tariffs decrease between 5 and 10 percent in each five-year period, 1–2 percent a year. Notwithstanding the prominence of the Corn Laws in the historiography, their repeal in 1846 does not appear to be more important than any of the other reforms. Including corn has the effect of magnifying the trends in both directions, but protection of corn and of other items always move together.

The picture changes only slightly if I compare the nominal fiscal effects of liberalization under William Huskisson in the 1820s and Robert Peel in the 1840s. Peel's 1841 budget included revenue reductions of £1.3 million, a little less than what Huskisson had proposed in 1824; Peel's 1845 budget reduced the raw cotton duty by £3.3 million (Fay 1951: 122–23). Taken as a whole, then,

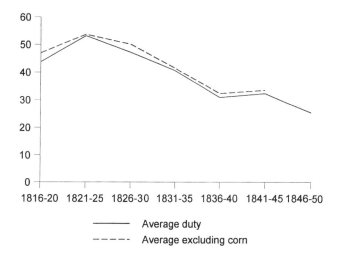

2. Tariffs in nineteenth-century Britain. (Five-year averages as percentage of import volume.)

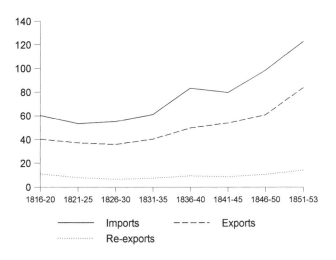

3. British trade volumes. (Five-year averages, millions of pounds.)

Peel's reforms had a greater effect than Huskisson's. Each exceeded the Whigs' reforms in the 1830s; for instance, Poulett Thompson's liberalizations in 1832 entailed a revenue loss of about £110,000, and his reductions in 1831, 1833, 1835, and 1836 were comparable.

As these data show, the only period with a qualitative change in policy is that of Huskisson's reforms in the mid–1820s. At that time, the government succeeded in halting and then reversing the postwar trend toward higher tariffs. While the entire period from 1815 to 1854 is of interest, this critical time from 1822 to 1827 warrants the greatest attention. As Britain lost allies, it switched its policy dramatically from protectionism to freer trade.

Economic Strategies, 1815–27

Having documented when the real change in tariff and trade outcomes occurred, the next task is to find out whether I can attribute it to conscious policy choices. The model predicts predatory hegemony between 1815 and 1821, benevolent hegemony thereafter. This section considers economic strategies over 1815–27, straddling this predicted change. Though Tories controlled the government throughout, these years saw remarkable change in economic policy. Beyond providing qualitative evidence for the theory, the history also helps illuminate some of the causal mechanisms at work.

With the end of war in 1815, Britain turned more protectionist, in part by choice and in part through the unintended consequences of deflation. With the postwar deflation, the burden of existing duties—most of which were specific duties rather than ad valorem—increased greatly. This represented the start of a return to mercantilism and the imposition of some restrictions on competition. Whenever anyone proposed lower tariffs, complained Frederick J. Robinson, then president of the Board of Trade, half of the manufacturers in the country presented petitions and sent delegations against any liberalization (Imlah 1958: 14).[4]

Protection was also intentionally increased in this period. By overwhelming majorities of 245–77 in the House of Commons and 144–17 in the House of Lords, Parliament passed a Corn Law in 1815, prohibiting the import of corn when the domestic price was below eighty shillings a quarter (Fetter 1980). Many of the bill's instigators were future reformers, such as Henry Parnell, Huskisson, Peel, and Robert Vansittart. When the Commons refused to

---

4. Robinson was Lord Goderich when he briefly became prime minister after Canning and before Wellington; he was president of the Board of Trade in the early 1840s as the Earl of Ripon.

continue the income tax in peacetime, fiscal reform required an increased tariff on other goods, which came in the 1819 budget (Imlah 1958).

These apparently popular policies were reversed at the precise moment the
theory predicts. In 1822, Castlereagh died, the Concert of Europe collapsed,
and moderate free traders began to take over the British cabinet. Stating these
facts in this manner exaggerates the relationship between them; in foreign policy, for example, Canning left unchanged Castlereagh's instructions to
Wellington for the Verona conference (Temperley 1925). Nonetheless, this
bald statement does highlight the kinds of changing trends centered in the span
of a few years near 1822, and the events are not without connection. The
impending collapse of his handiwork, in conjunction with the stress of the
diplomatic crises of these years, contributed to Castlereagh's suicide. Thereafter, the ultra Tories steadily lost ground in the cabinet, and some of these
changes in personnel were directly attributable to Castlereagh's departure and
Canning's resulting elevation to the Foreign Office. These events set off a chain
reaction, bringing Robinson to the Exchequer and Huskisson to the presidency
of the Board of Trade in 1823; Peel had already replaced Lord Sidmouth as
home secretary in 1822 (Brock 1941). All were now moderate free traders, and
in the next few years tariffs were greatly simplified and somewhat reduced.

The consolidation and future rise of these liberal Tories came as a direct
result of diplomatic developments. When the cabinet decided to begin negotiations and thereby implicitly recognize the independent republics of Buenos
Aires, Colombia, and Mexico in December 1824, Wellington and other ultra
Tories found themselves isolated and grew increasingly opposed to the government's policies (Temperley 1925). Some resigned and were replaced by more
liberals, strengthening the reformist coalition in the cabinet.

Even so, the specific makeup of the government was less important than
the changes in the circumstances in which any government would have found
itself; after all, Wellington's ultra Tory ministry at the end of the decade also
pursued reform. Furthermore, many of these moderates had only recently
changed their minds on foreign economic policy. Huskisson and Peel had even
served on the committees that recommended the restrictive Corn Law of 1815
(Hilton 1977).

Once this newer coalition was in place, Huskisson took the lead in trade
policy. He began major tariff reforms in 1822, committing the government to
rationalize tariffs and to replace prohibitions with duties (Brady 1928).
Huskisson endeavored to set these duties at a level that would force British producers to compete against foreign goods. For example, the import prohibition
on silk goods became a maximum duty of 30 percent (Gordon 1979: 19–21).

Huskisson also reduced the general duty on manufactured goods from 50 percent to 20 percent and passed the Warehousing Bill to ease the reexport trade. The 1825 budget made the most notable changes in tariffs while removing the customs barrier between Britain and Ireland; among the changes were tariff reductions on cotton goods, wool, woolens, linen, paper, glass, earthenware, metals, coal, rum, and silk (Brown 1958).

The reformists also began an attack on the Corn Law. In 1825–26, Canning, Huskisson, and Liverpool all favored relaxation or repeal of the law; even Wellington had, while in the cabinet, agreed to a new sliding-scale tariff on grain (Dixon 1976). The battle began in earnest in 1827, after Liverpool's death and Wellington's departure from the government, when Canning's government introduced a sliding-scale bill. The bill passed in the Commons, but Wellington successfully stopped it in the Lords. Aside from this failure, however, the reformists were remarkably successful and almost completely unconstrained by the growing domestic opposition to their liberalization.

Foreign Reactions in the 1820s

The theory predicts that when the leader increases contributions to public goods while losing allies, the followers will decrease their contributions. Using trade policy as a measure of these contributions, this means that British liberalization in the 1820s should be accompanied by foreign protectionism. To test this proposition, table 7 shows legislated tariff changes among those European countries for which I could find information as well as for the United States. While I have tried to be complete in collecting evidence from a sizable secondary literature (Haight 1941; Henderson 1939; Smith 1980; Judith Blow Williams 1972), the list of tariff changes is probably not exhaustive.

As I predict, most European countries turned protectionist in the 1820s. Depending on whether I include the inevitable ambiguous cases, the model predicts six of seven or eight countries correctly. Either is significantly better than we would expect by chance. With a null hypothesis of 50 percent, since tariffs can go either up or down, the probabilities of predicting this many correctly by chance are only 6.25 and 14.5 percent, respectively.

Spurious correlation is apparently not a problem. A spurious correlation would be likely if some excluded variable caused all tariffs to move in the same direction. What makes spurious correlation an unlikely problem is that hypothesis 2 expects non-British tariffs to move in the opposite direction from British tariffs. Anything that might explain the common movement of non-British tariffs could not explain the opposing movement of British tariffs that

TABLE 7. Foreign Reactions to British Liberalization: Changes in Legislated Tariffs

	Prediction, 1815–21	Pattern	Prediction, 1820s	Pattern
Austria	Lower	Unknown	Higher	Higher, 1824
France	Higher[b]	Higher, 1819, 1821	Higher	Higher, 1822, 1826
Netherlands	Lower	Lower, 1816, 1818, 1819, 1821	Higher	Higher, 1822
Portugal	Lower	Unknown	Not higher[a]	Not higher
Prussia	Lower	Lower, 1818, 1821	Higher	Slight trade diversion (*Zollverein*)
Sweden	Lower	Lower, 1817	Higher	Higher, 1823; Lower, 1826
Sicily	Lower	Lower	Higher	Higher, 1823, 1827
United States	Higher[b]	Higher, 1816, 1818	Higher	Higher, 1824, 1828
Correctly predicted	6 of 6, 100%, excluding unknown 6 of 8, 75%, counting unknown as anomalies		6 of 7, 85.7%, excluding Prussia 6 of 8, 75%, counting Prussia as anomaly	

Note: Throughout this table *legislated* does not necessarily mean "passed by a legislature." Many countries changed tariffs through administrative agencies; details vary by country. *Unknown* means that I have been unable to find evidence of a legislated change in tariffs.

[a]Britain and Portugal had a reciprocal trade treaty in effect from 1810 to 1836; see chapters 7 and 8.

[b]France and the United States were British rivals, not allies, after 1815, because of the Napoleonic Wars and War of 1812–15, respectively.

underlies the hypothesis. Thus, any rival explanation of tariff legislation in this period would have one more anomaly in each period than the theory here (that is, Britain itself).

Another check for spurious correlation is to look at the pattern in legislated tariffs before 1821. Holding the post-Napoleonic alliances constant, British protection should be met with liberalization among allies, protection among rivals. Because of the Chaumont coalition, only France and the United States were diplomatic rivals of Britain in this period, and these countries behave differently from the rest, just as the theory predicts. Depending on how one codes the two unknown cases, the theory predicts between three-fourths and all of the cases correctly. The likelihood of getting these correct by chance is only 14.5 and 0.4 percent, respectively.

One final piece of evidence for the theory comes from Portugal, which was allied with Britain across the 1821–22 divide.[5] Consistent with the hypothesis, Portugal did not turn protectionist with the other followers until after it withdrew from these treaties in 1836.

In short, the theory predicts these tariff changes remarkably well in the period of changing security relationships. After the 1820s, these diplomatic relations remain mostly constant except for the Anglo-French pair. Holding these relations constant, I then expect a positive relationship between Britain's policies and the policies of its rivals, a negative relation between Britain's policy and the policy of its allies. Because Great Britain has far more rivals than friends after 1821, British leadership led to a virtuous circle of liberalization after the 1820s.

Changing Governments and Unchanging Policies, 1827–41

A period of stable security relations lets me test a different implication of the theory. Just as losing allies should change British policy, continuity in alliance politics should lead to continuity in economic policy. With the security relations (p) relatively constant, British policy depends on the other parameters— namely, British and foreign resource constraints. With British economic growth I expect continued British liberalization because contributions to public goods are a normal good. This section will outline the policy continuity from Tory to Whig government. The following section presents some quantitative tests of the argument here, which are possible because the Austrian and French data series begin in 1831.

---

5. Portugal was also the only country to have a trade treaty in effect with Britain in this period. Chapter 8 will show that countries with a trade treaty in effect should liberalize together.

The outlook was bleak for the new liberal policy when Wellington replaced Canning as prime minister in 1827. *Blackwood's* rejoiced, "We have at last, thank God, got rid of the Liberals, and once more we have the happiness to live under a pure Tory Government" (cited in Gordon 1979: 57). Surprisingly for mainstream domestic-politics explanations, the change in governments did not change policy. Indeed, policy was remarkably constant over the next fourteen years despite several changes of government and a major change of electoral system in 1832.

Wellington's president of the Board of Trade, Vesey Fitzgerald, maintained the same policy direction as his late predecessor (who had become history's first railroad fatality); most strikingly, Fitzgerald refused silk workers' demands for a return to protection (Gordon 1979). Wellington also changed his mind about the Corn Laws once in power, passing a sliding scale for corn in 1828. Despite his reputation as an ultra, Wellington was not hostile to Huskisson's reforms, which "have gone a little too far, or not far enough in some cases; but this is very certain, that in principle he is right" (Gordon 1979: 108). Indeed, Wellington's 1830 budget proposed to repeal duties on beer and leather and to reduce the West India sugar duty by three shillings per hundredweight, with an estimated cost of £4 million.

Wellington's shifts from a reluctant reformer to an opponent and back to a reformer suggest that something came over his domestic political instincts whenever he sat in the cabinet. This behavior was typical of a pattern found throughout the period. When in government, figures such as Wellington, Canning, Liverpool, Huskisson, Robinson, Melbourne, and Peel all support the policies I predict the state should choose for systemic reasons, and they do so apparently without regard for consistency.[6] Wellington's double flip-flop in 1827–28 is an extreme case; Peel's behavior before and after the election of 1841 is perhaps another. In government, their preferences reflect the interests of the state that my theory identifies.[7]

There was no change in policy under the Whigs, who held office throughout most of the 1830s. After an abortive attempt in 1831,[8] the Whigs did not

---

6. Deacon Hume, who aided Huskisson's reforms from his post at Customs from 1822 to 1825, had also been a protectionist in 1815, having written a tract on the subject (see Brown 1958: 29–32). David Lake (1988: 173) describes similar shifts in the policies of Warren G. Harding and William McKinley before and after each became president.

7. Some suggestive evidence for this position is Aydelotte's (1967) finding that the only obvious difference between Protectionists and Peelites when they split in 1846 was that the latter were much more likely to have had experience in office.

8. They had proposed reducing tobacco duties, the colonial preference on timber and wines, and repealing duties on seaborne coal, slate, candles, glass, calico, and cotton (Brown 1958: 46–51).

launch any full-fledged tariff reform, though they were nominally pledged to further liberalization. Lord Althorp, chancellor of the Exchequer for the incoming Whig government, announced in 1831 that his "general view of finance" would be based on the generally liberal principles of Henry Parnell's *On Financial Reform* (Semmel 1970).[9] Yet, faced with revenue difficulties and a shortage of political will, Althorp did little along these lines. Viscount Melbourne, home secretary in 1830–34 and prime minister in 1835–41, was bored by tariffs (Cecil 1954: 401); no pressure would come from that quarter.

Conversely, the Whigs did not need to launch a full program of tariff reform because Huskisson's reforms remained in place. Keeping many specific duties in place during a period of moderate inflation lowered effective tariffs and encouraged trade, so that many sectors of the English economy faced increasing levels of foreign competition. Civil servants at the Board of Trade also reduced tariffs (Brown 1958). Poulett Thomson, a dogmatic Ricardian and free trader, led the senior civil service officials at the board, first as vice president between 1830 and 1834 and subsequently succeeding Lord Auckland as president. He continued the reform work that Huskisson began, reducing duties on a host of minor goods: barilla, food and drugs, cordage, tanning bark, dyestuffs, paints, varnishes and gums, canes, coconut, madder, ginger, pickles, dried fruits, hides and skins, and hardwoods. He also reduced the export duty on coal and slates. These reforms did not stem from political pressure, because "the Board of Trade was leading a new movement of opinion, rather than expressing one which was already there" (Brown 1958: 183).

The Whigs did not get around to the most politically sensitive elements of trade policy until 1841, as part of a broader attack on the tariff system. A select committee reported in 1840 that only seventeen articles[10] (of a total of 1,146) supplied 94.5 percent of the customs revenue. Lowering tariffs could actually raise revenue by increasing imports (Gash 1972: 251–64; Irwin 1988). Lord John Russell, now leading the government, had previously given notice that he would move for a committee of the whole to consider the Corn Laws. Yet rather than take on corn, the Whigs began with sugar (Crosby 1976; Stewart 1969). After defeating the sugar proposal, Peel's Conservatives brought the government down. Thereupon followed the election of 1841, the first British election in which a disciplined opposition defeated a majority government in an election to the Commons.

---

9. The book attacked tariffs on raw materials, foodstuffs, and manufactured goods and proposed an income tax or a property tax to cover the revenue loss from lower duties.

10. Butter, cheese, coffee, corn, cotton, currants, raisins, seeds, silk manufactures, spirits, sugar, tallow, tea, timber, tobacco, wine, and wool.

Despite the circumstances of the Whigs' fall, Peel was careful not to commit himself against free trade in the election campaign. He reserved himself

the liberty of proposing to Parliament those measures which I believe conducive to the public weal. . . . Free as the wind, I tell every man in the country that he has imposed no personal obligations upon me by having placed me in this office.[11] (cited in Imlah 1958: 150–51)

Privately, Peel was already moving toward further liberalization.

Curiously, then, 1841 ended with the leadership of both parties favoring tariff reductions; even Wellington thought this "must be the first thing to do" (cited in Imlah 1958: 152). For any domestic-level explanation, it is certainly strange that once the Whigs were persuaded to support free trade, they fell from power and the protectionist Conservatives actually did the deed.[12]

When Peel took office in the autumn of 1841, there was war in China, an expeditionary force in Afghanistan, a Canadian-border dispute with the United States, a crisis with France over Syria, a looming famine in Ireland, and an economic downswing at home. All these events put severe pressure on the Exchequer, particularly since imposing an income tax had been a political anathema since 1816. Lowering tariffs would help ease this pressure if, as the 1840 select committee had argued, it would increase customs revenue. For this reason, many have argued that financial concerns were a key reason for Peel's liberalization in the 1840s (e.g., Stein 1984). However, Peel reduced tariffs below the revenue-maximizing level and reimposed the income tax for three years to make up the difference. Here is a clear instance of the state's flexibility in its choice of taxes, even in the face of significant domestic opposition. Even when revenue picked up in 1844, Peel renewed the income tax to reduce tariffs still further in 1845. Reform also continued at the Board of Trade, where William Gladstone was vice president beginning in 1841 and president beginning in 1843.

The immediate occasion for repeal of the Corn Laws was the Irish potato famine; according to Wellington, "Rotten potatoes have done it; they put Peel

---

11. Such claims were common at the time, though many members of Parliament also availed themselves of the opportunity to state in *Dod's Parliamentary Companion* that they were publicly pledged to one course of action or another.

12. Historians have often viewed this period through Whig-colored glasses, though the policies praised were usually passed by liberal Tories, who should be their true heroes. Since historians almost always use domestic-level explanations, this persistent distortion should be suggestive.

in his d——d fright" (cited in Trevelyan 1926/1952: 189). Peel brought the Corn Laws to the cabinet in November 1845, suggesting that the government admit grain at a reduced rate to cope with the immediate emergency and that further action be taken on the Corn Laws after Christmas (Gash 1972). Only Aberdeen, Graham, and Herbert supported Peel, though some cabinet members did not commit either way. Wellington opposed the plan unless Peel thought it absolutely necessary; Ripon wished to compensate agriculture for the loss of its protection. Stanley (later Lord Derby) and Buccleuch were the only steadfast protectionists, but both refused to lead a protectionist ministry. (Stanley thought repeal inevitable but believed that the Whigs should carry it out.)

Peel resigned in December because he could not convince his cabinet to move on the Corn Law question. Russell next tried and failed to form a Whig minority government, though assured of Peel's support on the Corn Laws.[13] Peel then formed a new government, announcing that he would pursue repeal without or without his colleagues. He introduced his final proposal on January 27, 1846, beginning with a long list of other articles whose duties were also to be reduced or eliminated.[14] Colonial corn was to enter at a nominal duty, while other corn received a variable rate that would decrease over three years.

The resignation had strengthened Peel's hand: he could now rally hesitant Tories around his government as the only alternative to the Radicals. While Stanley refused to join him, Wellington stayed in: "It was not a question of measures, but of Government, of support of the Queen." The hero of Waterloo also tried to persuade Tory mutineers to stay with Peel: he told Salisbury, "A good Government is more important than Corn Laws." Redesdale was asked to give Victoria another Tory government, learning that he had a duty to "rescue the lady from Cobden" (all cited in Longford 1972: 363–64). Wellington also did his part in the Lords, ultimately moving repeal through on a show of hands.

While scholars have found the drama of the Corn Laws fascinating (see McLean 1992; Schonhardt-Bailey 1996 inter alia), their repeal reflects policy continuity over two decades. Far from a novel departure in trade policy, repeal was the culmination of the work begun by Huskisson in the early 1820s. Contemporaries realized this fact; for Peel in 1841,

---

13. The ostensible reason for the failure was that Lord Grey would not serve if Palmerston returned to the Foreign Office, and Palmerston would not accept the Colonial Office instead.

14. Tallow, timber, cloth, paper, carriages, candles and soap, dressed hides, straw hats, sugar, tobacco, maize, buckwheat, butter, cheese, hops, cured fish, and meat. The speech is reprinted in Schonhardt-Bailey 1996.

in economic affairs the precedents and traditions to which he looked back were those of Liverpool, Huskisson, Herries and Robinson in the eighteen-twenties. Office in 1841 was an opportunity to pick up the threads snapped short in 1830. (Gash 1972: 299)

Repeal of the Corn Laws represents continuity rather than change in British policy (see also Pahre 1996a).

Quantitative Tests

Quantitative tests of some hypotheses become possible in the 1830s. As in the other chapters, the qualitative definition of hegemony eliminates any variation in this independent variable, since I posit that a hegemon is always present. While this counterfactual rules out direct statistical test of the central proposition, other indirect tests of the model are possible.

In particular, I can test to see whether the relationship between openness in Britain and elsewhere is consistent with the model. The comparative statics of the theory predict that U.K. imports are positively related to foreign GDPs after the transition in the early 1820s.[15] Equivalently, U.K. openness is positively related to the ratio of foreign GDP to U.K. GDP. Whereas I showed the results of both the import and the openness tests in chapter 4, I show only the openness results here. As in chapter 4, the openness test is generally immune to problems of serial correlation and heteroskedacity; it also happens to yield smaller standard errors and thus more statistically significant results.

Changing security relations can change the sign of the relationship between British and foreign openness. Whereas the Troppau countries are friendly to Britain only in 1815–21, Britain's relationship with France varies a bit. Anglo-French relations grew cordial in 1830–32. It looked as if this situation would continue after the Russo-Turkish Treaty of Unkiar Skelessi in July 1833, which led to greater Anglo-French cooperation in the Near East. However, real disagreements persisted in the West, and Palmerston turned down Talleyrand's offer of a general defensive alliance in 1833. Relations deteriorated until Aberdeen replaced Palmerston in 1841. Aberdeen was pro-French, and his entente cordiale lasted until Palmerston returned to office in 1846 (see Bullen 1974: 66–68, 94–95). Based on this history, I have coded the years 1830–32 and 1841–46 as entente and other years as animosity.

---

15. Holding resources constant, losing allies leads to greater British imports and less foreign imports around 1821; holding allies constant thereafter, British and foreign imports should be positively related to one another's resources and thus to each other.

The theory predicts that there will be a negative relationship between British openness and the French-U.K. GNP ratio during ententes, a positive relationship otherwise. I test the hypothesis with a dummy variable equal to one in periods of entente; I multiply this dummy variable with the GNP ratio to generate an interactive variable. Then I regress both the GNP ratio and the interactive variable against British imports. This means that the net effect of the GNP ratio on British openness is equal to the GNP ratio plus the interactive term during ententes, the GNP ratio alone otherwise (because the interactive term is equal to zero). An *F*-test shows whether the sum effect of these two variables is positive and greater than zero.

Because of data limitations, I can test this hypothesis only for 1830–53 and only for Britain, France, and Austria. In addition, Austrian GNP is unavailable, so I use Austrian imports instead of the GNP ratio. (Austrian imports should be positively related to the unobserved Austrian GNP.) U.K. openness depends positively on Austrian imports because Austria and the United Kingdom are rivals throughout this period. Finally, the theory predicts a positive constant in the openness-against-GNP-ratio test here.

Table 8 shows the results, with and without the control variable *Year*. The estimates for the French-British GNP ratio are wrongly signed and statistically insignificant. (Note that alternative theories such as gravity models of trade would also predict a positive relationship for this variable.) All the other variables are rightly signed and significant. However, because of the large standard errors on the French-British ratio, the *F*-test for the sum of this ratio and the interactive term is not significant at conventional levels.

The estimates suggest that the variables are all substantively important. The data are in nominal national currency units, and the pound sterling was worth about twenty-five French francs or Austrian crowns in this period. Changes in French GNP have a little less than one-to-one effect on British imports; every two-pound change in Austrian imports has about a one-pound effect on British imports.

The results show that changes in Britain's most important security relationship has the predicted effects on behavior. This is especially useful because John Vincent Nye (1990) has argued that the relationship between British and French tariffs in the nineteenth century is anomalous for hegemonic-stability theory. Imre Lakatos (1970) argues that elimination of such anomalies, along with the prediction of new facts, is an important test of whether modifications in a given research program are "progressive." Because this negative relationship between allies is one of the most counterintuitive hypotheses of the model, the empirical results are striking.

Military Restraint

In addition to its speculations about foreign and domestic economic policy, the model makes subsidiary predictions about British military policy in this period. I expect military restraint by the hegemon when it lacks allies. Moving first, the Stackelberg leader does not want to set off an arms race by large military spending. Instead, low spending, conditioned on similarly low spending by others, is the best strategy. As Peel told Wellington in the 1840s, Britain "must neither appear to threaten other powers by hostile preparations nor appear so weak as to invite their aggression" (cited in Gash 1972: 520). Though commonplace for status quo powers, such a claim well captures the leader's incentives found in the model.

History bears out the model's prediction. British spending on the military was about 2 or 3 percent of GNP throughout this period. Paul Kennedy (1987: 153) notes that

These would have been impressively low figures for a country of modest means and ambitions. For a state which managed to "rule the waves,"

TABLE 8.   British Openness

	Predict	U.K. Openness	U.K. Openness
Constant	+	14.****	−170.*
		(3.8)	(110.)
France/U.K. GNP ratio	+	−.13	−.068
		(.15)	(.15)
Entente × (France/U.K. ratio)	−	−20.	−24.*
		(17.)	(16.)
Austrian imports	+	.026****	.019****
		(.0031)	(.0053)
Year			.10
			(.060)
France/U.K. + Entente × France/U.K.	+	$F = 1.5$ $p < .25$	$F = 2.14$ $p < .20$
N		24	24
(Years)		(1831–54)	(1831–54)
Adjusted R^2		.80	.81
F		30.8	26.1
Durbin-Watson		2.11	2.24

Note: Standard errors in parentheses. Data sources in appendix B.
†$p < .10$, two-tailed; ††$p < .05$, two-tailed; †††$p < .01$, two-tailed; ††††$p < .001$, two-tailed.
*$p < .10$, one-tailed; **$p < .05$, one-tailed; ***$p < .01$, one-tailed; ****$p < .001$, one-tailed.

which possessed an enormous, far-flung empire, and which still claimed a large interest in preserving the European balance of power, they were truly remarkable.

The navy even declined in size from eighty ships of the line in 1817 to sixty-eight in 1828 to fifty-eight in 1835 (Kennedy 1976: 150).

I can add a quantitative test, looking at the contrast between the military spending I expect during malevolent hegemony versus that during benevolent hegemony. A leader surrounded by allies will pick up the alliance's military burdens, while a leader surrounded by adversaries will exercise military restraint and reallocate resources to economic openness. This implies that the leader's military expenditures relative to the other great powers' expenditures will be higher when these other states are allies than when they are not.

Table 9 presents a test of this hypothesis, examining whether Britain's share of great-power military spending is significantly different during the Quadruple Alliance than after the alliance breaks down.[16] I use two different terminal dates for the Quadruple Alliance, the Troppau Protocol of 1820 and Britain's formal withdrawal at Verona in 1822. The evidence is consistent with the hypothesis in both cases, although much more impressive if we use the Troppau Protocol cutoff date.

The result supports the Stackelberg logic that is central to the theory here, since this result does not characterize the Cournot model. The quantitative evidence contrasting the two periods is especially useful, since I am aware of no other theory that might predict exactly this pattern of expenditure. Indeed, balancing logic would require Britain to compensate for its loss of external balancing (alliances) by increasing its internal balancing, or the conversion of internal resources into external power (Waltz 1979). As a result, neo-Realists

TABLE 9.   Alliance Leadership and Military Spending

	1815–19	1820–53	1815–21	1822–53
Average share of British	14.0	9.6	12.3	9.7
military spending in total	(2.0)	(1.2)	(2.9)	(1.2)
	$F = 17.69$		$F = 3.81$	
	$p < .001$		$p < .10$	

Note: Standard errors in parentheses. Data sources in appendix B.

---

16. This hypothesis follows informally from the intuition and follows formally with some messy algebra. Define the ratio R of U.K. spending to rest-of-world spending as $R = g_i^S/(g_i^S + g_j^S)$. If we simplify the algebra by letting $\alpha = \beta$, it can be shown that $\partial R/\partial p > 0$ iff $p > (1 - \alpha)^2$. This condition holds for all $p > 0$ and for almost all $p < 0$ if, as I argued in chapter 5, α is small.

would predict greater British military spending in the 1820s than immediately after the Napoleonic Wars.

The result also helps rule out a plausible rival explanation for openness, which might reflect the freeing-up of national resources after the Napoleonic Wars.[17] This demobilization hypothesis explains openness but not Britain's military spending relative to other countries, which were also demobilizing, of course.

In summary, Britain's military restraint is consistent with the theory. Because there are better data earlier than exist for trade, I can date the change in policy precisely to 1820–22, exactly as the theory predicts.

The Navigation Acts and the Sinking Fund

Another implication of Britain's policy of military restraint is that economic policies serving primarily military ends could be reversed after 1821. The Navigation Acts—which generally prohibited imports into Britain and trade with its colonies on third-party ships—had always been intimately connected with defense. Adam Smith, no friend of mercantilism, praised the acts because "defence was of more importance than opulence." Lord Brougham, an apostle of Smith and the leader of the free-trade forces before Cobden, supported the Navigation Laws as late as 1849. It was a question of defense, he argued, and "on the best interests of the country, her defence, her very existence." The more protectionist Members of Parliament naturally did not disagree; Disraeli warned of the danger to "the empire of the seas" posed by repeal of the acts (all cited in Semmel 1970: 200). In other words, the Navigation Acts were less an act of protection than a matter of defense, though English shipowners obviously benefited from them.

Changes in the Navigation Acts began in 1822, with a regulation allowing Latin American republics to export goods to Britain on Latin American ships. Provisions for reciprocity in shipping followed in 1823, and an 1825 act opened trade with British colonies on a reciprocal basis. Prussia was one of the first to take advantage of these provisions, signing a reciprocity treaty in 1824 that equalized harbor dues. Prussia also agreed to MFN treatment of English navigators in 1826 in exchange for being allowed to trade with English colonies (see also chap. 8). By the 1830s, only intraempire trade was still a monopoly of British bottoms. The Navigation Acts were finally repealed in 1849, and in 1854

---

17. The fullest models of demobilization rest on intertemporal allocations of consumption through sovereign debt and predict greater taxation, debt repayment, and deflation after a war than before (Grossman and Van Huyck 1988; Grossman 1990; Grossman and Han 1993).

foreign ships were even allowed to participate in the coasting trade (Gordon 1979; Semmel 1970).

Alternative explanations of the Navigation Acts are problematic. An explanation based on the ideology of free trade would have trouble explaining why this ideology should extend to something that many free traders—and their patron saint, Smith—considered a military issue. A domestic-group explanation would also prove inadequate; exporters would obviously expect to benefit from lower rates if the acts were abolished, but the only significant domestic groups with an interest in repealing the acts were the colonial government of Canada and those with economic interests in Jamaica. Moreover, the shipowners, the major losers, were a potent political force. They complained that their industry had been the most disadvantaged of all in the recent reforms, and a petition from London shipowners had lobbied for renewed protection in 1825.[18] The "imperialism of free trade" argument (e.g., Gallagher and Robinson 1953), which insists that British naval dominance was an essential component of the informal empire, also cannot explain the decision against this de facto subsidization of the merchant marine with an eye toward its use in war.

The shippers petitioned for relief again in 1827, with the support of General Isaac Gascoyne, Huskisson's fellow member from Liverpool. The protectionists had clearly pulled out all the stops, appealing to Huskisson's political constituency as well as bringing a military man to their aid. Huskisson remained unmoved, arguing that the share of British shipping in both the export and import trades had increased since the changes in regulation. If current profits were too low, he suggested, the shipowners had none to blame but themselves, for they had engaged in a building spree that had produced an oversupply of vessels. Peel, Viscount Milton, and Poulett Thomson all supported Huskisson; even Alexander Baring, by then a leading opponent of Huskisson's reforms, admitted that the shippers had not yet made a convincing case for aid.

Interest-group explanations cannot explain such a defeat of a powerful group, which had the added advantage of being able to appeal to military policy. Without reference to the change in military strategy, the defeat of the shippers is inexplicable. As Barry Gordon (1979: 105) points out, "The rout of the protectionist forces on this occasion betokened the emergence of a new attitude to the significance of the merchant marine since the cessation of hostilities with Napoleon." I would add that the key variable was not merely Napoleon's

18. Indeed, petitions on the 1849 bill were running 182 to 6 against in May (Schuyler 1945: 198).

defeat (which would have presaged a change in 1815–20), but the collapse of the anti-Napoleonic coalition.

The shift in military policy also affected the outcome of a more obscure debate, that on the "sinking fund" (Gordon 1979). Building on some of Walpole's policies, Pitt had begun this fund in the 1780s; it was now ostensibly designed to pay off the national debt resulting from the Napoleonic Wars. Under the system, budget surpluses were allocated to a board that purchased public stock from the holders of that stock. The board then collected the interest due on this stock in lieu of the original holders and used these revenues to purchase still more stock. In practice, the government often issued new stock to buy up old stock through the sinking fund. In all, it was a curious way of retiring the public debt, and it is better seen as an enforced saving plan for the government. By accumulating government savings in the form of public stock, the fund provided a reserve for future military spending.

David Ricardo campaigned tirelessly against the fund, both because he wanted the state to pay off the debt and because he was suspicious of its potential for military uses. Since the time of Walpole, he argued in 1822, it had served "only to encourage ministers to engage in new wars by facilitating the contraction of new loans" (cited in Gordon 1979: 127). Ricardo's opponents argued, naturally, that the fund was necessary for defense. Alexander Baring attacked Ricardo's "almost absurd" position that, as Baring understood it, "The country would be better able to engage in any contest, or cope with any difficulties with a strong finance than with a strong military or naval establishment" (cited in Gordon 1979: 115).

With the deemphasis of military spending, Ricardo's views triumphed, and the fund was closed in the 1828 budget. Aside from military policy, this change had the advantage of applying budget surpluses to tariff reductions rather than to the fund. One might see the end of the sinking fund, like tariff reform, as an attempt to make the financial machinery of the government as efficient as possible. However, this would prove unable to explain those policies unconnected with finance, such as repeal of the Navigation Acts. Seeing the question of the sinking fund in tandem with the other policies of the period, as part of a policy of military restraint, is more satisfactory because it is more powerful, explaining a wider range of behavior.

Rival Explanations

While I have touched on some alternative explanations of these events above, this section will look at them more closely. Interest-group theories argue that

British liberalization before and after the repeal of the Corn Laws stemmed from the sustained expansion of an internationally competitive manufacturing sector, gradually increasing the political power of free-trade interests. With the help of the 1832 Reform Act, the story goes, the manufacturers were eventually able to impose the strategy of free trade, with grain imports and manufacturing exports, making England the "workshop of the world" (Brawley 1993: 110–17; Briggs 1959; Gallagher and Robinson 1953; Gordon 1976, 1979; Hilton 1977; Hobsbawm 1969; Irwin 1989; Kindleberger 1975; Kitson Clark 1951; Platt 1968; Polanyi 1944; Schonhardt-Bailey 1991a, 1991b, 1994; Semmel 1970; see also Schonhardt-Bailey 1996: vol. 4).

This makes for a nice story, but cannot explain the changing Tory policies of 1815–30. Manufacturing, shipping, and finance, strengthened by their role in the Napoleonic Wars, should have been politically powerful on behalf of freer trade even earlier. Factory owners, such as a group of Manchester mill owners, opposed the Corn Laws from 1815. So, too, did mobs of rioting workers in London, with one group attacking Robinson's home because he had sponsored the bill in the Commons. In a famous example of the opposition, a group of London merchants petitioned the Commons for a change of strategy toward free trade in May 1820. Robinson opposed that petition on the government's behalf, though he became a reformer a few years later. Further petitions came a week later from the Glasgow Chamber of Commerce and the Hawick woolen manufacturers, but these groups also petitioned in vain.

In the 1820s, Huskisson's reforms engendered a flood of hostile petitions, especially from landlords and farmers, but they achieved nothing. Other petitions succeeded only in achieving some minor delays in implementation. One from the silk workers of Bethnal Green "thanked the House and the Chancellor of the Exchequer for the postponement of their destruction till 1826, and prayed it might be further postponed till 1829" (cited in Gordon 1979: 21). All these unsuccessful petitions, with relatively few liberal petitions against them, call domestic explanations into question.

Huskisson did not face reformist pressure from Parliament, which was not particularly responsive to the needs of industry. All the Lords and much of the Commons were aristocrats. In 1826, 232 of the 658 members of the Commons were baronets, Irish peers, or the sons of peers, and only 154 were businessmen (Gordon 1979: 4–5). Of the 154 businessmen, forty-four had interests in India (and presumably favored imperial preference), forty-two were bankers, and only eight were tied to manufacturing. The rise of a competitive manufacturing sector clearly is not reflected in the social background of MPs.

Even after the 1832 Reform Act, which admittedly augmented the power of the bourgeoisie, a bare majority of districts in the Commons were actually contested, and many rotten boroughs still existed. In the election of 1847, immediately after repeal, only 165 of 401 constituencies were contested. The electoral connection to policy, which is central to many domestic-level theories, can easily be exaggerated.

Another possible explanation is party politics and coalitions (Aydelotte 1966, 1977; Conacher 1972; Gash 1951). Yet this solution has problems explaining the nature of the coalition that repealed the Corn Laws in 1846. Once the Anti–Corn Law League had begun to win over the Whigs around 1840, the Whig government fell. Peel's Conservative ministry, based on a party with a protectionist majority, carried through repeal of the Corn Laws with overwhelming support from the opposing benches and without any compensatory gains for Peel's closest followers. Peel refused to construct a new ministry of Peelites and Whigs, which suggests that an interest in holding power (or reelection) was not important. Indeed, he split his own party for a generation, noting, "I must be insane if I could have been induced by anything but a sense of public duty to undertake what I have undertaken in this session" (cited in Briggs 1959: 325). No domestic-level theory can account for this remarkable independence of the cabinet's actions from domestic politics.

Kindleberger (1975) and others have argued that the influential ideology of the political economists can explain the policy (see also Anderson and Tollison 1985; Gordon 1976, 1979; Semmel 1970). Ricardo's works grew in popularity from the 1820s to the 1840s, and this increasing degree of acceptance may explain the steady liberalization of British foreign economic policy. The theorists—especially Ricardo and his law of comparative advantage—certainly were occasionally persuasive. Lord John Russell, a Whig leader of the 1840s, admitted to having been won over by the power of ideas. Henry Parnell announced in Parliament that he had been converted by the Ricardian theory of rent (Semmel 1970: 138).

Yet the ideological explanation has difficulty explaining why abstract doctrines, especially in a doctrinaire form, were generally frowned on. Alexander Baring—a free trader of 1820 who moved increasingly toward protectionism after 1824—could in 1826 refer to his late friend Ricardo as a man who "had some of the most fanciful theories that could possibly be imagined" (cited in Fetter 1980: 17). Sir Thomas Gooch, an advocate of the landed interest, was in 1827 "heartily sick of political economists altogether," and he wished that a clause be "inserted in the present bill, enacting that every vessel laden with foreign corn destined for this country should take back, instead of ballast, a cargo of political economists" (cited in Semmel 1970: 137). While that was sour grapes, even liberalizing Tories wished to disassociate themselves from the political economists. When prime minister, Lord Liverpool declared against "fanciful and impractical theories" before a group of shipowners in 1823 (cited in Semmel 1970: 138).

Explanations based on ideology also do not make satisfactory predictions about the timing of liberalization. After all, Adam Smith's *Wealth of Nations* did not immediately cause a change in policy in 1776, even if Ricardo's *Principles of Political Economy* (1817) certainly seems to have influenced the debates of the 1820s. But Smith's and Ricardo's ideas were a double-edged sword. By the 1840s, opponents of free trade were able to cite Smith and Ricardo against the doctrinaire free traders, correctly pointing out that these authors had recognized the need to protect agriculture and the merchant marine (Gordon 1976, 1979; Semmel 1970). A protectionist MP from Somersetshire argued that Smith was an "authority always quoted on the other side when it served their purpose," but when it did not, it "was treated as an old almanac" (cited in Semmel 1970: 143).

Moreover, ideology was by no means unambiguous. Physiocratic thought remained influential in England as on the Continent, and landowners used it to argue in favor of the Corn Laws (see Gordon 1979; Schonhardt-Bailey 1996 for overview). Noneconomic ideologies, such as constitutionalism or gradualism, also played an important role. Since we do not have a theory that predicts what ideas will triumph in a clash of doctrines, arguments based on ideology must be post hoc.

A different approach uses ideology only to condition an explanation based on interests. Bernard Semmel (1970: 206–7) admits that "the influence of the early theorists upon policy was most directly effective when substantial interests were not threatened thereby." Gordon (1979) argues that ideology was the driving force behind tariff reductions but suggests that the order in which tariffs were reduced is the result of interest-group politics: Canadian timber producers, British shipowners, and London silk weavers were the first victims, the powerful agricultural interest last. By reintroducing interest groups in this way, the ideological explanation begins to suffer from the problems of those theories discussed previously.

Conclusion

This chapter has suggested that a number of trade, military, and domestic policies chosen by British governments between 1815 and 1850 are unexpectedly coherent. Protectionism from 1815 to the early 1820s, trade liberalization from

Huskisson on, the modest role of commercial negotiations, the end of imperial preference, and an unusually low level of military spending can be interpreted together as the individual components in a state-centered strategy.

Against the historiography, this account exalts Huskisson at the expense of Cobden and Ricardo. Government policy was remarkably consistent from the early 1820s through the 1840s, albeit with differences in emphasis from Tory to Whig, in a period of extraordinarily rapid social, political, and economic change. Analysis should therefore not stress the domestic changes, because such change in the independent variable cannot explain why policy was so consistent. Instead, focus should be directed toward what was relatively constant after 1822: a system in which Britain faced more rivals than allies.

The quantitative tests presented here are also interesting with respect to the existing literature. While there are several different imaginable alternative explanations for each of the results, the logical rigor of a formal theory unites these disparate hypotheses and empirical results. Thus, parsimony dictates that any set of alternative explanations also be logically interconnected, and it is hard to see how they might be. While of limited usefulness against ad hoc rivals, the tests are useful placed against previous tests of hegemonic-stability theory. These tests, using the concentration-based definition of hegemony that does not apply here, have usually found that hegemony does not affect systemic openness (Conybeare 1984; McKeown 1983, 1991; but see also Mansfield 1994: chap. 5). Here, I ground hypotheses firmly in a theory using a qualitative definition of hegemony and find statistically significant results.

Moreover, my account relies on analyzing the choices made in the cabinet and the manner in which politicians' opinions on public policy change when in the cabinet. Changes in public opinion, or even in the balance of opinion in the Commons and the Lords, do not loom very large in comparison with the initiative taken by a succession of governments. This is not to argue in favor of a return to "great man" theories of history, of course, because the members of these governments faced similar choices and similar constraints throughout and therefore made the same broad choices. When we observe that most members of the 1815 commission changed their minds on trade policy within a few years of one another in the 1820s, we can suspect that rational choice under external constraint, and not personal predilections, is primary.

Part 3
Hegemony and Cooperation

CHAPTER 7

Bargaining and Cooperation

The first six chapters examined hegemonic provision of public goods in a sin-gle-play game. Despite the insight this model gives us, it leaves out the role of cooperation, by which two or more countries jointly agree to act in a way that they would not do separately.[1] After this joint decision, each country indepen-dently decides whether to adhere to the bargain.

Studies of cooperation have been a central part of mainstream hegemonic theory (Keohane 1979, 1980, 1982a, 1982b; Yarbrough and Yarbrough 1985, 1986, 1987), though some strands of the theory ignore it (e.g., Krasner 1976). An increasingly important part of this literature has been a hegemon's leader-ship of a small group of cooperators, which many believe is especially impor-tant as a hegemon declines (Keohane 1984; Lake 1983, 1988; Snidal 1985b).

Some mainstream analysis of the links between hegemony and coopera-tion have focused on international regimes. For example, Vinod Aggarwal (1985) distinguishes the strength, nature, and scope of a regime and shows how hegemony may affect these attributes in different ways. Robert Keohane (1984) looks in detail at the substance of international cooperation, discussing how regimes establish legal liability, reduce transaction costs, provide information, and reduce uncertainty. Others look at the role of hegemony in helping solve coordination problems (e.g., Martin 1993: 100). The theory in this chapter is more abstract than these works, though not in principle inconsistent with an analysis providing such details.

Other theorists have focused on repeated plays of the Prisoners' Dilemma as a metaphor for international bargaining, following a large body of coopera-

---

1. Throughout this chapter, I use *cooperation* in the informal sense found in the field of inter-national relations: the mutual adjustment of policies to achieve some common end (see Keohane 1984; Stein 1990 inter alia). This differs from its technical game-theoretic meaning, which refers to games in which it is possible to sign binding contracts. All of the games in this book are noncoop-erative in game-theoretic terms.

tion theory (Axelrod 1984, 1986; Axelrod and Dion 1988; Lipson 1984, 1986; Oye 1986a; Michael Taylor 1976, 1987). For example, some (e.g., Gowa 1994; Keohane 1984) argue that trade policy can be modeled as an indefinitely iterated game of Prisoners' Dilemma in which each actor would like to be protectionist but wants its trading partners to leave their economies open.[2] In such a game, states may choose a strategy of conditional cooperation (Axelrod 1984; Michael Taylor 1976, 1987), whereby they choose low tariffs while their trading partners do but retaliate with protection against protective tariffs.

The public-goods model of earlier chapters is well suited for such problems. As in the standard characterization of trade policy, each country wants to defect (not contribute to public goods) while wishing that others cooperate (provide the good). In public goods as in the Prisoners' Dilemma, mutual cooperation (joint provision of the good) is better for both than is mutual defection (suboptimal provision of the good).

This chapter will use a repeated-play version of the public-goods model to examine the role of leadership in international cooperation. Repeated play is necessary because a state will cooperate only if it expects not to be punished in future plays of the game. To capture the role of relative size that is important to hegemonic theory, I look first at the relative shares of each state to a given bargain. Presumably, large states make a larger share of the contributions to cooperative public-goods provision, though we can also treat these shares as a subject of negotiation. In contrast to chapter 2, changing the distribution of resources does affect the outcome in the cooperative model.

Stackelberg leadership, a second way to model hegemony, also affects cooperation. A leader is less likely to cooperate than are followers because the noncooperative outcome favors the leader. Again, this result stands in contrast to mainstream theory. As a result, either a quantitative or a qualitative definition of hegemony yields interesting results in the repeated-play game.

Next, I reintroduce security concerns in the cooperative model. This examination follows a growing literature on relative gains that argues that security relationships have an important effect on cooperation (e.g., Gowa 1989, 1994; Gowa and Mansfield 1993; Grieco 1988, 1990; Stein 1990). That literature arrives at the intuitive conclusion that economic cooperation is more likely among allies.[3] However, when we ground cooperation in a model that

---

2. Others use more subtle approaches to specifying the correct two-by-two game form, which might be Bully or Stag Hunt, among others (Conybeare 1984; Lake 1984). Michael Taylor (1976, 1987) rightly points out that collective-goods games may also resemble iterated Chicken.

3. I will look only at cooperation among allies, though it is easy to extend the model to cooperation among rivals (see Pahre 1990).

considers how the noncooperative equilibrium might also affect cooperation, this result no longer holds. Still, security concerns affect both the depth of cooperation and the effects of Stackelberg leadership.

A Basic Model of Cooperation: Size and Shares

Following the same procedure as chapters 3 and 5, I begin with a general model of cooperation and then introduce hegemony. After developing the model in this chapter, I then proceed to test the results in chapter 8. Recall that in chapter 2's two-actor, two-goods model,[4] states have utility functions in general form $U^i = U(m^i, Q)$ and $U^j = U(m^j, Q)$, with a private good (m^i, m^j), a public good (Q), and budget constraints $B^i = m^i + q^i$. The public good supplied equals the sum of contributions to the good, so that $Q = q^i + q^j$.

In the single-play game of chapters 2 and 3, these utility functions yielded a single Cournot-Nash equilibrium, with equilibrium values of the variables $m^{i'}$, $q^{i'}$, etc. If there are sufficiently few iterations, or if actors value the future sufficiently little, this will remain the sole equilibrium.[5]

If actors wish to improve on this nonbargaining outcome, they face a problem often modeled as a Prisoners' Dilemma (PD). If both states cooperate, they receive R (the reward for cooperation); if neither cooperates, they receive P (the punishment for mutual defection). If one cooperates and the other defects, they receive S (the sucker's payoff for unilateral cooperation), and T (the temptation to defect when the other player cooperates), respectively.

In addition to the simple choice of whether to cooperate, states can also choose how deeply they wish to cooperate. In other words, they may reach a bargain large or small. They can also negotiate over the distribution of costs, with one state paying more or less than the other. These two dimensions of a bargain are central to the model here—a bargain's size and the share of the costs paid by each state.

The concepts of size and shares have a natural empirical referent. To take one important example, the size of a trade agreement is the volume of trade covered by the agreement. Trade volume is also a common definition of a concession in the GATT (Curzon and Curzon 1976; Finlayson and Zacher 1983), suggesting that this concept captures something important to policymakers.

---

4. I change the notation for i and j from subscripts to superscripts to reserve subscripts for partial derivatives in this chapter; superscripts were used for exponents in the earlier chapters.

5. Throughout, I assume that the single-play equilibrium will result in the iterated game unless there is an explicit agreement on another point. I also rule out contingent strategies in which a player would contribute less than the single-play $q^{i'}$.

Shares are harder to operationalize but are also politically salient, since policy-makers do not wish to appear to make an unfair share of the concessions in an agreement.

To capture the size and shares of a bargain in the model, suppose that states i and j are considering making an agreement concerning the public good.[6] Under the proposed agreement, i will increase his spending on Q by αh, and j will increase hers by $(1 - \alpha)h$. The size of this bargain is h, which may be any positive real number. The two states' shares are α and $(1 - \alpha)$, respectively, both of which lie between zero and one. This increase costs resources, so i and j will also have to reduce spending on m by αh and $(1 - \alpha)h$, respectively.

There are two ways to think about cheating here, each of which affects only the one period in which a state cheats but before it has been punished. The game-theoretic approach would be to maximize one's utility, given the increased public-goods contributions the other state has agreed to make. In other words, a state cheats by finding $argmax\,(U_i/Q = Q' + (1 - \alpha)h)$. Then, anticipating the other state's punishment, the first state reverts in subsequent periods to the single-play reversion point m', q'. Alternatively, a state might cheat by reverting immediately to the single-play reversion point m', q'. In this approach, a state defects by taking away its concessions but not reducing its contributions below the reversion point level; in other words, q is constrained to be $q \geq q'$.

Because the analysis that follows rests on the comparative statics of the necessary condition for cooperation, it does not really matter which approach I choose. The two approaches yield slightly different starting points because they treat the first defection period differently, but they produce similar changes from this starting point in a comparative statics analysis. I use the second approach, constraining $q \geq q'$, for several reasons. First, doing so makes the analysis directly comparable to the PD case, in which an actor cheats by defecting to the reversion strategy (D). Because PD dominates the literature on international cooperation, this is an important consideration. Second, constraining $q \geq q'$ lets me treat the externalities case in exactly the same way as the public-goods problem because, as I will discuss below, we can think of any externalities problem as a special case of the general model in which $q' = 0$. Third, this approach makes the algebra much simpler, yielding the same Taylor-Axelrod condition that is used elsewhere in the literature (e.g., Gowa 1994; Gowa and Mansfield 1993; McGinnis 1986).

---

6. See appendix A for a model of tariff agreements in repeated play. Though not directly comparable to the public-goods model, it yields some similar results.

Given the utility functions assumed above, the payoffs for i in a Prisoners' Dilemma are (dropping superscripts to conserve notation):

$$P: U(m', Q') \qquad R: U(m' - \alpha h, Q' + h)$$
$$S: U(m' - \alpha h, Q' + \alpha h) \qquad T: U(m', Q' + (1 - \alpha)h) \qquad (7.1)$$

While still couched in terms of public goods, the assumption of a pure public good is not as important here as in chapters 2 and 3. For instance, if we relabel m' as the privately beneficial actions that an actor will take without taking externalities into account, then we redefine the equilibrium supply of those externalities as $Q' = 0$. This cooperation game is then capturing two actors negotiating over how much to change their privately beneficial actions so that the positive externalities for one another (Q) are taken into account.

In repeated play, both sides may stick to the bargain and receive the payoff R, if both are willing to punish the other for deviating from it. When these states successfully achieve R, their contributions to the public good will be positively correlated because the two states jointly increase their contributions contingent on one another's increases.[7]

Instead of cooperating, one or both sides may cheat on the agreement, yielding outcomes S, T, or P. To prevent such cheating, I assume, states use the metastrategy of Grim Trigger (GT) as a deterrent (or enforcement mechanism).[8] If the other state cheats, a state using GT will never cooperate again. While this may seem to be an unduly harsh punishment metastrategy, these are good reasons why most game theorists model this enforcement mechanism. After all, if GT is not strong enough to deter cheating, then it is hard to see what will. In this way, GT delineates the set of agreements that might imaginably be enforced, even if most agreements states actually negotiate are enforced less harshly.[9]

Strong as it is, GT may or may not be sufficient to support the bargain.

---

7. This positive correlation complicates my ability to draw inferences from some empirical patterns. A positive correlation between two states' policies may depend on a security rivalry (as in chapter 5), on successful cooperation, or on both. Neither security rivalry nor cooperation was found in chapter 3, which was unable to explain the positive correlation between states' imports sometimes found in chapter 4. In principle, such patterns are not inexplicable in either this chapter or chapter 5. See also chapter 8.

8. Any number of conditional strategies can support cooperation (see inter alia Axelrod 1984; Hirshleifer and Martinez Coll 1988; Kreps et al. 1982; Michael Taylor 1976, 1987; Tsebelis 1990). Other variations include sequential reciprocity (Calvert 1989), matching behavior (Guttman 1978, 1987), or the hegemonic enforcement that I analyze in chapter 9.

9. Problems of incomplete monitoring and accidental cheating help explain why states prefer less harsh enforcement mechanisms.

Whether cooperation occurs depends on each player's discount parameter w^i $\in [0,1]$, which measures the extent to which future payoffs are important. The higher the discount parameter, the more the player weighs future payoffs; when $w^i = 0$, i does not value the future at all, while at $w^i = 1$, i values tomorrow's interactions as much as today's.

Cooperation enforced by GT in repeated PD is stable if the Taylor-Axelrod condition holds—that is, if $w^i \geq (T - R)/(T - P)$.[10] I will label the ratio on the right-hand side of this inequality X. Cooperation based on GT is more likely as w increases and as X decreases, since these changes make it more likely that the inequality will be satisfied. Because discount rates are unobservable and we do not have a theory of where they come from, I examine only changes in X.

There are two sources of change in X, which is a function of α and h. The next two sections will examine changes in these two parameters by solving for the partial derivatives X_α and X_h. Changes that reduce X make cooperation more likely, since cooperation requires that $X \leq w^i$. Where $X_\alpha > 0$, cooperation is more likely as a state's share of a bargain decreases (for a bargain of constant size h); where $X_h < 0$, cooperation is more likely as the aggregate bargain (contributions by all states) increases, with the share of each state in the contributions constant at α. Because the cross partials (i.e., $X_{\alpha h}$) are nonzero, it is also true that changing one state's share of a bargain (α) influences whether larger or smaller bargains are more likely to be stable.

In all these cases, I couch the comparative statics results in probabilistic terms, though the comparative statics examine changes in a necessary condition. The Taylor-Axelrod condition states that $w^i > (T - R)/(T - P)$ is a necessary condition for cooperation.[11] For a known set of parameters, this condition leads to deterministic predictions: either cooperation is feasible or it is not. Because w^i and the other parameters are unobservable, I operationalize the condition probabilistically: increasing w^i makes cooperation more likely, while increasing $X = (T - R)/(T - P)$ makes cooperation less likely.

While there is no practical alternative, this operationalization does mean that falsifying these probabilistic hypotheses does not (directly) falsify the

---

10. The derivation of this condition is straightforward. A state will cooperate if the payoff for indefinite cooperation, $R + wR + w^2R + \ldots = R/(1 - w)$, is greater than the incentive to defect, $T + wP + w^2P + \ldots = T + wP/(1 - w)$. Rearranging this inequality yields the Taylor-Axelrod condition. It must also be true that $T > R > P > S$ to define the game as PD. Cooperation of this form also requires that $(T + S) < 2R$ so that there is no incentive for alternating between exploiting and being exploited (Axelrod 1984; Michael Taylor 1976, 1987). Because S does not matter in the Taylor-Axelrod condition, I drop it from further analysis.

11. Formal theorists can debate the point, but this is probably also a sufficient condition for cooperation because the strategies supporting any bargain that meets this condition Pareto-dominate the strategies supporting noncooperation.

model.[12] For a sufficiently high discount factor, all states cooperate regardless of the comparative statics analysis here, while for a sufficiently low discount factor, no state ever cooperates. This means that the comparative statics look at changes that might not make a difference between satisfying or not satisfying the Taylor-Axelrod condition.

Changing States' Shares in a Bargain

I begin with the derivative X_α to find out how changes in states' shares affect the likelihood of cooperation. First, I find that

$$X_\alpha = \frac{(T-P)(T_\alpha - R_\alpha) - (T-R)(T_\alpha - P_\alpha)}{(T-P)^2} \tag{7.2}$$

$$= \frac{(T-R)P_\alpha + (R-P)T_\alpha - (T-P)R_\alpha}{(T-P)^2}$$

This equation translates X_α into the effects of α on the PD payoffs P, R, and T. Now, I calculate how the payoffs P, R, and T are affected by changes in α:

$$P_\alpha = 0 \qquad R_\alpha = -hU_m|_R < 0 \qquad T_\alpha = -h\,U_Q|_T < 0 \tag{7.3}$$

In the notation here, $U_m|_R$ is the partial derivative of U^i with respect to m^i evaluated at R, and so on. Where we evaluate each partial derivative matters because of diminishing marginal utility. For example, $U_Q|_T > U_Q|_R$ because more public goods (Q) are supplied in R than in T; this means that the marginal utility of Q is greater in T than in R.

Substituting the values from equations 7.3 into equation 7.2 and rearranging, I find that $X_\alpha > 0$ if and only if:

$$\frac{U_Q|_T}{U_m|_R} < \frac{T-P}{R-P} \tag{7.4}$$

Because $T > R$, it will be true that $(T-P)/(R-P) > 1$. This means that the right-hand side of equation 7.4 is always greater than one. In the single-play equilibrium at P, the marginal utility of m and Q will be equal because each actor trades these goods off against each other at the margin. Reducing one's alloca-

---

12. See Lakatos 1970 for the general issues; Snidal 1986 for a compatible discussion of game theory; Pahre 1996b for the distinction between mathematical language and operationalizations applied to political economy.

tion to m and increasing the contributions to Q therefore increase the marginal utility of m and decrease that of Q. As a result, $U_m|_R > U_m|_P = U_Q|_P > U_Q|_T$. Consequently, the left-hand side of equation 7.4, $U_Q|_T / U_m|_R < 1$. As a result, the inequality in equation 7.4 always holds.

This finding means that reducing a state's share in a bargain (α) always makes its cooperation more likely. The intuition is straightforward: reducing the cost to a state of a given level of benefits (h) reduces the temptation to defect. It also increases that state's utility when cooperation occurs (R). Both of these changes make cooperation easier.

At the same time, reducing one state's share (α) must necessarily increase the other's share ($1 - \alpha$). By the same logic, this makes cooperation less likely for the other state. Given this interdependence, it is important to note that decreasing α does not make cooperation inevitable, though it does mean that the necessary condition is more likely to hold for i. Analogously, increasing ($1 - \alpha$) does not necessarily make j unable to cooperate. The best way to state the result is that lowering a noncooperative state's share of the bargain (α) is a necessary but not sufficient condition for cooperation because reducing may not suffice to make X^i less than w^i. Similarly, raising the other state's share ($1 - \alpha$) may make it less likely to cooperate but might also leave X^j less than w^j.

There is substantial indeterminacy in the model, as many possible values of α may make cooperation feasible for both states. (Depending on the discount factors and other parameters, it might also be true that no value of α makes cooperation possible for both states.) Again, this means that the best operationalization of the theory is probabilistic, since it explicitly allows for this indeterminacy.

Finally, the result in this section is consistent with a recurrent pattern in international relations. Small states, which pay a very small share of the costs of collective goods in most international regimes, almost always find such cooperation attractive.[13] Indeed, small-state support for international cooperation is a commonplace in theories of small states (e.g., East 1973; Katzenstein 1986). In this way the result captures a widely-observed empirical regularity in the international system.

Changing the Size of a Bargain

While changing a state's share has unambiguous effects, it is more difficult to analyze a bargain's size, h. Increasing the size of the bargain obviously increases

---

13. These regimes are multilateral, of course, not two-player games, as modeled here. However, the result follows whether we think of the two-player game as a small state against the rest of the world or whether we use the multilateral model in chapter 9.

the rewards of cooperation; intuitively, then, it is common for analysts to assume that doing so makes cooperation more likely. Conversely, increasing the size of the bargain also increases the temptation to defect, because both partners are contributing more than they had previously. Defecting saves the cost of one's own contributions while the partner picks up the slack. These changes intuitively make cooperation less likely. For this reason, previous analysts could not reach any conclusions about the likelihood of cooperation in the general PD model (see inter alia Jervis 1978, 1986; Van Evera 1986: 99–108).

Formalization lets me capture the net effects of these simultaneous changes in R and T. First, I find the derivative X_h to see how size affects the Taylor-Axelrod condition:

$$X_h = \frac{(T-P)(T_h - R_h) - (T-R)(T_h - P_h)}{(T-P)^2}$$

$$= \frac{(R-P)T_h - (T-P)R_h - (T-R)P_h}{(T-P)^2} \tag{7.5}$$

If $X_h < 0$, then increasing the size of a proposed bargain reduces X, making it more likely that the Taylor-Axelrod condition ($X \leq w$) will hold. If positive, then the reverse is true, and smaller bargains are more likely to be stable.

To find X_h, I take the derivatives of the PD payoffs with respect to h:

$$P_h = 0 \qquad\qquad R_h = -\alpha U_m|_R + U_Q|_R > 0$$

$$T_h = (1 - \alpha) U_Q|_T > 0 \tag{7.6}$$

It is easily verified that $R_h > 0$ and $T_h > 0$ up to the Pareto frontier, meaning that the bigger the bargain, the greater the rewards of cooperation and the greater the temptation to defect. This accords with the intuition. Yet again, the effect on $X = (T-R)/(T-P)$ is not obvious and requires further analysis.

Because its denominator is always positive and $P_h = 0$, X_h has the same sign as $(R-P)T_h (T-P)R_h$. Substituting the values in equations 7.6 for the derivatives in equation 7.5 and rearranging terms produces the following condition:

$$X_h < 0 \text{ iff}$$

$$\frac{(R-P) - (T-P)U_Q|_R}{(R-P)U_Q|_T - (T-P)U_m|_R} > \alpha \tag{7.7}$$

The denominator of the ratio on the left-hand side of equation 7.7 is negative because $(T-P)/(R-P)$ by definition and because $U_m|_R > U_Q|_T$ by diminishing marginal utility (as discussed earlier). If we normalize $U_Q|_R = 1$, then the numerator is also negative, making the ratio a positive number. The left-hand side and right-hand side of equation 7.7 are both positive, then, so neither is obviously larger than the other. The inequality may or may not hold.[14]

Whether equation 7.7 holds depends not only on unobservables such as $U_m|_R$ but also on α, a state's share in the bargain. Ceteris paribus, as α decreases, it is increasingly likely that the condition will be met, because α is the sole term on the right-hand side and does not appear on the left. This means that if a state's share of a bargain (α) is sufficiently small, it will be more likely to cooperate as the size of the total bargain (h) increases; conversely, if a state's share of a bargain is sufficiently large, it will be more likely to cooperate as the total size of the bargain decreases.[15]

While this is a fairly subtle result, the intuition is straightforward. Where a state's share of a bargain is small, it makes relatively small contributions in exchange for relatively large benefits from the contributions of the other party. If j defects, then i has made a relatively small supraequilibrium contribution and is not hurt too much. Similarly, the incentives for i to defect are relatively small, since the contribution is small and the potential gains large. This reasoning implies that T will be small relative to R. Inspection of the Taylor-Axelrod condition shows that this makes it more likely to hold.

The result may be confusing in the light of the previous section, which showed that reducing α made cooperation easier. Here, for a sufficiently small value of α, increasing the size of the bargain (h) makes cooperation easier.[16] While all states are more likely to cooperate if they pay a smaller share of a bargain (α), some are more likely to cooperate as a bargain becomes larger while others are more likely to cooperate as a bargain becomes smaller.

Again, the result is consistent with casual observation of some international regimes. In the European Union, for instance, the smaller members generally favor deeper integration, while the larger members are more reluctant and often prefer smaller bargains. Exceptions such as prointegration Germany

---

14. Because α is always less than 1, the inequality would always hold if the LHS were greater than 1. The LHS is greater than 1 iff $(R - P) - (T - P)U_Q|_R < (R - P)U_Q|_T - (T - P)U_M|_R$. Rearranging, this condition is $(U_Q|_T - 1)/(U_M|_R - U_Q|_R) > (T - P)/(R - P)$. Because $U_M|_R > U_Q|_R$ and $U_Q|_T > U_Q|_R = 1$, this condition may or may not hold.

15. The definition of "sufficiently" large or small depends on the unobservables in the LHS fraction of equation 7.7. This means that the only available operationalization is probabilistic.

16. Note that h as a measure of size is independent of the size of the parties. For example, any particular bargain over externalities such as NAFTA has some size h such as the increased trade volume its parties anticipate. This trade volume and the contributions necessary to achieve it may look big to Canada and Mexico and small to the United States, but these perceptions are outside the model here.

and a skeptical Denmark only highlight the general pattern.[17] As I will show in chapter 8, there is a similar pattern in negotiations over reciprocal colonial preferences at the turn of the century. The largest state, the United Kingdom, favored little or no bargain, while the smaller dominions favored extensive mutual concessions.

The analysis here bodes poorly for hegemon-led cooperation, since a hegemon is likely to pay a large share of any bargain. For a state paying a sufficiently large share of the bargain (α), cooperation is less likely to be stable as the size of the bargain increases. Instead, such a state is more likely to cooperate as the size of the bargain decreases. In other words, hegemony makes smaller bargains more likely, at least for the hegemon.

To avoid this effect, the nonhegemonic states might obtain the hegemon's cooperation by reducing the hegemon's share (α). Because $X_\alpha > 0$ for all states, this makes the leader more likely to agree to any such bargain. Still, reducing α forces the nonhegemonic states to increase their share of the bargain $(1 - \alpha)$. Nonhegemonic states will end up paying an unfair share of the costs of public-goods provision if they wish larger bargains. This parallels the noncooperative result, where the hegemon shifts the costs of public goods onto others when it can.

Both of these results challenge the existing literature, which argues that leadership of international cooperation is an important way that hegemons can act benevolently (Keohane 1984; Lake 1988). It is true in the model here that hegemonic cooperation is benevolent in the sense that everyone is better off with cooperation than without it. Still, this cooperation is a different kind of hegemonic benevolence than that in chapter 5, since it depends on mutual consent.

While mutual cooperation may be benevolent, the precise terms of this cooperation are less advantageous for others when there is a hegemon (or other large state) than when there is not. Because it pays a large share, a hegemon is less likely to cooperate. This implies that a hegemon will often demand reducing its share of the costs of any bargain. Moreover, since smaller bargains are more likely to be stable for a large state, a hegemon will typically want to reduce the size of a bargain. Applied to tariff negotiations, for example, these results suggest that a hegemon or other small state will want agreements that make relatively small cuts on a narrow range of tariff lines and will ask other states to increase their share of the total volume of tariff cuts in the agreement. All these effects bode poorly for others, even when hegemons are willing in principle to cooperate.

---

17. For a test of these hypotheses against Britain's renegotiation of the terms of entry into the EU, see Pahre 1995.

Stackelberg Leadership and Cooperation

The results of the previous section depend on the Cournot-Nash (non-Stackelberg) equilibrium. Chapter 3 showed that Stackelberg leadership will change the nonbargaining outcome.[18] By changing the single-play equilibrium, Stackelberg leadership also changes the reversion point or punishment payoff P in repeated play. Increasing P increases the ratio $(T - R)/(T - P)$ and makes cooperation less likely because $X_P > 0$;[19] decreasing P has the reverse effect. As a result, leadership affects the likelihood of stable bargaining outcomes.

Specifically, the leader's utility in the Stackelberg equilibrium is greater than in the Cournot-Nash, so for the leader i, $P^S > P^C$. The follower's utility is less, so for follower j, $P^C > P^S$. Because $X_P > 0$, the leader is less likely to cooperate in the Stackelberg equilibrium than in the Cournot-Nash. The follower, in contrast, is more likely to cooperate. Phrased differently, the leader's ability to free ride on the followers makes the leader less likely to cooperate.

This result has a simple intuition. Because the Stackelberg equilibrium reversion point is favorable for the leader, the follower's retaliation is not as menacing. Conversely, the reversion point is worse for the follower, so she is more likely to cooperate to avoid it.

However, this claim ignores any changes in T and R that may also occur as a result of the changed Stackelberg reversion point.[20] Thus, I will also consider the *Stackelberg bargain,* a term I use as a shorthand for "bargains with a single-play Stackelberg reversion point" (which are not Stackelberg in the sense that one state moves first). To focus attention on the changed reversion point, I examine a bargain of the same size and shares as in the Cournot-Nash case.

---

18. Stackelberg leadership might have two additional effects. First, a leader might be able to move first in negotiations and always make the first offer. This may give the leader a valuable negotiating advantage, which I ignore here (see Rubinstein 1982 for analysis of such a model). Second, defection and punishment might be sequential, with the leader being the first to choose whether to defect. If the sequence in each round is (1) leader defects, (2) follower defects, (3) both receive payoff, then the leader never faces a temptation to defect, which makes its choice completely uninteresting. If the sequence is (1) leader defects, (2) both receive payoff, (3) follower defects, (4) both receive payoff, then the analysis is the same as in the text.

19. Specifically, $X_P = (T - R)/(T - P)^2 > 0$.

20. This need not be a problem if we are willing to make some unusual additional assumptions. Even with the new P^S, we could construct a bargain guaranteeing both states the same utility as before, $R^S = R^C$, in which actors cheat by choosing some $T^S = T^C$, because if they cheat with some other T the other state punishes them with P. By the wonders of the Folk Theorem, this would be an equilibrium with sufficiently little discounting of the future. Though it relies on odd assumptions, this means that looking at changes in P without considering changes in T and R is at least theoretically possible.

General results are difficult, and I will summarize the following analysis at the end of this section for readers who wish to skip the mathematical details. In the rest of this section I compare the payoffs T and R and their effects on the ratio $X = (T - R)/(T - P)$ across bargains. Anything that increases T makes cooperation less likely, while anything that increases R makes cooperation more likely.[21] Similarly, decreasing $(T - R)$ and increasing $(T - P)$ makes cooperation more likely by the effect on X.

The follower's utility is less in P^S than in P^C. By assumption, we now add to this P a bargain of constant size and shares to obtain R. This effectively retains the cost-shifting effects on P found in chapter 3.[22] As a result, for an identical bargain (α and h), the follower's utility is less in the Stackelberg bargain than in the non-Stackelberg bargain (i.e., $R^S < R^C$). The temptation to defect also retains the underlying cost-shifting effects so that $T^S < T^C$. In other words, by holding the bargain constant, the Stackelberg bargain simply shifts both R^S from R^C and T^S from T^C in the same direction as hegemony shifts P^S from P^C. This has ambiguous effects on the Taylor-Axelrod condition because reducing R makes cooperation less likely while reducing T makes cooperation more likely.

To resolve this ambiguity, consider $(T - R)$ and $(T - P)$, which are the numerator and denominator (respectively) of X. Because of diminishing marginal utility, a bargain of constant size αh will produce different net utility effects in the Stackelberg bargain than in the Cournot bargain. In either equilibrium, the only difference for j between T and P is i's contribution αh in T. When added to a lower base such as P^S, αh will be valued more highly than when it is added to a higher base such as P^C, because of diminishing marginal utility. Because this αh makes T different from P, the difference between the temptation and punishment payoffs is greater in the Stackelberg bargain than in the Cournot bargain. Algebraically, then, $(T^S - P^S) > (T^C - P^C)$. This increase in $(T - P)$ reduces the fraction X. By reducing X, it makes the follower more likely to cooperate.

I also need to consider changes in the numerator, $(T - R)$. It is possible to compare $(T - R)$ in the Cournot and Stackelberg equilibria with a little algebra. Given that $(T^S - P^S) > (T^C - P^C)$ and $R^S < R^C$, subtracting the latter inequality from the former implies that $(T^S - R^S - P^S) > (T^C - R^C - P^C)$. Rearranging, $(T^S - R^S) > (T^C - R^C) + (P^S - P^C)$.

---

21. Formally, $X_T = (R - P)/(T - P)^2 > 0$, while $X_R = -(T - P)/(T - P)^2 < 0$.

22. When cooperating, j contributes $q^{j'} + (1 - \alpha)h$ and its allocation to private goods is $m^{jS'} - (1 - \alpha)h$.

This inequality shows how the effect of leadership in the numerator of X, $(T - R)$, depends on the cost-shifting effect of leadership in the reversion point. When the cost-shifting effect $|P^S - P^C|$ is sufficiently small, $(T^S - R^S) > (T^C - R^C)$. In contrast, if the cost-shifting effect is sufficiently large, $(T^S - R^S) < (T^C - R^C)$.

Chapter 3 showed that the size of the cost-shifting effect depends on how much states value private goods relative to public goods. If both states place great weight on private goods, the cost-shifting effect is large, while if both states weigh public goods heavily, the cost-shifting effect is small.[23] As I discussed in chapter 3, states probably weigh private goods heavily, so the cost-shifting effect is large. When this effect is sufficiently large, the numerator in X is less in the Stackelberg bargain than in the Cournot-Nash bargain, so X is less and cooperation is more likely.

What does all this mean? For the follower, the denominator of X is always larger in the Stackelberg bargain than in the Cournot-Nash, making cooperation more likely. The numerator $(T - R)$ may be either larger or smaller in the Stackelberg equilibrium, depending on how states' preferences influence the cost-shifting effect. While I can make no definite claim, state preferences are probably such that followers are more likely to cooperate when there is a Stackelberg leader than when there is not. Because this is the same conclusion I reached by comparing only P across the two equilibria, holding T and R constant, it is probably fairly robust.

An analogous analysis is possible for the leader, though it produces different conclusions. For i, $T^S > T^C$ because the gains from shifting the costs of the public good onto others affect not only the reversion point (P) but also the utility from the follower's increased contributions of $(1 - \alpha)h$. No unambiguous comparison of R^S and R^C is possible, since the leader benefits from greater consumption of private goods at the cost of lower public-good provision than in the Cournot-Nash. For a sufficiently small share (α) of the total contributions, $R^S > R^C$ because the leader gains from the underlying cost shifting and from large gains in public-goods provision at small cost; for a sufficiently large share α, $R^S < R^C$ for the reverse reason. In short, for a hegemon paying a sufficiently large share of the bargain, $T^S > T^C$, $P^S > P^C$, and $R^S < R^C$, all of which make cooperation less likely. Since hegemons presumably pay a large share of bargains, Stackelberg leadership makes their cooperation less likely.[24]

---

23. In the notation of that chapter, $Q^S = Q^C/(1 - \alpha\beta)$. The Stackelberg level Q^S becomes small relative to Q^C as $\alpha\beta \to 1$, where α and β are the two states' Cobb-Douglas weightings of private goods relative to public goods.

24. One important exception to this is when a hegemon's share of a bargain is relatively small. Chapters 9 and 10 argue that multilateral bargains can do this, so they may make a hegemon more likely to cooperate.

In short, when the leader pays a sufficiently large share of the bargain, I can unambiguously say that cooperation is less likely for the leader. As in the Cournot bargain analyzed in the previous section, a large state paying a large share of a bargain is less likely to cooperate. Moreover, this is the same conclusion I reached by comparing only P while holding T and R constant. The conclusion is most likely robust.

To summarize this section, I have found that malevolent hegemony makes cooperation less likely for the leader and more likely for the follower. Moreover, this result will generalize to a game with multiple followers.[25] Each follower will face a worse reversion point when there is a leader, giving each follower a greater incentive to cooperate with someone. Since the leader's incentive to cooperate is less, it only stands to reason that the followers will find themselves cooperating with each other.

This suggests that followers cooperate with one another as a response to malevolent hegemony. This result differs significantly from the conventional wisdom. Robert Keohane (1984: 244), like many others, argues, "Nonhegemonic cooperation is difficult, since it must take place among independent states that are motivated more by their own conceptions of self-interest than by a devotion to the common good." Lisa Martin (1992: 86–90) rightly counts as a falsification of existing hegemony theory her finding that the hegemon obtains less cooperation on economic sanctions than do other states. In the face of these problems, mainstream theory has tried to figure out what kinds of states will or will not cooperate with the hegemon in support of its leadership (Brawley 1993; Lake 1988; Stein 1984; Yarbrough and Yarbrough 1985, 1987). The absence of such cooperation is important to Timothy J. McKeown's (1983) critique of the theory.

This literature overlooks the possibility that nonhegemonic states may cooperate with each other and, even more striking, that the leader may make such nonhegemonic cooperation more likely. Hegemony may indeed make cooperation more likely—by everyone but the leader!

Alliances and Economic Cooperation

Having worked through the effects of size, shares, and hegemony, I am now in a position to reintegrate security concerns into the model of cooperation. To do so, I return to the model of chapter 5, which analyzed a three-way trade-off

---

25. Consider a model with leader i and followers $\{j, k, \ldots, n\}$. The effects of Stackelberg leadership on $X = (T - R)/(T - P)$ will remain for bargains of i and any j, or between any two or more followers.

of guns, butter, and contributions to public goods. Recall that this analysis assumed the following utility functions and resource constraints:

$$U^i = U(G, m^i, Q) \qquad Q = \Sigma q^i$$
$$B^i = m^i + g^i + q^i \qquad G = g^i + pg^j \tag{7.8}$$

Because of the budget constraint, increased contributions to the public good require lower allocations to some other goods. There are three choices: the increase in public goods can come out of private goods, out of spending on guns, or out of both. Reducing military spending to pay for public goods would be a strange choice among allies, since each benefits from the military spending of the other. This leaves private goods alone as a source for the greater contributions to public goods.

Yet if the increased contributions come solely out of private goods, the model reduces to the simpler model analyzed so far in this chapter. In this case, security concerns are irrelevant and do not raise any further theoretical questions.

There is a third possibility, however. The allies could agree to increase spending on both public goods and on the military, reducing both states' spending on private goods to pay for this bargain. In other words, security concerns may affect economic cooperation when there is linkage between bargains in the economic and military realms.[26] In this model, then, linkage is a necessary condition for security considerations to affect economic cooperation.

This focus on linkage differs from the literature on relative gains (Gowa 1989, 1994; Gowa and Mansfield 1993; Grieco 1988, 1990; Snidal 1991a, 1991b; Stein 1984). That literature argues that states in an anarchic environment cannot only look to the absolute gains from cooperation but also must worry about how cooperation benefits them relative to their rivals. Cooperation among allies, for example, should be more likely because it makes both parties better off against third-party adversaries. This is not what drives the model here, where alliances affect economic cooperation only when there is linkage between military cooperation and economic cooperation.

To model this linkage, suppose that two allies come to a comprehensive agreement to increase contributions to the collective good and to increase joint military spending. Since I wish to examine the effects of changing the size of the total bargain, I will assume that each state's concessions in each issue area are

---

26. For different kinds of linkage models, see Lohmann 1997; McGinnis 1986; Tollison and Willett 1979; Stein 1980.

proportional by a factor $\beta > 0$. State i's increased contributions to the collective good are αh, and its increased military spending $\alpha \beta h$; state j's increased contributions to the collective good are again $(1 - \alpha)h$, and the increased military spending $(1 - \alpha)\beta h$. The payoffs in a Prisoners' Dilemma are:

$$P: U[g^{i\prime} + pg^{j\prime}; m^{i\prime}; Q']$$

$$R: U[g^{i\prime} + \alpha\beta h + p(g^{j\prime} + (1 - \alpha)\beta h); m^{i\prime} - \alpha (1 + \beta)h; Q' + h] \qquad (7.9)$$

$$T: U[g^{i\prime} + p(g^{j\prime} + (1 - \alpha)\beta h); m^{i\prime}; Q' + (1 - \alpha)h]$$

A glance at these utility functions makes it evident that the algebra in this section will be rather involved. Again, I will summarize the results at the end of the section for readers who wish to skip the mathematical details.

Both the size of the bargain (h) and the relative shares of each state in the bargain (α) affect the payoffs. The two new variables also play a role, alliance tightness (p) and the variable (β) that captures the relative weight of economic and security cooperation in the total bargain.

Changes in alliance tightness (p) have several distinct effects on cooperation. First, p changes the payoffs directly, affecting the ratio X. Second, p may make larger or smaller bargains more likely by affecting how changes in h change X. Third, p may affect how linkage (β) affects X. This multiplicity of effects is richer than the relative-gains literature, which looks solely at p and cooperation.

I begin by looking at the direct effects. As p changes, the payoffs change as follows:

$$P_p: g^{j\prime} U_G|_P > 0 \qquad\qquad R_p: (g^{j\prime} + (1 - \alpha)\beta h) U_G|_R > 0$$

$$T_p: (g^{j\prime} + (1 - \alpha)\beta h) U_G|_T > 0 \qquad\qquad (7.10)$$

Because of diminishing marginality utility, $U_G|_P > U_G|_T > U_G|_R$; the more guns produced, the less the marginal utility from an additional increment.

Once again, the sign of the partial derivative X_p will depend on the sign of the expression $(R - P)T_p - (T - P)R_p + (T - R)P_p$. Unlike the other derivatives of P discussed so far, the derivative of P with respect to p is nonzero (recall that $P_\alpha = P_h = 0$). Changes in the size or shares of a bargain do not affect the non-cooperative level of P, but changing alliances or animosities (p) do affect P. As in the preceding section, changing the reversion point has important effects on the likelihood of cooperation.

After substituting and rearranging, I find that $X_p < 0$ iff

$$(T - R)g^{i'} U_G|_P + [g^{i'} + (1 - \alpha)\beta h] [U_G|_T(R - P) \ U_G|_R(T - P)] < 0 \qquad (7.11)$$

Perhaps surprisingly, this condition may or may not hold. The first term and the first bracketed term are both positive, while the second bracketed term may be positive or negative.[27] This means that closer security ties may make cooperation either more or less likely. (The intuition behind this result is discussed shortly.) An alliance, for example, might have either a positive or negative effect on a particular bargain.[28] A population of such alliances might show that there is a systematic positive relationship between alliances and cooperation, a systematic negative relationship between alliances and cooperation, or no systematic relationship at all.[29]

The ambiguity in this result contradicts the relative-gains literature, which argues that increasing alliance tightness has an unambiguously positive effect on the likelihood of cooperation. The ambiguity stems from the fact that alliance tightness (p) affects the noncooperative equilibrium (P) in the model here, an effect that is ignored in this literature. By making the noncooperative outcome better for both allies, alliance tightness may make cooperation less likely. Cooperation is easier when states threaten each other with reversion to an unattractive single-play equilibrium, but allies only threaten each other with a relatively attractive P. Even though alliance tightness increases the rewards of cooperation (R), looking solely at changes in T and R leads to misleading results.

Because it distinguishes the effects of p on the noncooperative game from the effects on GT enforcement of cooperation, the model also lets me make a clear distinction between trade and cooperation. In the mainstream literature, as here, cooperation is the mutual adjustment of policies (Keohane 1984; Stein 1982, 1990). Countries make nonzero contributions to public goods in both P and R, but they cooperate by adjusting policies only in the latter. In contrast, the relative-gains literature generally conflates the two, treating trade and cooperation as the same thing (see esp. Gowa 1989, 1994; Gowa and Mansfield 1993). Alliances may well increase trade, as in the single-play model of chapter 5. However, this increase in trade makes cooperation less likely by making noncooperation more attractive. At the same time, it is reasonable to suppose

---

27. Because $(T - P) > (R - P)$ but $U_G|_R < U_G|_T$, the term $U_G|_T(R - P) - U_G|_R(T - P)$ may be greater or less than zero.

28. Note that I have made no claims about security rivalries and either the presence or absence of cooperation.

29. Interestingly, the result is consistent with Martin's (1992) finding that Cold War allies were no more likely to cooperate against their Cold War adversaries on economic sanctions than were states in North-South sanctioning episodes.

that cooperation—when it occurs—leads to increased trade. Simply using trade as a measure of cooperation, which is ostensibly more likely among allies, can easily lead to misleading results.[30]

Even though it does not affect the probability of cooperation, alliance tightness (p) does have other interesting effects on cooperation in the model here. To see these, I examine the direct effect of size (h) on the Taylor-Axelrod condition (X). As the size of the bargain (h) changes, these payoffs change as follows:

$$P_h = 0$$
$$R_h = \beta[\alpha + p(1 - \alpha)]U_G|_R (1 + \beta)U_m|_R + U_Q|_R > 0 \tag{7.12}$$
$$T_h = \beta p(1 - \alpha)U_G|_T + (1 - \alpha)U_Q|_T > 0$$

Because p affects these derivatives, it will also affect X_h. To see how, I examine how changes in h affect the Taylor-Axelrod condition for stable cooperation,

$$X_h < 0 \text{ iff} \tag{7.13}$$

$$(R-P)U_Q|_T + \frac{T-P}{1-\alpha}[\alpha(1+\beta)U_M|_R - U_Q|_R - \alpha\beta] < \beta p[(T-P)U_G|_R - (R-P)U_G|_T]$$

Though it is hardly obvious at a glance, increasing p increases the likelihood that these conditions will be met.[31] This means that, as an alliance grows tighter, states will prefer larger and larger bargains. Conversely, as p decreases, smaller bargains will make it more likely that this stability condition holds.

This is intuitive. When states link cooperation in economic and security affairs, a closer security relationship makes deeper cooperation easier in both issues. It is interesting that tighter alliances make larger linked bargains more likely, even if alliances do not make such bargains either more or less likely.

A good illustration of the logic at work here is allied export-control policy in the postwar period (see Long 1989; Mastanduno 1988). Throughout the Cold War, the United States and its NATO allies cooperated in restricting the export of certain technologies to the Soviet Union and its allies. Changes in the

---

30. Some earlier studies of security externalities theorized directly about trade without considering cooperation as an intervening variable (e.g., Polachek 1980; Pollins 1989), so this point does not apply to them. Martin's (1992) analysis of sanctions is also compatible with the analysis here since she looks directly at cooperation.

31. By diminishing marginal utility, $U_G|_R > U_G|_T$, and $(T - P) > (R - P)$ because $T > R > P$, so the bracketed term on the RHS is greater than zero; thus, increasing p unambiguously makes the condition more likely to hold.

alliance, such as a tightening during the Korean War or a loosening in the 1970s, did not affect the presence or absence of cooperation, since the allies cooperated on export controls throughout the period. However, the size of the bargain did vary over time with changes in the Cold War and in alliance politics. A simple measure of this size is the number of goods covered by the regime, and the literature agrees that this number increased in times of Cold War tension, decreased in times of detente. This is exactly the distinction that the theory tells me to examine.

Changing β, which captures the importance of military cooperation relative to economic cooperation, also has an interesting effect on X_h. To analyze this effect, first move all the terms with β to the right-hand side of equation 7.13. Then the derivative of the new right-hand side with respect to β is

$$\alpha(T-P)(1 - U_m|_R)/(1-\alpha) + p[(T-P)U_G|_R (R-P)U_G|_T] \tag{7.14}$$

Because I have normalized $U_Q|_R = 1$, and because $U_m|_R > U_Q|_R$, then $(1 - U_m|_R)$ < 0. This means that the first of the terms in equation 7.14 is always negative, the second always positive. The negative term will be small if α is small, large if α is large. As a result, for a sufficiently small state (small α), increasing β makes it more likely that $X_h < 0$.

Translated, this means that a sufficiently small state will be more likely to agree to larger bargains as military cooperation makes up a greater share of a linked bargain. By the same token, a sufficiently large state will be less likely to agree to larger bargains as military cooperation makes up a greater share of a linked bargain.

An example, which I discuss in greater length in chapter 8, can help illuminate this complex proposition.[32] As joint military concerns became increasingly important in the South Pacific around the turn of the century, the (small) Australian colonies sought larger comprehensive bargains. This concern eventually helped lead to Australian Federation (Patterson 1968). However, this increased role played by military cooperation did not make the much larger United Kingdom more likely to cooperate in comprehensive bargains. Indeed, the mother country explicitly rejected economic cooperation linked to the empire. This cooperation, which went under the name of tariff reform, would have raised British tariffs against some nonempire goods as part of a general system of intraempire tariff preferences. Economic cooperation occurred

---

32. I also use the proposition to explain intertemporal and cross-national variation in Scandinavian economic cooperation with Western Europe after World War II (see chap. 10).

within the empire, but the forms that interested Britain remained small. This pattern is consistent with the result here.[33]

Linkage (β) also affects the Taylor-Axelrod condition (X) directly, not just by affecting h. The relevant derivatives are:

$$P_\beta = 0$$

$$R_\beta = [hp + \alpha h(1 - p)] U_G|_R - \alpha h U_m|_R \qquad T_\beta = hp(1 - \alpha) U_G|_T > 0] \quad (7.15)$$

The direct effect β of on X indicates whether greater military cooperation makes linked bargains more likely. When $X_\beta > 0$, making military cooperation more prominent increases X, making cooperation more difficult. When $X_\beta < 0$, making military cooperation more prominent makes cooperation easier.

Rearranging, $X_\beta < 0$ when $p(1 - \alpha) U_G|_T (R - P)/(T - P) + \alpha (U_m|_R - U_G|_R) - p(1 - \alpha) U_G|_R < 0$. Increasing makes this condition less likely to be true, while decreasing α makes this condition more likely. In other words, as a country's share of the linked bargain decreases, it is more likely that increasing the share of military cooperation in the bargain makes cooperation more likely to be stable. Phrased differently, making military cooperation more important can make cooperation more likely for states contributing sufficiently small shares to the linked bargain. Large states are less likely to cooperate as military cooperation becomes more salient because they pay the cost of providing both public goods and semipublic military goods. These results concerning the probability of cooperation parallel the earlier result, that greater linkage makes small states more likely to agree to larger bargains. A small state is more likely to cooperate, and more likely to cooperate in a large bargain, as military linkage becomes more important.

This result is subtly different from the conventional wisdom. Mainstream hegemonic theory has argued that American leadership of the Atlantic alliance was an important cause of postwar economic cooperation, since it made American participation in European affairs more likely.[34] The model here suggests that this claim holds only for smaller follower states, since only a state making a sufficiently small share of the contributions will find that greater military cooperation makes a linked bargain more attractive. For this reason, chapter 10

---

33. Chapter 9 shows that a large state can get around this problem by making cooperation multilateral; this reduces its share in the bargain. Chapter 10 argues that this effect, not alliances per se, explains the Marshall Plan and other forms of postwar cooperation.

34. Opinions are not unanimous on this point, however. Robert Keohane (1984: 137) has argued, "American military power served as a shield protecting the international political economy that it dominated, and it remained an important factor in the background of bargaining on economic issues; but it did not frequently impinge directly on such bargaining."

provides a brief test of these propositions against the states of northern Europe, which are small and provide variation in their postwar security relations. This argument leaves only American willingness to cooperate as a puzzle to explain, a problem that I solve through the theory of multilateralism in chapter 9.

This section has derived several results concerning the effects of alliances on economic cooperation. First, I argue that an alliance may make economic cooperation either more or less likely. By improving the reversion point for both players, an alliance makes punishing defectors less effective and therefore may make cooperation less likely, even though alliances also make the benefits of cooperation greater. Second, an alliance makes deeper cooperation more likely by increasing the rewards of cooperation. Placed next to the first result, this suggests a rethinking of the relative-gains literature because alliances affect the size of cooperation but not its likelihood. Third, increasing the importance of military cooperation in a linked bargain has two related effects, both of which depend on a state's share of the costs of the bargain. Greater military cooperation will make a small state more likely to cooperate and will make larger bargains more likely for them. These changes have the reverse effects on large states.

Alliances, Hegemony, and Cooperation

By introducing security considerations, chapter 5 showed that the systemwide pattern of alliances determines whether hegemony is malevolent or benevolent. A leader with more friends than rivals is malevolent, while one with more rivals than friends is benevolent. Like Stackelberg leadership itself, these outcomes of the single-play game change the reversion point, affecting the likelihood of cooperation.

This section will sketch out these effects nonformally, relying on the logic of the results to this point. First, having more friends than rivals leads to malevolent hegemony. This malevolent hegemony, in turn, makes cooperation among followers likely. The logic is the same as the model without alliance considerations presented in this chapter. However, this coincidence of hegemony and cooperation makes it look as if the leader acts benevolently among allies, a common claim in mainstream theory. In contrast, the theory here shows how hegemonic malevolence in the single-play game creates an incentive for the followers to cooperate with each other. Though the observed correlation resembles mainstream theory, the causal mechanism differs substantially.

Second, having more rivals than friends makes leadership benevolent. This raises the followers' utility in P, the reversion point. Following the logic of earlier sections, cooperation becomes less likely. As a result, we should see a general absence of cooperation in periods of benevolent hegemony. Moreover, there should be no systematic difference between the leader's and the followers' willingness to cooperate, since benevolent hegemony raises the reversion points of both. For this reason, it was possible to analyze British hegemony in chapter 6 without discussing cooperation among followers or between Britain and other states in 1815–54. Chapter 8 will provide some evidence showing that this theoretical claim about the nonimportance of cooperation in this period has substantial empirical support.

This effect of benevolent hegemony on cooperation is quite different from that posited by the conventional wisdom. Most scholars have presumed that bargaining is a sign of benevolent leadership, because states only enter into agreements that make them better off. The implication is clear: if hegemons make cooperation more likely, then hegemons are good. In contrast, this chapter finds that malevolent hegemons may make it more likely that other states will cooperate. States are more likely to seek cooperative outcomes if the world without cooperation is especially unattractive. When leadership worsens the nonbargaining outcomes, it may make international bargaining more successful, simply because the hegemon-led outcome makes everyone worse off. When leadership is benevolent, improving everyone's nonbargaining outcomes, cooperation is less likely.

Given these seemingly paradoxical results, we must be careful to distinguish cooperative leadership (analyzed in this chapter) from benevolent noncooperative leadership (analyzed in chapter 5). Table 10 shows these analytic distinctions and how they interact. For example, American leadership in chapter 4 was malevolent with little cooperation, British leadership in chapter 6 benevolent with little cooperation. Chapter 8 will show that British leadership in the second half of the nineteenth century was malevolent with widespread cooperation among followers.

Because they do not clearly distinguish "cooperation" from "welfare improving," other theories of hegemony collapse these two kinds of leadership. However, some mainstream theories argue that cooperation may be a substi-

TABLE 10.   Hegemony and Cooperation

	Benevolent Hegemony	Malevolent Hegemony
Cooperation	Leadership	"The followers shall lead"
Little Cooperation	Tacit hegemony	(Systemic) power

tute for (benevolent) leadership (e.g., Keohane 1984; Snidal 1985b), and this contention is consistent with the theory here.

Finally, it should be noted that this section analyzes how the systemwide pattern of alliances affects the likelihood of cooperation. Cooperation depends on whether the leader has more rivals than friends rather than on whether any particular dyad is friendly or hostile. Benevolent hegemony depends on having fewer allies than rivals. This also makes cooperation less likely, which means that trade is less than it could be if states would cooperate to increase trade. Malevolent hegemony, conversely, makes cooperation more likely, perhaps making it possible to achieve greater joint gains from trade. For this reason, the relationship among hegemony, alliances, cooperation, and trade is more subtle than the existing literature has realized. In the relative-gains literature, for example, alliances affect cooperation at the dyadic level in that two allies are more likely to cooperate than two nonallies.

Despite this analytical difference, the hypotheses here may be difficult to distinguish empirically from the relative-gains argument. If the hegemon is surrounded by rivals, both theories predict an absence of cooperation; if the hegemon has more allies than rivals, both theories predict cooperation is more likely. Looking at trade and cooperation together, as the relative-gains literature does (see Gowa and Mansfield 1993; Gowa 1994), misses the subtlety of the relationship found here. Chapter 8 will attempt to untangle empirically these nuances.

Conclusion

This chapter has covered a lot of ground, looking at cost sharing and the size of cooperative bargains with and without leadership and with and without alliances. Though I used a model of public goods, the publicness assumption is more innocuous here because any externalities problem translates easily into the cooperation model.

The first variant of the model examined leadership solely in quantitative terms, as a state's share of a bargain relative to the share of others. First, decreasing a state's share of a bargain makes its cooperation more likely. Second, states paying a small share of the bargain are more likely to cooperate as the bargain gets larger, while states paying a large share are more likely to cooperate as the bargain gets smaller. Because a hegemon is large, these results imply that large bargains are possible only if other states are willing to reduce the hegemon's share of these bargains.

Alliances also affect cooperation. While having an alliance does not make cooperation more likely, it does make larger bargains more likely. When states link cooperation across economic and military spheres, increasing the importance of military cooperation makes large bargains more likely for small states and makes small bargains more likely for large states. Finally, when economic and military cooperation are linked, increasing the importance of military cooperation makes economic cooperation more likely for small states but not for large states.

While these effects hold without treating the hegemon as qualitatively different, Stackelberg leadership also affects cooperation. Malevolent hegemony makes it more likely that the followers will cooperate with each other, while benevolent hegemony makes cooperation less likely for all. These system-level effects may make it appear that alliances have a direct effect on a dyad's probability of cooperation, but this apparent relationship is spurious.

In contrast, benevolent hegemony makes cooperation less likely for everyone by making the noncooperation outcome more attractive. Benevolence is good for both leader and followers, so there should be no systematic difference between the extent to which the leader and the followers cooperate with each other or with third parties.

As I have noted throughout this chapter, there is also substantial indeterminacy in each variation of the model. This is true of any repeated-play game because of the Folk Theorem, which states (roughly) that anything can happen as long as it improves the noncooperation outcome for one player without making the other player worse off (see inter alia Fudenberg and Maskin 1986; Kreps et al. 1982). Although this infinity of possible outcomes might seem to justify a historian's thick description of events, this chapter has shown that predictions are still possible. The set of possible outcomes is infinite but bounded, and the boundaries may change.[35]

The results differ significantly from the conventional wisdom. Large states, including the hegemon, are less likely to cooperate in large bargains. A Stackelberg leader is less likely to cooperate than are followers. In short, a hegemon is less likely to cooperate with others whether we define hegemony in terms of size or Stackelberg leadership. Moreover, allies are no more likely to cooperate than nonallies. Because of this finding, some scholars' suggestion (e.g., Gowa 1994) that alliances play an important role in hegemonic leadership does not follow from the model here.

In some cases these differences come from making analytical distinctions

---

35. See also the distinction between feasible outcomes and implementable outcomes in Calvert 1989 and the conditions under which the boundaries of the latter set change.

not found in the mainstream literature. For example, I distinguish benevolence from cooperative leadership. Other differences stem from formalization, such as my analysis of the effect of the reversion point on cooperation. Whether the theory here does a better job of explaining the world is, of course, an empirical question, to which I turn in the next chapter.

CHAPTER 8

Hegemony and Commercial Negotiations, 1815–1913

This chapter shifts the focus of earlier empirical chapters to cooperation, the main dependent variable in chapter 7. The Taylor-Axelrod condition in the preceding chapter is a necessary condition that determines whether cooperation is stable. This presumes a dichotomous dependent variable. However, as that chapter showed, a cooperative bargain may be large or small and thus have continuous effects.

One measure of economic cooperation is the signature of international economic agreements. Trade agreements have been a common feature of the international political economy over the past two centuries (and more), so they are a readily available object of study. Moreover, these agreements are similar along many dimensions. This makes it straightforward to compile data concerning them (see appendix B for sources and definitions).

Trade agreement data are well suited for testing the theory. A reciprocal tariff treaty is a dichotomous variable; either two countries sign a treaty or they do not. Such agreements affect trade but do so only indirectly, so I can and should distinguish trade levels clearly from cooperation. However, the trade volume covered by a given treaty is then a reasonable measure of the size of a treaty, an important variable from chapter 7.

To study international cooperation, I need a period that provides variation in the variables examined by the theory.[1] As I will show, the "nineteenth century" (1815–1913) displays substantial cross-national and intertemporal variation in most of the independent and dependent variables of this theory. Alliances varied throughout the century, with Britain allied both with and

---

1. I do not examine assumptions such as Stackelberg leadership, having addressed them in chapter 6 for much of this period.

against France, Sardinia/Italy, Austria(-Hungary), Russia, Prussia/Germany, the Ottoman Empire, and many smaller powers. I limit this chapter to the nineteenth century to avoid tests across structural breaks such as world wars.

The theory in chapter 7 shows that relative size plays a role in cooperation—that is, that quantitative definitions of hegemony are relevant in the bargaining model though they are not in the single-play model. The century exhibits substantial variation along this dimension as well, since the rapid growth of Germany and the United States led to a significant decline in Britain's relative size over the course of the century.

Like the other periods studied here, the nineteenth century does not provide variation in hegemony defined as a Stackelberg leader. As a result, there is no good way to test the counterfactual argument that a leader is less likely to cooperate because it is a leader. To get around this problem, I will use cross-national variation between Britain and the other great powers, contrasting the patterns of their commercial negotiations.

To provide greater variation in the relative size of states, I will also look at cooperation within the British Empire as countries achieve control over their own commercial policies. When a large state cooperates, its bargains are more likely to be small. By looking at the negotiations leading up to a particular economic agreement, I should also find the United Kingdom making demands to reduce the size of the bargain. A good way to test this claim is to examine England's discussions with the dominions, all of whom were much smaller than it. I expect to see Britain trying to reduce the extent of any such cooperation while the dominions seek to expand it. In addition, the theory suggests that Great Britain will be less interested in intraempire cooperation than the dominions will be, because it is a leader and they are followers.

A second way to get at the effects of hegemony is to contrast periods of malevolent and benevolent hegemony. Chapter 7 makes different predictions depending on whether hegemony is malevolent or benevolent in the single-play game, because this serves as the reversion point for the repeated-play model of cooperation. The nineteenth century provides variation in this variable as well, especially if I revisit the period discussed in chapter 6 (1815–54). At the same time, some simple tests help me reject the mainstream hypothesis that systemic concentration affects aggregate trade.

The systemwide pattern of alliances also varied. The United Kingdom had more rivals than friends from 1821 until about 1866 but more friends than rivals in 1815–21 and in most of 1866–1913. As a result, British hegemony was benevolent in 1821–66, malevolent in most of 1866–1914.[2] However, this malevolence is less obvious in 1866–1914 than in 1815–20 because it led to a network of commercial treaties among follower states, led by Austria-Hungary, France, Germany, and Italy. These commercial treaties counteracted what would have been British malevolence. This nonhegemonic cooperation poses a major challenge to existing theory (e.g., Lake 1988: 92–96; cf. McKeown 1983) but is strikingly consistent with the theory here.

Concentration and Trade, 1866–1914

I begin by rejecting an important part of mainstream hegemony theory before moving to my interpretation of the period. The conventional wisdom is that hegemony is a form of concentration, and that concentration leads to higher levels of trade and public goods provision. Though I have already criticized this argument both theoretically and empirically in chapters 2 through 4, I briefly present another test here for completeness.

If the conventional wisdom is right, aggregate trade should depend on the concentration of resources in the system. Table 11 tests this concentration hypothesis. Data exist for six countries from 1881 on, five countries beginning in 1866.[3] I use the Hirschman measure of concentration, the sum of the squared shares of resources, and I include each country's GNP as a control variable. Initial tests showed high degrees of positive serial correlation, which disappeared when I used first differences. Unlike most of the other tests in this book, the control variable *Year* is irrelevant, but I show tests both with and without it for comparison.

The table finds no support at all for the concentration hypothesis. Of course, it is possible that including those major powers for which data are unavailable, such as Austria-Hungary or Russia, might change these results. However, the results are so consistently bad for the concentration hypothesis, and the standard errors so large, that I find this possibility unlikely. Concentration and the quantitative measures of hegemony that it implies do not matter

---

2. Because most previous tests of the theory assume benevolent hegemony, they should find no relationship between hegemony and openness during periods of malevolence. Mansfield (1994) finds that hegemony leads to openness if he defines British hegemony as having ended in 1873, but he finds no relationship between the two variables if he codes British hegemony as having ended in 1914. This is consistent with the claims here.

3. Norway and Sweden were not, strictly speaking, two countries in this period because they were united under the Swedish crown until 1905. However, Norway had autonomy in many areas and kept separate statistics.

for the system. In the next two sections I will show how diplomatic relations do and do not affect the international political economy in the nineteenth century.

British Hegemony, 1854–1870

Chapter 5 showed that the systemic pattern of alliances determines whether hegemony is malevolent or benevolent. Chapter 6 showed that I should divide the first half of the "nineteenth century" into two periods, the Quadruple

TABLE 11.   The Concentration Hypothesis, 1866–1913

	Six Countries		Five Countries	
	Total Imports	Total Imports	Total Imports	Total Imports
Constant	−350.††	−8800.	6.1	−3900.
	(140.)	(26000.)	(64.4)	(8500.)
Concentration (six)	−29.	−34.		
(in thousands)	(76.)	(78.)		
Concentration (five)			−17.	−21.
(in thousands)			(26.)	(28.)
U.K. GNP	4.9†	5.0†	−.087	−.14
	(2.5)	(2.5)	(1.2)	(1.2)
France GNP	.29†	.31†	.22	.25
	(.16)	(.17)	(.18)	(.19)
Germany NNP	.19	.18		
	(.12)	(.13)		
Italy GNP	.33	.30	.036	−.00081
	(.31)	(.34)	(.23)	(.25)
Norway GNP	−5.1†	−5.6	−1.3	−1.5
	(3.3)	(3.7)	(1.9)	(2.0)
Sweden GNP	2.0†	2.0†	1.2	1.1
	(1.1)	(1.1)	(.72)	(.76)
Year		4.5		2.1
		(13.8)		(4.5)
N	33	33	48	48
(Years)	(1881–1913)	(1881–1913)	(1866–1913)	(1866–1913)
Adjusted R^2	.76	.75	.44	.43
F	15.5	13.1	7.2	6.1
Durbin-Watson	2.42	2.45	2.07	2.07

Note: All data except Year are first differences. Standard errors in parentheses. Data sources in appendix B.

†$p < .10$, two-tailed; ††$p < .05$, two-tailed; †††$p < .01$, two-tailed; ††††$p < .001$, two-tailed.

*$p < .10$, one-tailed; **$p < .05$, one-tailed; ***$p < .01$, one-tailed; ****$p < .001$, one-tailed.

Alliance (1815–21) and European peace (1821–54). The first period saw malevolent hegemony, the second, benevolent hegemony

The second half of the century is more difficult to classify.[4] Coalitions shifted quite rapidly from the Crimean War through the wars of German and Italian unification. Still, aside from the Crimean War itself, the United Kingdom tended not to have many friends until about the late 1860s. As a result, I should expect continued benevolent hegemony through the 1860s, malevolent hegemony thereafter.

For convenience, I will divide the period in 1870, because it marks German unification and the end of this period of warfare. This section will examine the security relationships underlying British leadership between 1854 and 1870. The rest of the chapter examines the period of renewed peace from 1870 to 1914 characterized by both malevolent hegemony and extensive international cooperation in response to this malevolence.

This period of intermittent warfare (1854–70) begins with the Crimean War, in which Russia fought Britain, France, Piedmont-Sardinia, and Turkey. Though it did not fight, Austria supported this coalition against Russia and gained territory at Russian expense in the Balkans. However, this ungainly coalition fell apart almost immediately after the war, with particular animosity between Austria and both France and Russia. Britain and Turkey were happy to have stopped Russian expansion, while France and Piedmont-Sardinia had expansionist goals of their own. Russia and France enjoyed something of a rapprochement (see A. J. P. Taylor 1954: 96–98). Once again, Britain had few if any friends.

French and Sardinian intentions became evident in the war of 1859, in which they took on an isolated Austria in northern Italy. That war ended when Prussia, with support from an otherwise hostile Britain and Russia, forced both sides to accept international mediation (see Kennedy 1987: 176–77; A. J. P. Taylor 1954: 108–14).

Aside from this mediation effort, Britain remained diplomatically isolated from both the eastern monarchies and from France in most of the subsequent wars. The low point was the war over Schleswig-Holstein, in which England backed the losing Danes. Britain was unable to obtain French or Russian support for its position, since it was on bad terms with both, and Palmerston was unwilling to offer either country meaningful concessions in exchange (see

---

4. Again, I operationalize the theory with my own reading of diplomatic history instead of using databases that are at root someone else's reading of the same history. This has the advantage of capturing informal relationships that are necessarily excluded in any database that relies on formal relationships in the coding rules.

Kennedy 1987: 153; A. J. P. Taylor 1954: 13–17). Again, the hegemon had no friends.

The United Kingdom did enjoy some coincidence of interest with Russia. Both sought to contain France after it annexed Nice and Savoy in 1860 (A. J. P. Taylor 1954: 118). The United Kingdom and Russia were even willing to allow Prussia a greater role in Germany if doing so prevented France's expansion to the east or north. Britain and Russia therefore had a more sanguine view of the wars of German unification than we might otherwise expect. Bismarck had French and Italian support against Austria in 1866 and the approval of most great powers, including the United Kingdom, in his war with France (see Craig 1978: 15–26; Kennedy 1987: 185–86; A. J. P. Taylor 1954: 201–11). These wars marked the start of a period in which Great Britain had more friends than adversaries. I therefore expect malevolent hegemony.

If the claims here are correct, I should see a change in British policy around 1870. Figure 4 shows such a change, with British openness staying near a plateau after 1870 instead of continuing its previous upward trend (see also chap. 6). Unfortunately, the statistical authorities changed the data series in 1870, so that data before and after that date are not directly comparable. Still, the change in trends—which are comparable across data series—are consistent with the theoretical expectation.

This change in British policy presumably had negative effects on other countries. It is interesting that a global slump, the magnitude and length of which remains somewhat controversial among economic historians (see Gourevitch 1986: 72–76 for review), followed a few years after the switch in British policy. However, this slump is usually attributed to a bust in Germany following the *Gründerzeit* boom and to declines in the prices of many primary products stemming from rapid improvements in global transportation (see Craig 1978: 78–85; Rogowski 1989: 21–25; Trebilcock 1981: 46–50 for overviews).

Despite the slump, British openness remained higher in the 1870s than in earlier periods of malevolence. One reason is a secular increase in trade as a result of factors outside the theory, such as improved transportation, communication, and the spread of capitalist economic institutions outside Europe. Another more theoretically germane reason why British openness remains high is the commercial agreements between the United Kingdom and its major trading partners, especially France, Germany, and Belgium. This network of international cooperation neutralized the effects of British malevolence.

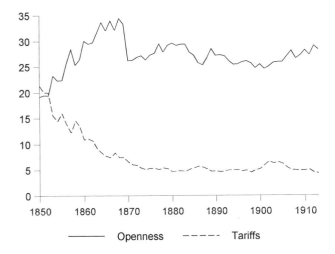

4. British openness and tariffs, 1850–1913. ("Openness" is imports as a percentage of GDP; "tariffs" are customs revenue as a percentage of imports. Sources in appendix B.)

Alliances and Adversaries, 1870–1914

Before turning to this cooperation, I must operationalize the security variables for this final period. The European system changed dramatically in 1871 as a result of German unification (my account draws from Bourne 1970; Craig 1978; Kennedy 1987: 249–56; Steiner 1977; A. J. P. Taylor 1954). Those who had previously acquiesced in Prussia's gains were now concerned lest the seizure of Alsace and Lorraine set a precedent for further expansion.

If the others were wary of Germany, Britain was on good terms with most great powers in the 1870s (Kennedy 1980, 1987: 186–93; A. J. P. Taylor 1954: 256–59). Italy had sought good relations with England as a counterbalance to France. Moreover, Anglo-French relations were quite friendly until 1881, as both shared an interest in containing Germany. There were really no outstanding issues between Germany and England as long as Germany was satisfied with the boundaries of 1871. Only Russia was a clear adversary, both in the eastern Mediterranean and in central Asia.

Though it had good relations with the other great powers in the 1870s, Britain became isolated from 1881 to 1885. Bismarck had brought Austria and Russia together in the Three Emperors' Alliance (*Dreikaiserbund*) of 1881, whose clauses on the Bosporus and Dardanelles were clearly directed against Britain (Craig 1978: 124–34). French rivalry with Italy over North Africa led Italy to join the Triple Alliance in 1882, leaving Britain and France isolated from the other great powers (A. J. P. Taylor 1954: 275–80). The Western powers were also isolated from one another because Gladstone's intervention in Egypt had alienated France (A. J. P. Taylor 1954: 290–92). Britain's isolation was especially clear in 1885, when Gladstone considered using force against Russia in retaliation for its expansion to the borders of Afghanistan. The Triple Alliance acted against Britain, heading off a repeat of the Crimean War by getting Turkey to close the Straits to British warships.

Though colonial problems had exposed Britain's lack of friends, they also helped lead to a new coalition in which the hegemon was to have more friends than adversaries. A colonial entente between Germany and Britain in 1885 gave Germany some colonies in East Africa. Then the Bulgarian crisis of 1886–87 broke the Three Emperors' Alliance apart (Craig 1978: 124–34). After the alliance's formal demise in 1888, Russia turned immediately to France. A Franco-Russian military convention in 1893 was soon followed by a formal alliance, with both accompanied by massive government-sponsored investment in Russia (Kennedy 1987: 221–22; Trebilcock 1981: 221–47).

Britain generally opposed the Franco-Russian alliance, while British interests in the Mediterranean loosely linked it with the other powers. These interests soon led to the First Mediterranean Agreement among Britain, Austria-Hungary, and Italy, with Germany's encouragement behind the scenes (Craig 1978: 131–32, 235–36). England once again had more friends than adversaries.

England and Germany began discussions about an alliance in 1885–89 (see Craig 1978: 117–24; Kennedy 1980; Steiner 1977). There was little colonial rivalry between these powers, and they often shared common interests. In 1890, for example, Britain gave Germany Heligoland in exchange for concessions in East Africa and Zanzibar (Craig 1978: 235–36). This cordial relationship had its effects on British relations with other powers. For example, in the mid–1890s Britain enjoyed the support of the Triple Alliance against France and Russia in Egypt. Again, England had more friends than adversaries.

By the late 1890s, however, events in Europe began to overshadow these colonial concerns (Craig 1978: 224–50). In the interests of a "global policy" (*Weltpolitik*), Kaiser Wilhelm II appointed new men to high positions, most notably Admiral Alfred von Tirpitz as the new state secretary of the *Reichsmarineamt*. Because Tirpitz believed that a conflict with Britain was inevitable, he launched a massive naval construction plan. The hostile German response to the Boer War, German denunciation of the 1900 Yangtze Agreement in China, and Tirpitz's naval program soon combined to turn Britain against Germany by 1901 or 1902 (see Steiner 1977: 25–30).

In response, England switched from one coalition to another (A. J. P. Taylor 1954: 403–26). A treaty with France in 1904 settled differences in Egypt, Morocco, and Newfoundland. England formally came to terms with the Russians in 1907, ending the "Great Game" in central Asia with an agreement covering Afghanistan, Tibet, and Persia. The United Kingdom also signed an alliance with Japan in 1902, while the Hay-Pauncefote treaty (1901) and the Alaskan boundary settlement (1903) contributed to a detente with the United States (Kennedy 1987: 250–52).

When this happened, Britain became part of a larger coalition against Germany and Austria-Hungary, including France, Russia and several non-European powers. The reality of the new diplomatic constellation was brought home during the Moroccan crisis of 1905–6. Britain supported France in Morocco not because of any British interest but to maintain the entente.

In sum, Great Britain had more friends than adversaries in 1887–1914; more adversaries in 1881–85; and probably also more friends in the fluid years between 1870 and 1881. There are minor fluctuations in each of these periods.[5] However, variations in alliance patterns do not affect British trade policy as dramatically as in 1821 because Britain was cooperating with its major trading partners (France, Belgium, Germany).

Without trade agreements, then, I would expect British openness beginning in the 1870s to be negatively correlated with other countries' openness. Because trade agreements entail mutual increases in openness, cooperation counteracts this effect. As I will show, the period from the late 1880s into the mid–1890s also sees a flurry of trade agreements by followers. This is what I expect from underlying malevolent hegemony.

Systemwide Patterns of Trade Agreements

As in chapter 6, I can distinguish claims about behavior at the systemic level from claims about dyads or individual states. These systemic claims include predictions about how a leader's pattern of cooperation will differ from a follower's, since these states vary only in the system-level characteristic of leader/follower.

---

5. There were minor fluctuations in between 1821 and 1854, of course, but the most important of these was limited to 1827, the British-French-Russian coalition that led to the battle of Navarino Bay.

The theory makes two major claims about the systemic pattern of trade agreements. First, Britain is less likely to cooperate than are other countries between 1870 and 1913 because Britain is a Stackelberg leader and they are not. Second, nonhegemonic countries are more likely to cooperate with each other in 1870–1913 than in 1821–54 because the conditions for malevolent hegemony were met in most of this period (especially from 1888 to 1913).

I begin with the cross-national claim that hegemons are less likely to cooperate than are other states. One simple measure of economic cooperation is the number of trade treaties signed with other countries (for more qualitative measures such as size or importance, see below). As figures 5 and 6 show, most follower states cooperated with each other from the 1860s on. The countries that were most active in signing trade treaties were Prussia until 1870 and Austria-Hungary, France, and Italy from the 1860s until World War I. Britain was the leading signer of trade treaties only briefly, from 1815 until the mid–1820s. Because Britain was a malevolent leader in this short period (see chapter 6), this pattern of treaties at the start of the century is anomalous for the theory. The rest of the century, conversely, exhibits exactly what the theory predicts. Followers take the lead in economic cooperation, especially under malevolent leadership in the latter half of the century.

The most important example is the *Zollverein,* or German customs union (Henderson 1939). In 1819–23 the states of Schwarzburg and Anhalt had adopted the Prussian tariff schedule by treaty. They were joined by the Grand Duchy of Hesse in 1828, Hesse-Cassel in 1831, and twelve other states by 1854. The rest of the German confederation joined in 1854–65 except for Austria, the Mecklenburgs, and the Hanse cities. A new customs union in 1867, between the North German Confederation and the south German states (Bavaria, Württemberg, Baden, and Hesse), ultimately became the basis of the fiscal system for the new empire in 1870. By eliminating all internal tariffs on goods, this customs union represented an important form of cooperation.[6]

Prussian success in negotiating trade treaties with the German states induced non-German nations to seek accommodation with it. In 1853, Prussia and a reluctant Austria agreed not to levy corn duties on each other. In 1862 Prussia and France signed a trade treaty, which was applied to the entire *Zollverein* in 1865. Even the United Kingdom sought accommodation with the German states. While it attempted to sign a treaty with the *Zollverein* in the 1830s, it did not succeed until 1841 (Henderson 1939: 127–38). However, this agreement was fairly small, consisting mostly of shipping clauses.

---

6. Other German customs unions in this period include Belgium-Luxemburg and Austria-Hungary-Liechtenstein.

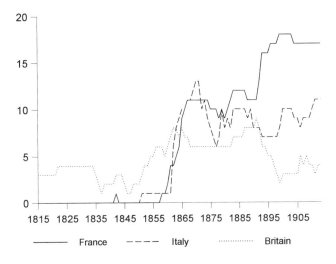

5. Trade treaties in effect, 1815–1913: Britain, France, and Italy

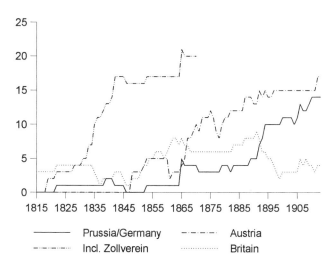

6. Trade treaties in effect, 1815–1913: Austria, Britain, and Germany. (Until unification in 1870, I show the count for Prussia both with and without those treaties signed with German states that made up the *Zollverein*.)

The most important follower nation, France, also cooperated extensively with others. Figure 5 contrasts the number of British and French trade treaties in effect between 1815 and 1913. Roughly speaking, Britain cooperates more with others before 1860, France more after 1860. This pattern is generally consistent with the theory, which expects a difference under malevolent hegemony after 1870. Indeed, the acceleration in the number of French trade treaties comes at roughly the same time that British hegemony turns malevolent, reaching eleven treaties around 1870 and eighteen around the turn of the century. However, since the theory predicts no systematic difference in economic cooperation from leader to follower under benevolent hegemony, the variation we see is unexplained.

Figure 6 shows a different intertemporal trend for Prussia, since the *Zollverein* enjoys a steady increase in cooperation until unification. Germany also saw a marked increase in trade treaties between 1890 and 1894, as part of Leo von Caprivi's *Neue Kurz* (Weitowitz 1978). Most of these commercial treaties lasted until World War I, despite the nominal opposition of subsequent German governments to them.

Italy and Austria-Hungary also signed more treaties than Britain after 1870.[7] Austria-Hungary had an increasingly active commercial policy from the 1870s, signing treaties not only with the traditional trading countries of the West but also with the newly independent Balkan countries. Though Sardinia did not sign a large number of treaties, the kingdom of Italy was active immediately after unification.

Not only did Britain sign treaties comparatively infrequently during most of the century, but those treaties that Britain signed were generally quite small. In the first half of the century, Britain was much more likely to enter into smaller treaties of shipping reciprocity than into larger treaties of tariff reciprocity (see fig. 7). A few shipping treaties made tariff concessions, but the focus of most was reciprocal MFN treatment in shipping regulations and port duties (see Brown 1958: 116–40). In the Prussian treaty of 1841, for instance, British ships could enter *Zollverein* ports on the same terms as German ships and could export rice and sugar to the *Zollverein* on an MFN basis. In exchange, Britain was to treat any *Zollverein* goods shipped through non-*Zollverein* ports from the Elbe to the Maas as if they came from a *Zollverein* port (Henderson 1939: 127–38). This meant that shipping *Zollverein* goods through nonmember entrepôts would not receive unfavorable treatment in

---

7. Russia, not shown in the figures, signed virtually no trade treaties until the Witte period in the 1890s. Smaller powers such as Belgium, the Netherlands, Spain, and Sweden are also not shown. They exhibit an increase in treaties from the 1860s but do not surpass the United Kingdom until the 1890s.

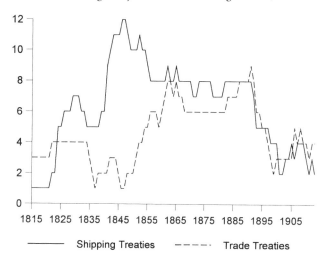

7. **British economic cooperation with Western Europe, 1815–1913**

England. In a treaty with Austria, Britain gave MFN treatment to Austrian articles shipped through the Elbe and Danube and granted a limited exemption from the Navigation Acts for Turkish timber and corn carried on Austrian ships to England.

Huskisson also signed shipping treaties with most states on or near the Baltic Sea, including Denmark, Hanover, the Hanse, Mecklenburg, Prussia, and Sweden. He failed to sign treaties with almost all other countries, including Belgium, Chile, Naples, Portugal, Russia, Spain, and the United States. The Whigs and then Peel added treaties with Greece (1834), Haiti (1838), the Netherlands (1837), Peru (1837), and Prussia (1841) but failed to renew the Swedish treaty.

All these shipping treaties are smaller than tariff treaties. They usually addressed the unintended tariff effects of shipping goods through third parties rather than tariff rates per se.[8] Contemporaries realized that these treaties were fairly insignificant, and the alleged unreasonableness of foreigners led Britain to choose unilateral free trade instead.[9] Robert Peel claimed that he sought unilateral liberalization in the 1840s because he was "wearied with our long and unavailing efforts to enter into satisfactory commercial treaties with other

---

8. Moreover, most MFN tariff treaties included shipping clauses, but shipping treaties did not generally include tariff concessions.

9. In George Canning's doggerel, "In matters of commerce, the fault of the Dutch / is offering too little and asking too much" (cited in Dixon 1976: 253–54).

nations" (cited in Semmel 1970: 141). William Gladstone came to a similar conclusion in the 1850s after his experience at the Board of Trade: "We were anxiously and eagerly endeavouring to make tariff treaties with many foreign countries. . . . we failed in every case. I doubt whether we advanced the cause of Free Trade by a single inch" (cited in Drage 1911: 129).

The claims in this section differ significantly from the conventional wisdom. Many have argued that the Cobden-Chevalier Treaty of 1860 was a watershed event in the Pax Britannica, signifying Britain's willingness to use its large market as a carrot with which to open foreign markets (Gourevitch 1986: 71–72; Stein 1984). This claim cannot explain the fact that France, not Britain, did the most to follow up on this policy by signing treaties with other countries (cf. McKeown 1983; see also Smith 1980: 28–34). In earlier periods, Prussia had done far more than Britain to construct a free-trading zone, while later in the century Austria-Hungary rivaled France in the number of treaties signed, as discussed later in this chapter. Moreover, the United Kingdom had had a moderately active commercial diplomacy in the 1820s, but it was focused on modest shipping treaties instead of more significant trade treaties.

The theory I present is really the only explanation of Britain's failure to use commercial negotiations in conjunction with unilateral liberalization. Britain attempted to negotiate tariff treaties in the 1820s and 1840s, but benevolent leadership is not conducive to major trade agreements. When hegemony is beneficial, the marginal utility of commercial negotiations is less than it otherwise would be.

Security Relations and Trade Agreements

Having looked at the systemwide pattern of cooperation, I can turn to dyadic variables that affect economic cooperation. The first hypothesis is a negative one. The model in chapter 7 suggests that an alliance may either increase or decrease the likelihood of signing a trade agreement. In addition, trade agreements among allies will be larger than trade agreements among nonallies. This claim stands in marked contrast to the relative-gains literature (Gowa 1989, 1994; Gowa and Mansfield 1993; Grieco 1988, 1990; Snidal 1991a, 1991b), which would expect that allies are more likely to sign trade agreements than are nonallies, because allies can benefit from the security externalities of trade.[10]

---

10. Gowa (1994) uses bilateral trade as a measure of economic cooperation, but her theory rests on a comparative statics analysis of the Taylor-Axelrod condition, which assumes a dichotomous distinction between cooperation and noncooperation. For this reason, data on trade agreements would be a better test of her theory.

I test these arguments for both Britain and France, for which good data are available throughout the century. The unit is the country year, where an alliance or treaty is considered in effect if it is operational for six months or more in that year.[11] Data exist for Britain's relations with seven countries: Austria(-Hungary), Belgium, France, Portugal, Prussia (Germany, *Zollverein*), Sweden, and Turkey; I look at France's relations with nine other countries, adding Italy (Piedmont-Sardinia), the Netherlands, Switzerland, and the United Kingdom while excluding Turkey (and France itself).[12]

The data on alliances come from the Correlates of War (COW) project, while the trade treaty data come from the Trade Agreements Database (see appendix B). Because COW distinguishes among defensive alliances, entente alliances, and neutrality alliances, I can examine the effects of different kinds of alliances. Varying alliances imply changing diplomatic relations (p), with defensive alliances the tightest and neutrality alliances the loosest.

I expect to find a significant relationship between alliances and trade agreements, though this relationship may be either positive or negative. Increasing alliance tightness may also have either a positive or negative effect on cooperation. In contrast, the relative-gains argument predicts that there will be a significant positive relationship between alliances and trade agreements and that increasing alliance tightness will also have a positive effect on cooperation. If most relationships are positive and significant, then of course relative-gains theory is more useful because it makes more precise predictions.

The findings, presented in tables 12 through 16, generally do not support the relative-gains argument.[13] For both Britain and France, signing a defensive alliance made signing a trade treaty less likely. For each country, defensive

---

11. An alternative measure would be the initiation of trade treaties instead of the period in which they were in effect. This is problematic because treaty initiation is very strongly clustered around the expiration dates of the old treaties and because of the common practice of having all agreements expire at roughly the same time. Another kind of clustering occurs when newly independent states, such as Bulgaria and Montenegro, start signing treaties. See the Trade Agreement Database, described in appendix B, for further details.

12. I include only those countries with which Britain (France) signed at least one alliance or treaty, and ignore *Zollverein* countries other than Prussia and Italian states other than Piedmont-Sardinia. I also exclude those countries that became independent only late in the period, such as Bulgaria, Montenegro, Romania, and Serbia. All treaties with the *Zollverein* were counted as being Prussian treaties. The Treaty of Frankfurt in 1871 is counted as a trade treaty because it bound French tariffs and guaranteed Germany MFN status. The country-years do not sum to 693 or 891 because Belgium did not exist prior to 1831.

13. Some versions of relative-gains theory argue that the effect should be weaker in a multipolar system or in a system with many great powers (e.g., Gowa 1989, 1994; Snidal 1991a, 1991b). This argument could not explain the consistently significant relationships found here.

alliances made up about one-tenth of all the dyad years, but the combination of a defensive alliance and a trade treaty makes up only about one-twentieth of all trade treaty dyad years. This pattern is inconsistent with the relative-gains argument but entirely consistent with the model of chapter 7.

Neutrality alliances and ententes, in contrast, make trade treaties more likely. Neutrality alliances seem to have the strongest positive effect on the likelihood of a trade treaty. This is perverse for the relative-gains literature, since neutrality alliances are often signed by hostile powers as a guarantee that they will not attack one another. Defensive alliances are generally tighter than either ententes or neutrality alliances; for example, Britain declined French overtures to upgrade their entente to an alliance prior to World War I. This pattern, in which the weakest alliances have a positive effect on cooperation while tighter alliances have a negative effect, directly contradicts relative-gains theory.[14]

The positive relationship between ententes and cooperation should also be treated with suspicion on causal grounds. If we looked only at Anglo-French ententes, the relative-gains hypothesis would fare pretty well (see table 17). However, most of the country years with both an entente and a trade treaty come at the end of the period, in the years leading up to World War I. The relevant trade treaty predates the entente by over a decade, casting doubt on the causal relationship. Even if one argues that Anglo-French security relations were growing closer well before the formal entente, one would be hard pressed to explain why a later treaty (signed in 1881 and honored after its expiration by mutual consent) covers fewer goods than earlier commercial agreements such as Cobden-Chevalier (see Dunham 1930; Smith 1984: 28–34, 184–88). In short, a closer look at the evidence fails to support the relative-gains argument even when a superficial examination looks promising.

In contrast, the evidence is consistent with the claims of chapter 7. All of the relationships are strongly significant, even though they may be positive or negative. Alliance tightness has a significantly negative effect on cooperation, at least when we move from an entente (strong positive effect) to a defensive alliance (strong negative effect).

The bargaining model in chapter 7 also suggests that while security ties may make economic cooperation either more or less likely, these ties do unambiguously make larger agreements more likely to be stable. Testing this proposition is simple in principle. A larger agreement would cover more goods, mak-

---

14. Other recent studies have also called the relative-gains argument into question on empirical grounds (see esp. Morrow, Siverson, and Tabares 1996).

TABLE 12.   Defensive Alliances and Trade Treaties: United Kingdom, 1815–1913

	No Trade Treaty	Trade Treaty	Total
No defensive alliance	505	360	865
Defensive alliance	94	15	109
Total	599	375	974

$\chi^2 = 31.99$ $p < .001$

TABLE 13.   Formal Ententes and Trade Treaties: United Kingdom, 1815–1913

	No Trade Treaty	Trade Treaty	Total
No entente	584	349	933
Entente	15	26	41
Total	599	375	974

$\chi^2 = 11.86$ $p < .001$

TABLE 14.   Defensive Alliances and Trade Treaties: France, 1815–1913

	No Trade Treaty	Trade Treaty	Total
No defensive alliance	389	383	772
Defensive alliance	84	19	103
Total	473	402	875

$\chi^2 = 34.98$ $p < .001$

TABLE 15.   Formal Ententes and Trade Treaties: France, 1815–1913

	No Trade Treaty	Trade Treaty	Total
No entente	461	380	841
Entente	10	24	34
Total	471	404	875

$\chi^2 = 8.30$ $p < .01$

TABLE 16.   Neutrality Alliances and Trade Treaties: France, 1815–1913

	No Trade Treaty	Trade Treaty	Total
No alliance of neutrality	466	391	857
Alliance of neutrality	5	13	18
Total	471	404	875

$\chi^2 = 5.19$ $p < .05$

ing up a larger share of bilateral trade, than a smaller agreement. Unfortunately, it is very difficult to collect systematic data about the size of trade agreements in the nineteenth century because trade data in the period are almost never broken down by commodity. I can test the proposition indirectly by using estimates of size in the next section. In the rest of this section, I make a brief qualitative argument about the pattern of British commercial agreements over the course of the nineteenth century.

Throughout the period, British trade treaties were often a simple guarantee of most-favored-nation status. The most significant exception by far is the famous Cobden-Chevalier treaty of 1860. It granted not only mutual MFN but also entailed important tariff concessions. France abolished import prohibitions and agreed to admit British goods at duties not to exceed 25 percent within five years. The treaty further reduced duties immediately on coal, coke, bar and pig iron, some steel, and machine tools; it also provided for a reduced duty on linens after the expiration of the Belgian treaty in June 1861. Nearly all French goods were already admitted free into Britain, but the government also agreed to reduce the wine duty from fifteen shillings on the gallon to a new scale based on alcohol content, with one or two shillings on wines, eight shillings/four pence on brandies and spirits. England also lowered the duty on silk by half and agreed to allow the free export of coal (Dunham 1930: 98–100).

The theory suggests that security concerns might be a reason why the 1860 treaty was large relative to others (see Stein 1984). This supposition makes sense if the treaty was linked to cooperation in security affairs. The evidence suggests that it was. France thought trade ties would forestall British intervention in Italy, while Britain saw a way to direct French resources from military expansion to trade. Michel Chevalier had argued in the press that England believed a French alliance was the best guarantee of peace, and a commercial agreement could complement Anglo-French cooperation in European affairs (Dunham 1930: 66). Prime Minister Gladstone's instructions to Richard Cobden had included the goal "to cement the friendship with France" (cited in Dunham 1930: 87). The traditionally Francophobe *Times* endorsed the treaty,

TABLE 17.   Anglo-French Ententes and Trade Treaties, 1815–1913

	No Trade Treaty	Trade Treaty	Total
No entente	41	43	84
Entente	4	11	15
Total	45	54	99
$\chi^2 = 2.517$ $p < .113$			

which, "by enabling us to lower the tariff . . . will also enable us to win the confidence of our neighbors, induce them to contract their armaments, and so allow us to contract ours also, and reduce our expenditure" (cited in Dunham 1930: 120).

Of course, a single treaty does not provide definitive support in favor of the hypothesis. Still, it does suggest that the causal mechanisms work in the way I expect. With the evidence in this section, it seems correct that alliances do not affect the probability of cooperation in economic affairs, though alliances do affect the size of an agreement. The next two sections will provide further evidence in support of the claim that allies sign larger bargains, with a quantitative study of Anglo-French trade treaties and then a qualitative examination of imperial preference.

The Effect of Trade Agreements: Quantitative Evidence

Though having an alliance has an ambiguous effect on the probability of a trade agreement between two countries, it has an unambiguous effect on the size of any agreement signed. As chapter 7 showed, alliances make large agreements more likely to be stable, so allies should be more likely to sign large agreements than should nonallies. To test this claim, I need an estimate of the size of trade agreements.

To estimate the size of an agreement, I compare a state's behavior with an agreement against its behavior without one. I can do so by using the same kind of tests as in earlier chapters, looking at how one state's policy affects another's. The public-goods model predicts that each state's imports are a positive function of its own resources and a negative function of other states' resources (see chapter 3; see also appendix A), at least among allies (see chapter 5); among adversaries, a state's imports are a positive function of an adversary's resources.[15] I also presented an alternative test, which predicted a negative relationship between British openness and the ratios of foreign to British GNP.

When two states agree to increase their contributions to public goods, each state's imports or openness will be positively related to the resources of the other or to the ratio between the two states' resources (chapter 7; see also appendix A). The coefficient on this positive relationship, less the positive or negative coefficient in the absence of any trade agreement, is then an estimate of an agreement's size.

There are four possible states of the world, summarized in table 18. Britain

---

15. As in chapter 4, but unlike the second-best solution in chapter 6, this chapter is able to use imports as a left-hand-side variable, GNP on the right-hand side.

and France may have signed neither an alliance nor a trade treaty, they may have signed both, or they may have signed one but not the other. In the absence of a trade treaty, the theory predicts that British imports (openness) will depend positively on French GNP (French/British GNP ratio) when they are security rivals but negatively when they are allies. When they have signed a trade treaty, British imports (openness) should depend positively on French GNP (French/British GNP ratio) regardless of whether they are allies. Finally, British imports depend positively on British GNP in the import model, while I expect a positive constant in the openness model.

To capture these effects, I estimate the effects on British imports of British GNP and four French variables: (1) French GNP; (2) A, an interactive term equal to French GNP when there is an Anglo-French alliance, zero otherwise; (3) T, an interactive term equal to French GNP when there is an Anglo-French trade treaty, zero otherwise; and (4) AT, an interactive term equal to French GNP when there are both an Anglo-French alliance and an Anglo-French trade treaty, zero otherwise. The logic is the same with the openness-and-GNP-ratio test because it is algebraically equivalent to the import-volume-and-GNP test.

The bargaining model predicts that allies will sign larger bargains than will nonallies, even though allies are no more likely to cooperate than nonallies. This implies that the difference between the (alliance, treaty) and (alliance, no treaty) states of the world should be larger than the difference between the (no alliance, treaty) and (no alliance, no treaty) states of the world. Table 18 shows the necessary algebra, which yields the simple prediction that there should be a positive estimate on the interactive variable AT (which is nonzero only when Britain and France have both an alliance and a trade treaty in effect).

TABLE 18.   Quantitative Tests of the Bargaining Theory

	State of the World	Total Estimated Effect	Predicted Sign
I	No alliance, no treaty	GNP	+
II	Alliance, no treaty	GNP + A	–
III	No alliance, treaty	GNP + T	+
IV	Alliance, treaty	GNP + A + T + AT	+
Hypothesis: Allies sign larger bargains than nonallies		$(IV - II) > (III - I)$ or $(IV - II) - (III - I) = AT$	+

Note: All listed variables are interactive variables resting on are dummy variables coded 1 when two states have an alliance or treaty, 0 otherwise. The interactive variables are: A = Alliance × GNP; T = Treaty × GNP; AT = Alliance × Treaty × GNP.

Table 19 presents the estimates for both the import-volume and openness tests.[16] As in chapter 4, the import-volume test suffered from problems of serial correlation and heteroskedacity that were eliminated by using first differences. Unlike that chapter, the openness test suffered from the same serial-correlation problem as the import test (Durbin-Watson = .42), so I used first differences for that test as well. For consistency, I present results with and without the control variable *Year* although it does not improve the estimates here as it did in earlier chapters.

TABLE 19.   The Effects of French Alliances and Trade Treaties on British Imports

	Predict	U.K. Imports (first differences)		U.K. Openness (first differences)	
Constant	(+)	.66	28.	.19	10.
		(1.8)	(130.)	(.16)	(12.)
U.K. GNP	+	.18****	.18****	N.A.	N.A.
		(.030)	(.032)		
France GNP	+	.0057****	.0057****	.36****	.36****
(France/U.K. GNP ratio)		(.0014)	(.0014)	(.10)	(.10)
Alliance Interaction	–	–.00055*	–.00055*	–.048***	–.047***
		(.00040)	(.00040)	(.023)	(.023)
Trade Treaty Interaction	+	.00065	.00065	.11**	.11**
		(.00073)	(.00074)	(.050)	(.050)
Alliance × Trade Treaty Interaction	+	.00052	.00053	.016	.016
		(.00050)	(.00051)	(.039)	(.039)
Year	N/A		–.015		–.0053
			(.069)		(.00065)
N (Years)		83	83	83	83
		(1831–1913)	(1831–1913)	(1831–1913)	(1831–1913)
Adjusted R^2		.51	.51	.26	.26
F		18.4	15.2	8.31	6.86

Note: The Interaction variables are a dummy variable (presence/absence of alliance/trade treaty) multiplied by French GNP (first two columns) or the France/U.K. GNP ratio (last two columns). The theory predicts a positive constant for the ratio test in the last two columns but makes no prediction for the constant in the import-volume test. Standard errors in parentheses. Data sources in appendix B.
†$p < .10$, two-tailed; ††$p < .05$, two-tailed; †††$p < .01$, two-tailed; ††††$p < .001$, two-tailed.
*$p < .10$, one-tailed; **$p < .05$, one-tailed; ***$p < .01$, one-tailed; ****$p < .001$, one-tailed.

---

16. While it would be nice to multiply table 19, for British relations with other countries, the treaties and GNP data both appear at the same time for most other countries, eliminating variation in the treaty variable for those years for which we have data.

The results are consistent with the hypotheses, though some estimates do not reach conventional levels of statistical significance. Just as it did in earlier chapters, the openness test yields consistently more significant results than the import-volume test.

The import test has a more natural interpretation, so I begin with it to discuss the substantive meaning of these estimates. Trade agreements seem to have a small effect. While a one-franc increase in French GDP increases British imports by about one and one-third pence when they are not allied, this effect is only a little over one and one-half pence with a trade treaty in effect.[17] In percentage terms, British imports grow by about 11 percent of any increase in French GDP without a treaty, 12.5 percent with a treaty. The effect of trade treaties is larger when Britain and France are allies than when they are not—more than half again as large, in fact. The openness test yields larger estimates for these variables, with a trade treaty increasing the dependence of British openness on French GNP by more than 30 percent above the level without a treaty. However, the openness test produces much smaller (and statistically insignificant) estimates for the combined alliance-treaty variable than does the import test.

These results are all consistent with the theory here, but they are not consistent with plausible alternatives such as relative-gains theory. Trade treaties, like alliances, affect how Britain responds to France in the direction that the theory predicts. With the evidence from the previous section, these findings also support my claim that alliances affect the size but not the likelihood of cooperation.

Imperial Preference

One of chapter 7's more subtle results is the claim that, for a sufficiently small state, increasing the salience of military cooperation in a linked military-economic bargain will make larger bargains more likely to be stable. For a sufficiently large state, in contrast, increasing military salience makes smaller bargains more likely.

The best way to test this is to find a group of states, both large and small, that regularly made linked bargains in both economic and military affairs. The British Empire is an excellent candidate, especially as the dominions gain self-governing status through the century (see Beloff 1970; Drage 1911; Russell 1947; Schuyler 1945: 132–62). Testing the hypothesis also requires variation in

---

17. Trade treaties have a much more dramatic effect if we look at the reaction functions, where foreign openness affects British openness.

the importance of military cooperation within the empire as well as variation in size among the would-be cooperators. There are periods in which the empire faced lesser or greater military threats in particular parts of the world, leading to more or less military cooperation within the empire. Finally, Great Britain qualifies as sufficiently large by any useful operationalization of that concept, and I will assume that all of the colonies are sufficiently small.

This case selection is also interesting on substantive grounds. One mainstream theory of hegemonic stability argues that a hegemon will be willing and able to coerce other countries to choose free trade. If this claim is correct, surely the very first places to be forced open should be the hegemon's own colonies.

This is not at all what we observe. Indeed, Britain gave up precisely this coercive power as it gave colonies self-governing status, because "the principle of self-government was even more important than the principle of free trade" (Shaw 1955/1983: 145). An 1846 act allowed colonial legislatures to set new duties as long as they were nondiscriminatory; British governors retained the power to reserve (veto) such bills, but this power was used against only one tariff bill, a Tasmanian act of 1867.[18] Hurt by losing its preferential access to the British wheat and timber markets in 1846, Canada took immediate advantage of this provision, passing its first tariff in 1847.[19] It even began to discriminate de facto through tariff reciprocity with the United States beginning in 1854 (Brebner 1945: 150–62; U.S. Tariff Commission 1920). Shortly thereafter, in 1858 and 1859, Canada imposed new duties on manufactures, many imported from Great Britain.

The Australian colonies also gained trade autonomy in this period. The New South Wales Constitution of 1850 granted the right to impose nondiscriminatory tariffs, a power extended in the revised constitutions of 1855–56 for New South Wales, Victoria, South Australia, and Tasmania (Van Dieman's Land). In 1866 the Imperial Parliament repealed governors' powers to reserve tariff bills (Patterson 1968: xiii–xiv). The Australian colonies used their tariffs largely for revenue purposes at first, applying them to tobacco, spirits, sugar, tea, and coffee. By the 1860s and 1870s, all of the colonies began to be more clearly and more explicitly protective. This trend began in Victoria and then

---

18. Britain was changing its system of colonial differentials at this time. In 1842, 375 of the 825 items in the tariff had preferential levels. For example, foreign and colonial timber had paid duties of fifty-five shillings and ten shillings, respectively; Peel lowered these to thirty shillings/one shilling in 1842, twenty-five shillings/one shilling in 1843, and fifteen shillings/one shilling in 1847. Sugar and coffee preferences disappeared between 1846 and 1854.

19. Recall that this includes only Upper and Lower Canada—that is, Ontario and Quebec—at the start. Most other provinces joined the federation later in the century, though Newfoundland remained outside until 1949.

spread to Tasmania, Queensland, West Australia, and South Australia. The dominions also received the power to impose discriminatory tariffs in 1873.[20]

In other words, the dominions' tariff policy toward the outside world, one another, and the mother country itself had become a live issue by 1860s and 1870s. One possible response to this new environment would have been a network of trade treaties among the members of the empire.[21] Such a network would have maintained traditional trading relationships by giving preference to intra-imperial trade over external trade. If the relative-gains argument is correct, such a network would also have given each country security externalities from the prosperity of the others, all of whom were certain to be one another's allies in any imaginable major conflict (as they were in World War I).

Mainstream hegemonic theory would suppose that Britain, as leader of both this alliance and the international economy as a whole, would advocate such a solution. This did not occur. Instead, chapter 7's hypothesis that follower states seek cooperation with one another better accounts for events. The bargaining model of chapter 7 predicts that Britain should be generally uninterested in economic cooperation, even with its closest allies. Moreover, because Britain would have to pay a large share of any bargain, it would demand smaller bargains.

This is consistent with events. Canada, not Britain, first sought an imperial network of discriminatory trade treaties. Canada introduced imperial preference in 1897 and was the prime mover behind several Colonial Conferences that recommended that the rest of the empire follow suit.[22] Canada discriminated by lowering intraempire tariffs, which kept it from alienating the giant to the south (U.S. Tariff Commission 1920).

The Australian colonies also sought cooperation with one another. Tariffs had been a major obstacle to Australian unity after the granting of self-government, and the obvious gains from a customs union were, for decades, insufficient to induce federation. German moves in New Guinea and Samoa around the turn of the century provided an external threat that was previously

---

20. They were constrained a bit by the 1865 commercial agreement with Belgium and the 1867 agreement with the *Zollverein,* which gave the signatories the right to be treated as well as Britain by the dominions.

21. As an interesting comparison, recall that the German confederation had developed exactly such a treaty network, the *Zollverein,* in the new environment after the Napoleonic Wars.

22. Introducing preference required that Britain renounce the clause of the Belgian and *Zollverein* treaties prohibiting such preference. Germany protested, setting off a tariff war with Canada but not the mother country (Ashley 1926: 75–76). This suggests that Germany and others knew exactly who had made the decision to renounce the treaty.

lacking. As joint military concerns became increasingly important in the South Pacific, the Australian colonies sought larger comprehensive bargains (see Greenwood 1955; Shaw 1955/1983: 182).[23] This eventually culminated in Australian federation in 1901, which naturally included a customs union.

Federation also led to Australian discrimination in favor of other members of the empire. In 1908, Australia granted Britain preference in all tariff classes except spirits and tobacco, with the result that about 65 percent of imports from the United Kingdom received preference. In contrast to Canada, Australia gave preference by raising nonempire tariffs, thereby retaining high levels of protection (see Drage 1911: 75–78).

Other colonies also decided to grant imperial preference at about this time. New Zealand introduced some preferences in 1903, although this action had little effect because almost all of its trade was with the empire. In the same year, South Africa granted preference in the form of a 3 percent rebate on tariffs for most empire goods (Drage 1911: 79–90).

The introduction of preference in the dominions came as a result of ongoing consultation between the governments, highlighted by the quintennial Colonial Conferences (see Sykes 1979). The Third (1897), Fourth (1902), and Fifth (1907) Colonial Conferences all passed resolutions in favor of preference. These were not mere words: Canada used the first conference to get the Belgian and *Zollverein* treaties renounced; the second led directly to preferences in New Zealand and South Africa; the third to Australian preference. Nevertheless, aside from the act of Australian federation, none of this tacit cooperation was enshrined in formal treaties.

However, the increased role of military cooperation in the empire after 1900 did not make the (much larger) United Kingdom more likely to cooperate in comprehensive bargains. Indeed, the mother country explicitly rejected economic cooperation linked to the empire in the form of tariff reform. When Joseph Chamberlain made imperial preference a hot political issue in England as part of his campaign for tariff reform, he failed entirely (see Sykes 1979). The rise of imperial sentiment resulting from the Boer War, repeated resolutions of Colonial Conferences, and a German-Canadian tariff war could not incite the Parliament or the public to pursue preference.

This failure is especially striking when we recall that imperial preference was often set forth as a weapon against Britain's growing rival, Germany.

---

23. The economic crisis of 1893 was another important spur, weakening liberal New South Wales's resistance to the duties a common tariff policy would bring.

Goschen, a leading free-trade Unionist, conceded that "the keen will to forge a weapon by which to defeat those d——d Germans is very strong" (cited in Kennedy 1980: 263). Though tariff reform and a fear of Germany generally went together, these security issues could not induce Britain to cooperate more deeply with its imperial partners.

Though large bargains were impossible, Britain did agree to small, even obscure, bargains that strengthened the empire. In the midst of the Boer War in 1900, amendments to the Colonial Stocks Act made the securities of colonial and dominion governments eligible as "Trustee Securities," and therefore purchasable by trust bodies. Because trusts made up a large share of the overall London money market, all securities on the list of approved assets for trustees were in greater demand than they would otherwise be. This allowed British overseas possessions to raise loans in London at a noticeably lower cost than before (Feis 1950: 93; Russell 1947: 19). While such imperial cooperation was not very large, it was more than Britain had been willing to do before the turn of the century. In this very narrow sense, closer military cooperation with the dominions in the Committee on Imperial Defence made larger—but still small—bargains more likely for Britain.

In short, the case of imperial preference nicely illustrates the differences between the model of cooperation here and the arguments of mainstream hegemonic theory. Large states seek to reduce the size of cooperation. When negotiating with small states, they will pay a large share of the bargain. Small states may wish deeper cooperation, especially as the link to military cooperation grows stronger. Like other follower states, they will be likely to cooperate with each other whether or not the hegemon joins them. The link to military cooperation, important as it is for small states, may be insufficient to induce a large state's cooperation. Instead, the large state will cooperate only in small ways. None of these claims follow from mainstream theory, but all are consistent with both the theory here and the historical record.

Conclusion

Existing hegemonic theory has argued that Britain was an ineffective hegemon because it did not use reciprocity in trade (Keohane 1984: 37; Stein 1984). This meant that it sacrificed an important form of leverage over the policy of others. Trade treaties did not help Britain persuade other countries to open their markets (McKeown 1983), and Britain did not use treaties to insist that others lower their tariffs if they were to be admitted to England duty free.

By explaining both cooperation and noncooperation, this chapter better accounts for the evidence. Nonhegemonic cooperation should occur under malevolent hegemony. The leader may or may not cooperate with others. It will cooperate less than followers when it is malevolent. When benevolent, there should be no systematic difference between the leader's frequency of cooperation and the followers'.

However, this period points out some limits to my distinction between malevolent and benevolent leadership. Voluntary international cooperation is benevolent, making both countries better off. However, such benevolence is most likely as a response to malevolent leadership in the single-play game. This stretching of categories is also evident when I examine multilateral cooperation in the post–1945 period in the next two chapters.

This chapter has also examined the ways in which security concerns do and do not affect international cooperation. Alliances do not make cooperation more likely, and cooperation is not more likely as alliances grow tighter. However, alliances do make bargains larger, and greater security cooperation also makes larger bargains more likely. The historical evidence is consistent with each of these propositions. Moreover, security considerations play an important role in determining whether hegemony is malevolent or benevolent.

Much of the argument in this chapter turns mainstream hegemonic theory on its head. Having an alliance does not lead two states to cooperate more frequently. Benevolent leadership lacks cooperation, while malevolent leadership induces followers to cooperate. Large states prefer small bargains, even with their closest friends. Hegemony is important for the international system, but not in the way that existing theory expects.

CHAPTER 9

Multilateral Cooperation

International negotiations and regimes vary along several dimensions. They may encompass many issues or cover only one, involve two states or many, adjust policy only slightly or infringe deeply on each state's sovereignty. Chapter 7 modeled some of these dimensions, including the size of the bargain and the possibility of linkage between economic and security issues.

One major negotiating question in that chapter's two-actor model is whether the size of a bargain should be increased or decreased. I found that hegemons want to decrease the size of bargains because they pay a large share of the costs. To achieve a leader's participation in international cooperation, other states may need to reduce the leader's share of a bargain. Unfortunately for cooperation, lowering the leader's share raises everyone else's share, making their cooperation less likely. However, multilateralization might lower everyone's share simultaneously. By increasing the number of participants, a multilateral agreement necessarily reduces the average share of each state. Though this lower average share does not necessarily reduce the leader's share, multilateralization nonetheless provides an opportunity to reduce the hegemon's share of a bargain.

One natural referent for extensive multilateral cooperation is the postwar period. Postwar cooperation has centered on a series of multilateral regimes, such as the GATT, World Bank, and IMF (see Baldwin and Lage 1971; Bhagwati 1990; Curzon and Curzon 1976; Keohane 1990; Nogués 1990; Ruggie 1993). Moreover, traditional hegemonic theory has long been concerned with understanding these multilateral regimes (e.g., Keohane 1984).

These multilateral agreements fly in the face of a remarkable consensus that increasing the number of states concerned with a given issue makes cooperation less likely (see Pahre 1994 for review). Many argue that it is easier to punish defectors bilaterally than multilaterally, as does John A. C. Conybeare (1987: 55–56):

Large numbers in the Prisoners' Dilemma make it unlikely that iteration of the game will result in cooperation, since large numbers introduce one aspect of a public good, namely the inability to punish defection. . . . Since the actions of any one actor now have a much smaller effect on any other actor, it is hard for any one individual actor to punish another actor who defects, so that iteration of the game has no cooperation-inducing effect.

Multilateralism is especially problematic for hegemonic theory. As Steve Weber (1992: 637) argues with reference to NATO:

Multilateralism . . . minimizes the hegemon's coercive power and its ability to extract payment for protection. It makes the sanctioning of free riders difficult and threats of abandonment almost impossible. From a choice-theoretic perspective, multilateralism does not seem a convincing bargain or a determinate solution.

In these ways, multilateralism makes international cooperation even more of a public good than it otherwise would be.

This conventional wisdom overstates the problem of multilateralism. The rational existence of multilateralism follows directly from the Folk Theorem. By this theorem, any cooperation in the set of individually rational outcomes can be justified in an indefinitely iterated game with sufficiently little discounting; at least one proof of the Folk Theorem specifically includes multilateral cooperation (see Fudenberg and Maskin 1986; cf. Lohmann 1997; Pahre 1994; Michael Taylor 1976, 1987). However, the existence of multilateralism as a plausible equilibrium in an infinite set of equilibria does not tell us when it will be more or less likely than bilateralism.

This chapter looks at the role of international leadership in multilateral regimes. I will investigate the conditions under which states may rationally prefer multilateralism to bilateralism or vice versa and the role of leadership in this choice.[1] This analysis of multilateralism depends critically on the definitions of *multilateralism* and *bilateralism* and on additional assumptions about enforcement mechanisms and conjectures. One finding is that the distinction between multilateralism and bilateralism is irrelevant under conventional assumptions, while some less conventional assumptions yield interesting results. For this

---

1. My approach to this problem looks at the enforcement problems of multilateralism, not the negotiation issues (see Bueno de Mesquita 1990). For analogous studies looking at n-player enforcement problems in very different political economy settings, see Greif, Milgrom, and Weingast 1990; Veitch 1986.

reason, the following sections analyze multilateralism under several different sets of assumptions. While the analysis differs from other scholars' focus on the normative content of multilateralism (see esp. Ruggie 1993), it shares with them a focus on the common beliefs that underlie multilateral institutions.

Multilateral Cooperation and "Necessary Multilateralism"

Some nonformal analyses of multilateralism suppose that one incentive for multilateral bargains is that they provide greater benefits than bilateral bargains because more states are members, because regimes benefit from economies of scale, or because they reduce transaction costs (Bureau and Champsaur 1992; Caporaso 1992: 609–10; Keohane 1984: 90; Lipson 1986: 223; Martin 1993: 100; Oye 1986b: 20). However, this does not explain why multilateralism is more attractive than an equivalent set of bilateral bargains.

While the Folk Theorem shows that multilateral cooperation is possible, it says nothing about whether some range of discount rates makes bilateral cooperation, but not multilateral cooperation, possible. This is the more important question for international relations, where a consensus recommends breaking multilateral cooperation into bilateral deals to make enforcement easier. Moreover, the Folk Theorem is not very useful as an empirical statement: since any individually rational outcome can be justified as an equilibrium, we cannot predict which outcome will occur. The Folk Theorem does not even guide us in whittling down the infinite set of outcomes to a smaller set.

Instead, I will investigate whether multilateralism is a necessary part of a given bargain, regardless of whether multilateralism is an equilibrium. Moreover, earlier chapters have already examined the way that changing the size of a bargain might make cooperation more or less likely. For these reasons, this chapter looks only at equivalent bargains where the size and shares are held constant across both the multilateral bargain and the set of bilateral bargains.

As in chapters 2, 3, and 7, I assume a simple public-goods game with each state's utility $U^i = U(m^i, Q)$, where m^i is a basket of private goods and Q is the public good, subject to a budget constraint $m^i + q^i = B^i$, and $Q = \Sigma q^i$ where q^i is the contribution of each state to the public good. Equilibrium occurs at $\partial U^i/\partial m^i = \partial U^i/\partial Q \ \forall i$, with equilibrium values $m^{i'}$, etc. The publicness assumption implies rejection of one plausible multilateral alternative, in which states sanction cheaters by excluding them from any benefits. This would mean analyzing our public good as a club good instead, since a club good is a public good from which actors may be excluded (see Cornes and Sandler 1986 for an accessible introduction). Unfortunately, this club-goods solution eliminates key theoretical problems: states will not cheat on club-good provision under perfect information and will not join a club if the costs to them outweigh the benefits. Neither free riding nor sanctioning, which many believe to be important problems in international relations, enter into such a game. For this reason, I continue to assume public goods.

If states agree to increase their contributions to the good, i will increase her spending on Q by α^i, and all other cooperators will increase theirs by $\Sigma \alpha^j \, \forall j \neq i$. Because fixed contributions are part of the definition of equivalence, I no longer break contributions into size and shares but capture each state's contributions in a single variable α^i. The variables $(\alpha^i, \alpha^j, \ldots, \alpha^n)$ are exogenous and fixed, thus holding all features of the bargain constant except multilateralism itself. Thus, the payoffs in a two-country prisoner's dilemma for i are:

$$
\begin{array}{ll}
P^i\colon U^i(m', Q') & R^i\colon Ui(m' - \alpha^i, Q' + \alpha^i + \alpha^j) \\
S^i\colon U^i(m' - \alpha^i, Q' + \alpha^i) & T^i\colon U^i(m', Q' + \alpha^i)
\end{array} \tag{9.1}
$$

Bargains are evaluated as a choice between contributing the full α^i or zero. I assume throughout that no state ever contributes less than the single-shot level $q^{i'}$. This rules out free riding on other states' bargains by decreasing one's own contributions only in the existence of bargains among others.[2]

I want to know if there exist bargains that are either necessarily bilateral or necessarily multilateral. A necessarily multilateral bargain is feasible when multilateral yet would not be feasible if broken up into an exactly equivalent set of bilateral bargains.[3] A necessarily bilateral set of bargains, in contrast, would no longer be feasible if packaged multilaterally instead of bilaterally.[4] Where a

---

2. I exclude such free riding because any $q^i < q^{i'}$ would require analysis of second-order punishment problems involving whether or not this reduction lowers other actors' utility below the single-play equilibrium; I exclude these calculations for simplicity. As I argued in chapter 7, excluding any $q^i < q^{i'}$ also makes the externalities problem (where often $q^{i'} = 0$) directly comparable to the public-goods problem.

3. The bargain is necessarily multilateral if the Taylor-Axelrod condition holds for the multilateral bargain but not for at least one bilateral bargain Q^{ij}. In other words, this requires that for at least one bilateral bargain, $X^i_B > w^i > X^i_M$ or simply $X^i_B > X^i_M$. Solving this inequality for various values of X^i_B and X^i_M lies behind my analysis in this chapter.

4. Formally, the multilateral bargain Q_M is "equivalent" to the set of bilateral bargains Q_B iff the contributions of i (α^i) to the public good Q are the same in both cases $\forall i$. A bargain Q_M is "necessarily multilateral" if it is feasible $\forall i$ and if the equivalent set of bilateral bargains is not feasible for some i. A set of bilateral bargains Q_B is "necessarily bilateral" if it is feasible $\forall i$ and if the equivalent multilateral bargain Q_M is not feasible for some i. Notice that this entails a purely nominal definition of multilateralism, "the practice of coordinating national policies in groups of three or more states" (Keohane 1990: 731).

given set of bargains is neither necessarily bilateral nor necessarily multilateral, then both kinds of bargains are equilibria, and I cannot predict whether we will see one or the other.

As in earlier chapters, I assume that whether or not a bargain is feasible depends on whether it can be enforced by the metastrategy of Grim Trigger. Even here, multilateral enforcement is inherently complicated. Under one set of conditions, which I call *symmetric conjectures,* multilateralism is not an issue. After discussing this, I turn attention to two variations, *individually feasible bargains* and *hegemonic enforcement.* In individually feasible bargains, states consider signing agreements one at a time; a multilateral deal is not compared to a set of bilateral deals but to one bilateral deal at a time. In hegemonic enforcement there is only one state that enforces a bargain instead of the multilateral enforcement assumed under symmetric conjectures.

Symmetric Conjectures and Individually Feasible Bargains

To analyze multilateralism I begin with a point of reference in which multilateralism is irrelevant. A state must consider two feasibility questions: first, will I want to cheat on this bargain, and second, will anyone else want to cheat? If any other state would cheat, then all states know it (under complete information) and will themselves defect to avoid being a sucker. Moreover, a state considering whether to cheat on one bilateral bargain recognizes that this will affect its reputation in all such bargains. As a result, if it cheats on one, it cheats on all. These two lines of reasoning define symmetric conjectures. Each state conjectures (symmetrically) that if any state cooperates, all cooperate; if a state defects, it defects against all and not just one; and so on.[5]

With symmetric conjectures, for all sets of equivalent bargains, $P_B{}^i = P_M{}^i$, $R_B{}^i = R_M{}^i$, $T_B{}^i = T_M{}^i$ for all i. If a state cooperates with one, it cooperates with all ($R_B{}^i = R_M{}^i$); if it cheats on one, it cheats on all ($T_B{}^i = T_M{}^i$); if it is punished by one, it is punished by all ($P_B{}^i = P_M{}^i$). Neither necessary multilateralism nor necessary bilateralism exist because the Taylor-Axelrod condition is the same under both bilateral and multilateral bargains. In this way, symmetry erases the

---

5. Formally, under symmetric conjectures, each i assumes that if any j cheats, all $j \neq i$ cheat. An alternative assumption is asymmetric conjectures, under which each i assumes that if any j cheats, no other $k \neq j$ cheats; each i also assumes that it can cheat on a given bargain Q^{ij} without affecting the behavior of all $k \neq j$ in the set of bilateral bargains $Q^{-i}{}_B = \{Q^{ik}, \ldots, Q^{in}\}$. For additional analysis of these differences, see Pahre 1994. For a different way to model multilateralism, see Lohmann 1997.

difference between bilateralism and multilateralism, making the puzzle in the nonformal literature (e.g., Ruggie 1994) a nonissue.

This result stems from strong assumptions about the set of bilateral bargains. Specifically, each state evaluates each bilateral bargain on the assumption that all other bilaterals will succeed in providing the agreed-on level of public goods. Since all states evaluate all of the bilateral bargains simultaneously in this model, this assumption is problematic. It is possible that states evaluate bilateral bargains sequentially, since some bilateral bargain is negotiated first. In this case, a state will evaluate early bargains as if no others exist. In contrast, a multilateral bargain encompasses all the would-be bilaterals at a single moment in time.

To capture this, consider whether a bilateral bargain might be individually feasible—that is, feasible when considered as the first of all bilaterals.[6] This is a nonstandard conjecture in that it excludes consideration of other bilateral bargains that the state might rationally anticipate.[7] However, this kind of assumption lends itself to historical analysis, where sequence affects the play of each game because some bargain is generally negotiated first. As I will discuss later, this assumption of individual feasibility also makes it possible to consider historical context, in that a state's evaluation of bilateralism and multilateralism may depend in part on the prior existence of a network of bilateral cooperation.

Define α^{ij} as i's contribution in its bilateral contract with j, and α^{ji} as j's contribution in its bilateral contract with i, and $\alpha^i = \sum_j^n \alpha^{ij}$. For simplicity, I examine the three-player game, but it can be extended to more actors without any qualitative change in the results. A state must compare the following set of payoffs in the bilateral bargain Q^{ij} and multilateral bargain Q_M:

$$P_B^i: U(m', Q') \qquad\qquad P_M^i: U(m', Q')$$
$$R_B^i: U(m' - \alpha^{ij}, Q' + \alpha^{ij} + \alpha^{ji}) \qquad R_M^i: U(m' - \alpha^i, Q' + \Sigma\alpha^i) \qquad (9.2)$$
$$T_B^i: U(m', Q' + \alpha^{ji}) \qquad\qquad T_M^i: U(m', Q' + \alpha^j + \alpha^k)$$

By inspection, $P_B^i = P_M^i$ because a state faces the same reversion point regardless of whether it is reverting from a multilateral agreement or a single bilateral agreement. It is also true that $R_B^i < R_M^i$ because the rewards of cooperating with many states are greater than the rewards of cooperating with a single state.

---

6. Formally, a bilateral bargain is individually feasible if it can be enforced by GT in the absence of any other bilateral bargain.

7. Analysis of non-Nash conjectures is not unusual in public-goods theory (see esp. Cornes and Sandler 1986: 51–55; Guttman 1987; Sugden 1985).

Finally, $T_B{}^i < T_M{}^i$ because the temptation to cheat on many states is greater than the temptation to cheat on only one.

Using these values in the formula for necessary multilateralism and rearranging, I find that under symmetric conjectures with individually feasible bargains, necessary multilateralism exists if the following condition is satisfied for any bilateral Q^{ij}:

$$R_B{}^i(T_M{}^i - P^i) - R_M{}^i(T_B{}^i - P^i) < P^i(T_M{}^i - T_B{}^i) \tag{9.3}$$

This condition may or may not hold.

Equation 9.3 allows for some comparative statics. Increasing the size of the multilateral bargain (R_M) makes multilateralism more likely, as does decreasing the size of bilateral bargain (R_B). These results are intuitive. The rewards of cooperation may suffice to draw countries into a multilateral agreement despite the greater temptation to defect from it.

Increasing the value of the single-shot status quo (P^i) also makes multilateralism more likely.[8] This is interesting because a malevolent leader raises its own noncooperative payoff (P^i) while lowering that of others (P^j). Under symmetric conjectures with individually feasible bargains, Stackelberg leadership therefore makes multilateralism more likely for the hegemon.[9] By the same token, Stackelberg leadership makes multilateralism less likely for the follower countries. Because of this situation, I expect to find the hegemon advocating multilateral solutions to problems, while nonhegemonic states prefer bilateral cooperation.

More speculatively, this has an interesting dynamic effect. If followers cooperate bilaterally with each other, their network of cooperation raises $P_B{}^i$. This makes multilateralism more likely if the leader is to cooperate. If cooperation raises the leader's utility in the first place, then entering multilateral cooperation and the unified sanction of many followers makes the leader more likely to cooperate.

In sum, relaxing the usual game-theoretic assumption to consider sequence yields some interesting results about multilateralism. A leader is more likely to favor multilateral bargains than are followers, especially where follower states have already negotiated bilaterally with one another.

---

8. This claim also requires that $(T^i{}_M - R^i{}_M)/(T^i{}_B - R^i{}_B) > 1$, or that the temptation to defect on a multilateral bargain is greater than the temptation to defect on any individual bilateral bargain. This is a reasonable assumption.

9. Stackelberg leadership also affects $T^i{}_B$, etc., with unclear implications for equation 9.3. However, the discussion in chapter 7 suggests that analysis of P^i alone is informative.

Hegemonic Enforcement

Because the increasing sanction of multilateralism drives the previous result, it may also be possible for some less-than-total sanction to support multilateralism. For example, some subgroup might punish defecting states for any defection. If sufficiently large, a single state could enforce multilateralism. This makes hegemon-led provision of a multilateral public good a special case of a general theory.

To consider this possibility, I treat the actors asymmetrically. First, everyone holds the conjecture that the leader (i) is the only enforcer. Second, each state decides whether to defect under the conjecture that if it cheats, no other state will cheat in that same round (this is the Nash conjecture). Together these assumptions mean that all $k \neq i, j$ sit passively by and do not react to others.[10]

To find out if hegemonic enforcement can work, I need to know two things: first, is it rational for i to punish j for any defection, and second, can j be deterred from defecting on a multilateral bargain through punishment by a single state i? The first condition is simple: is i at least as well off when punishing j, regardless of whether j changes her behavior? The answer is yes, because i would prefer not to contribute α^i if it can do so without being punished.[11] Since k contributes regardless of i's action, i is not punished; thus, enforcement is rational.

The hegemon's incentive to punish defectors relies on the forbearance of all k. This forbearance raises serious questions in itself, since it eliminates the incentive for i to contribute at all.[12] This special treatment resembles Andrew Shonfield's (1976: 33) notion of hegemony in a gold-currency monetary system:

> that the other members accept that the rules which apply to them do not necessarily bind the nation which dominates the system. It supplies the initiatives and is chiefly responsible for ensuring that sanctions against those who break the rules are effectively applied, but it has itself the option whether to obey the rules or not in any particular instance.

---

10. Formally, under hegemonic enforcement, only state i punishes each cheater j in GT; no k ever cheats or punishes. I assume complete information; for the signaling problems of hegemonic enforcement under incomplete information, see Alt, Calvert, and Humes 1988.

11. Formally, hegemonic enforcement by i is rational when $U^i(m^{i'}, Q + \alpha^k) > U^i(m^{i'} - \alpha', Q' + \alpha^k)$. This condition always holds.

12. The conjectures supporting this result resemble the set of conjectures that make punishing defectors in repeated-play PD subgame perfect (as in Fudenberg and Maskin 1986). While apparently strange, these conjectures are no more arbitrary than this conventional standard.

Understanding k's forbearance when i punishes j points us toward the rules or norms that specify when i's noncontributions are to be labeled enforcement, and when they are to be labeled defection (cf. Axelrod 1986). Still, there is a need for someone to enforce the commitments of the enforcer. If we move beyond the trilateral bargain here to consider multiple k, then clearly it would be possible for the forbearance of some k to support the enforcement action of other k against i and for i to enforce the bargain against any k. However, I set this problem aside here.

Now consider the feasibility conditions for j, which chooses between a bilateral agreement with i under asymmetric conjectures and a multilateral bargain with hegemonic enforcement. The payoffs are:

$$
\begin{aligned}
P_B &= U(m' - \alpha^{jk}, Q' + \alpha^{jk} + \alpha^{ki} + \alpha^{ik} + \alpha^{kj}) \\
P_M &= U(m', Q' + \alpha^k) \\
R_B &= U(m' - \alpha^j, Q' + \Sigma\alpha^i) \\
R_M &= U(m' - \alpha^j, Q' + \Sigma\alpha^i) \\
T_B &= U(m' - \alpha^{jk}, Q' + \alpha^{ij} + \alpha^{jk} + \alpha^{ki} + \alpha^{ik} + \alpha^{kj}) \\
T_M &= U(m', Q' + \alpha^i + \alpha^k)
\end{aligned}
\tag{9.4}
$$

Given these payoffs, necessary multilateralism may exist whenever j faces hegemonic enforcement. The two bargains are equivalent when everyone cooperates, so $R_B = R_M$. By inspection, $T_B < T_M$ since the temptation to cheat on everyone is greater than the incentive to cheat on only one. After algebraic manipulation, I find that necessary multilateralism exists if, for a feasible multilateral bargain, the following condition holds:

$$
\frac{P_B^j T_M^j - T_B^j P_M^j}{T_M^j - T_B^j + P_B^j - P_M^j} > R^j \qquad \text{when } P_B^j > P_M^j
\tag{9.5}
$$

For any i making sufficiently large contributions (α^i), $P_B^j > P_M^j$ because α^{ik} raises j's utility in P_B but not in P_M. When this is true, equation 9.5 may or may not hold, recalling that $P_B > P_M$ and $T_M > T_B$.

For sufficiently large α^{jk}, j's contribution to third-party bilateral bargains, then $P_B^j < P_M^j$. This may make the denominator of equation 9.4 negative, which complicates my analysis of the inequality because the derivation of equation 9.5 involves dividing both sides of an inequality by this term. This is a problem if and only if $P_B^j < P_M^j$ and $P_M^j - P_B^j > T_M^j - T_B^j$. In this case, equation 9.5 becomes:

$$\frac{P_B{}^j T_M{}^j - T_B{}^j P_M{}^j}{T_M{}^j - T_B{}^j + P_B{}^j - P_M{}^j} < R^j \tag{9.6}$$

Both the denominator and numerator of the left-hand-side fraction are negative,[13] so equation 9.6 may or may not hold. Thus, regardless of whether $P_M{}^j - P_B{}^j > T_M{}^j - T_B{}^j > 0$, necessary multilateralism may or may not exist for j even under hegemonic enforcement. Phrased differently, hegemonic enforcement can indeed suffice to support multilateralism, though it also might not suffice.

Comparative statics are difficult, since the direction of the inequality in equations 9.5 and 9.6 depends on an unobservable condition $P_M{}^j - P_B{}^j > T_M{}^j - T_B{}^j > 0$. Since changing the sign of the inequality changes all the comparative statics, I cannot determine whether, for example, increasing the rewards of cooperation makes multilateralism with hegemonic enforcement either more or less likely. Instead, I am left with an existence result that hegemonic enforcement of multilateralism may indeed occur.

Summary

The central finding of this chapter is that multilateral cooperation makes sense in a rational-choice model, despite the contrary claims of mainstream theories of both hegemony and multilateralism. Multilateralism might create greater rewards for cooperation and a more severe punishment for defecting from a regime, though it also furnishes a greater incentive to cheat. When I consider all these factors simultaneously, I find that multilateral cooperation may make the Taylor-Axelrod condition either more or less likely to hold. As a result, there is no particular reason to privilege either bilateral or multilateral cooperation. Indeed, there is no difference at all with the assumption of symmetric conjectures.

However, by assuming a collective-goods or externalities problem, this chapter cannot explain variation by issue. In particular, the model cannot distinguish problems of multilateral coordination, which differ from the multilateral collaboration problem analyzed here (see Martin 1993). Multilateral institutions are apparently well suited to solve noncontroversial coordination problems, such as international telegraphy, European river transport, and public health (Ruggie 1993: 16–17; see also Stein 1984).

---

13. Because $P_M{}^j - P_B{}^j > T_M{}^j - T_B{}^j$ and $P_B{}^j < T_B{}^j$, then clearly $(P_M{}^j - P_B{}^j)/P_B{}^j > (T_M{}^j - T_B{}^j)/T_B{}^j$. This simplifies to $P_M{}^j/P_B{}^j - 1 > T_M{}^j/T_B{}^j - 1$, and thus to $P_M{}^j/P_B{}^j > T_M{}^j/T_B{}^j$. When this condition holds, the numerator in equation 9.6 is less than zero (as is the denominator, by assumption).

The analysis in this chapter highlights the importance of conjectures, each actor's beliefs about how others react. Theorists who reject rational-choice models routinely emphasize the role of beliefs in multilateral cooperation (see esp. Ruggie 1993), so it is interesting that a rational model can also address some such beliefs. While these theorists give greater attention to the normative content of multilateralism than I do, they have difficulty explaining variation in outcomes, such as that between multilateral and bilateral institutions. Combining conjectures and interests in a formal model can better explain this variation.

There are three major results. First, increasing the rewards of multilateral cooperation makes multilateralism more likely. While this result may seem obvious, it implies that tight alliances that raise the benefits of linked economic and security bargains will make it more likely that these bargains are multilateral. Second, the leader is more likely to prefer multilateral cooperation than are followers. Third, in a context where followers have already negotiated bilateral agreements, the leader is more likely to cooperate if cooperation is multilateral. Together, these hypotheses explain important features of the postwar world, which I examine in the next chapter.

CHAPTER 10

From Malevolence to Multilateralism, 1945–1967

This chapter examines American economic leadership after World War II. This period has played an important role in the development of hegemonic theory. Even more than the Pax Britannica, it is the major example of hegemony. The breakdown of postwar regimes such as the gold-dollar standard in the 1970s gave the theory a major spur, focusing special attention on hegemonic decline (e.g., Avery and Rapkin 1982; Calleo 1987; Calleo and Rowland 1973; Keohane 1977, 1984; Lipson 1983; Nau 1990). The coincidence of hegemony and the Cold War provided a motive for extension of the theory to include security externalities (e.g., Gowa 1989, 1994). Arguably, the entire theory of hegemonic stability would never have been important in the field of international political economy had there not been a (declining) hegemon in the field's formative years. Providing a reinterpretation of this period would add to the plausibility of the theory here.

Perhaps surprisingly, given the unprecedented economic growth of the 1950s and 1960s, I will argue that American leadership was malevolent throughout this period. As in chapter 8, however, mere malevolence inadequately characterizes what is happening. Cooperation to overcome malevolence, not noncooperative malevolence itself, dominates the period.

The first few "postwar" years, from approximately 1944 through 1946–47, exhibited malevolence analogous to the 1920s (see also Nau 1990: chap. 3). Bilateral cooperation was a common response among the countries of Western Europe and the United States itself. After 1947, American-led multilateral cooperation, especially the Marshall Plan, was important. This cooperation, and not American policy per se, is responsible for the postwar era's remarkable growth. To understand this cooperation, we need the bargaining model of chapter 7 and the model of multilateralism from chapter 9.

American malevolence stemmed from having too many friends and allies—namely, the wartime coalition against the Axis powers. The wartime "United Nations" collapsed, like the Quadruple Alliance, but its demise did not leave the hegemon without friends. Instead, the Soviet Union became a strong foe in 1947–48. This led in turn to much stronger security ties between the United States and Western Europe (as well as several countries in the Far East).

There is no reason to believe that these closer security ties between the United States and Western Europe made cooperation any more (or less) likely. Cooperation was common both before and after the start of the Cold War. However, closer security ties did affect cooperation in other ways. In particular, increasingly close security ties made larger bargains more likely. We see a large increase in the size of bargains with the start of the Cold War, most notably from large public loans to even larger public grants in the Marshall Plan.

For states evaluating individually feasible bargains, the greater rewards made multilateral cooperation more likely. By making cooperation among allies deeper, the Cold War made cooperation among allies more likely to take a multilateral form. The existence of a prior network of bilateral cooperation also increased the likelihood of multilateralism, in which hegemonic enforcement came to play a large role.

The share of military cooperation in linked bargains also affected the likelihood of cooperation. One way to find this pattern is to look at countries on the European periphery, where there is significant variation in participation in the NATO alliance. A brief study of Scandinavia's changing participation in postwar economic cooperation tests some of the more subtle claims of the bargaining model. Though they are of similar size and wealth, the Scandinavian countries vary significantly in security policy, making them a good test of the hypothesis.

Because it relies on indeterminate models of interstate bargaining and multilateralism, this chapter is the most historically contingent of the empirical chapters in this book. This indeterminacy stems from the nature of the bargaining model. For example, while followers are more likely to cooperate than is the leader, we might observe cooperation by both, as we do in this period. However, this theoretical indeterminacy has its advantages. The countries of Western Europe and North America faced real choices in this period, and several different choices would have been consistent with the theory. As a result, this chapter partakes of much more thick description than other chapters and has much less explicit theory testing (either qualitative or quantitative).

Externalities and Public Goods in Postwar Reconstruction

As in earlier chapters, I want the assumptions of the model to be reasonable generalizations about the situation at hand. These include the claim that the United States was a hegemon in the period, the assumption that nations negotiate over an issue similar to a public good, and that states used enforcement strategies similar to those modeled in chapter 9. Because the conjectures about enforcement strategies raise a host of questions, I postpone these to a later section.

It is easy to define the United States as a Stackelberg leader in this period. Its numerical dominance was overwhelming. It accounted for roughly half of the world's manufacturing, half the merchant marine, one-third of the world's total production, one-third of global exports, two-thirds of the world's gold reserves, and all of the world's nuclear weapons (Kennedy 1987: 358). The U.S. Navy and Air Force were without equals. These facts could not help but shape everyone's conjectures.

As in other periods, the public-goods assumption exaggerates the semi-public goods and externalities associated with private goods that we actually find, such as economic recovery. The problems of postwar recovery meant that each country's policies had significant externalities for the others. One example of this is Alan Milward's (1984: 92) argument that Marshall aid to Belgium had virtually no direct effect on the Belgian economy; nonetheless, "the contribution of Marshall Aid to economies other than Belgium is of serious importance in estimating its importance for Belgium's own economic and political life." What was true for Belgium was true for many others. Marshall aid to Europe as a whole had public effects on other countries, even if direct aid appears to be a purely private good.

There were also smaller-scale problems entailing externalities. For instance, to save Germany's foreign exchange, the American and British occupation authorities used Hamburg and Bremen for imports instead of lower-cost Dutch and Belgian ports; loosening the Bizone's currency constraint helped not only German consumers but Benelux traders as well. To take a very different example, many countries' plans involved capital investments that duplicated those elsewhere, especially in heavy industry. This overcapacity affected everyone's profitability. Similar inefficiencies and coordination problems were ubiquitous (Kindleberger 1987: 10–11). Eliminating these inefficiencies created joint gains from the positive externalities (or removal of negative externalities) associated with the actions of the participating countries—hence, they included quasi-public goods.

Another example of the public-good aspect of European recovery is evident when we look at the effects of capital investment. Marshall aid allowed European countries to continue high levels of investment and imports, thereby avoiding deflation or further trade controls (Milward 1984: 98–99). This made it a vehicle for expansion on both the production and demand sides. For example, Marshall aid enabled Britain to continue importing dollar capital goods of the kind that had provoked the 1947 balance-of-payments crisis. The direct demand for imports and the increased demand for all goods stemming from growing incomes served as a demand stimulus for imports from other countries.

A second-order question is whether we should think of these externalities as quasi-public or as club goods. Direct aid was obviously excludable, as were institutions such as payments unions. Still, some externalities were nonexcludable. For example, an important technical problem throughout postwar planning was the allies' inability to exclude Germany from the benefits of European cooperation. Even more important were the difficulties of Europe-wide recovery without substantial German growth. For instance, because the Italian and German economies were largely complementary, the Italians supported "reconstruction of the German economy within the framework of European cooperation" (cited in Mee 1984: 166). Finally, because one American motive for proposing the European Recovery Program (ERP) was to reduce the expenses of the German occupation, German participation was essential.[1]

A final issue concerning the fit between model and reality is the assumption that each country makes contributions to a public good such as Europe-wide production (or recovery). Obviously, the United States made the major fiscal contributions to European recovery, once the ERP took effect. However, the United States and Western Europe ultimately agreed on a package that included direct American aid, mutual liberalization of trade, and a regional payments union. The first round of trade liberalization came in October 1949, when each European country eliminated many of its quotas on imports from other Europeans. This first liberalization encompassed only about 10 percent of total British and French imports and about 15 percent of Italian and West German imports. In contrast, Denmark removed quotas on 28 percent of total imports, while Switzerland, Belgium and Luxemburg each liberalized about 40 percent (Milward 1984).

As a result, each European country made important concessions, includ-

---

1. The State Department was the major advocate of this position (Gimbel 1976: 255–56). This is an interesting example of how publicness can be constructed and is not just a technical property of goods.

ing a partial grant of sovereignty.[2] These sovereignty concessions were the Soviets' primary objection to joining the program (Mee 1984: 131–33). The essentially standardized agreement that each nation signed with the United States as part of the ERP committed the country to currency stabilization and limited convertibility, a balanced budget, and the maintenance of monetary confidence. These clauses contradicted some existing policies, such as Norway's policy of expansionary fiscal deficits (Lundestad 1980: 145). The European Cooperation Agency (ECA) later encouraged countries to devalue their currencies, in order to increase exports and to make direct investment by American multinationals less expensive (Milward 1984).

There were also more narrow concerns. Congress required that one-fourth of all wheat financed by ERP be exported as American milled flour, a proportion it reduced to 12.5 percent in 1949 (Milward 1984: 121). Another clause of the ERP legislation required that at least 50 percent of Marshall goods be shipped on American vessels. Norway, whose merchant marine was one of those most severely affected by this legislation, strenuously objected, without success (Lundestad 1980: 150).

One widely criticized concession was the establishment of counterpart funds (Arkes 1972: 292–94; Hogan 1987: 152–53; Lundestad 1980: 151–54; Pollard 1985: 160). The ECA required that recipients deposit in a counterpart fund local currency equal to the amount of grant assistance received. These funds could be used only with American consent; Congress reserved 5 percent of the total for the expenses of U.S. embassies and as a slush fund for congressional junkets (Kindleberger 1987: 113). The norm was to earmark these funds for approved investment projects, but Britain and Denmark used them largely for fiscal deficit reduction, while Norway used them to reduce the inflationary German occupation account. American veto power influenced the goals for which these funds were used, forcing trade-offs with other goals.

Moreover, counterpart funds were taken out of circulation, so these accounts had a deflationary effect on each country. One result was drastic deflations in France, Germany, and Italy (Block 1977: 90), as well as in Norway (by using the counterpart funds to buy up the occupation account) (Bjerve 1959). One effect of the deflations was unemployment, which obviously had real political costs that these governments would not otherwise have borne.

Related to the question of European contributions to quasi-public goods is the existence of trade-offs among national and international goals. States recognized these trade-offs more explicitly than in previous periods, thanks to the

---

2. Losses of autonomy are a significant cost to states (Morrow 1991).

existence of national planning agencies. Whether they used indicative or imperative planning models, politicians made policy with an eye to the allocation effects made evident through their plan (see Shonfield 1965 inter alia).

One particular kind of trade-off is that between defense spending and contributions to international public goods. Planners recognized these and tried to minimize them, devising plans that would increase both alliance military spending and joint economic recovery. George Kennan had warned in 1948 against "a general pre-occupation with military affairs, to the detriment of economic recovery" and insisted that the North Atlantic Treaty must not preclude the "real unification of Europe" (cited in Hogan 1987: 192) To make these goals complementary, American policymakers tried to make rearmament a part of economic recovery, structured along similar lines: mutual aid, coordinated planning, and standardized production, with American aid supplementing European resources (Hogan 1987: 193–94).

In summary, the Europeans made substantial contributions to the ERP.[3] Moreover, these contributions entailed real trade-offs among different goals. Because the European governments agreed to policies that they would not otherwise have followed, there were potential problems of compliance and enforcement, as follows from any iterated prisoners' dilemma. Moreover, these contributions all entailed problems of externalities and even public goods. The model is a reasonable simplification of the actual situation.

Changing Security Relations, 1944–47

As in chapters 6 and 8, examining security relations in this period is an essential precondition for an analysis of leadership. The outline of security relations after World War II is well known (see Gaddis 1982; Kolko and Kolko 1972; LaFeber 1980; Lundestad 1980, 1986; Pogue 1987; William Appleman Williams 1959/1972; for memoirs see Clay 1950; Kindleberger 1987; Truman 1956). Three major powers survived the war, along with a very much weakened France. Most observers, like most policy makers, expected a tripolar world; William Fox's influential book *The Super Powers* (1944) coined a term that he and others applied to the big three (Ruggie 1993: 29). Anglo-American ties had been close during the war, but most observers expected renewed economic rivalries and a loosening of the security relationship. One sign of this was Tru-

---

3. The Vandenberg Resolution (passed June 11, 1948) also required that countries that received American guarantees for Atlantic security would provide benefits to the United States as well as receiving them. Kennan (1967: 406) claims, "This last principle was borrowed from the Marshall Plan legislation."

man's refusal to share nuclear weapons secrets with the British despite his earlier commitments to do so.

People were less sure what to expect of the Russian-American relationship. Fraying became evident in 1946, with a more serious rupture in 1947 and a definitive break by 1949. Stalin had announced in February 1946 that war was inevitable as long as capitalism existed. In March 1946, Winston Churchill announced the existence of an "Iron Curtain" from Stettin to Trieste. Presumably as a result of the growing tensions this speech reflected, the Soviets soon rejected a long-desired $1 billion American loan, and they refused to join the IMF and IBRD. In May, American zone commander General Lucius Clay stopped sending the Soviets reparations from the western zones.

By March 1947, the Cold War had essentially begun. Truman announced the Truman Doctrine to Congress, by which the United States was to fill the void left by British withdrawal from Greece and Turkey. Given Soviet behavior in Europe, Secretary of State George Marshall concluded that the Soviet-American rift was inevitable and irreversible (Pogue 1987: 196). Even William Fulbright, a leading internationalist, admitted that he saw the Soviet Union as a menace in May 1947: "There are doubts in the minds of many of us that Russia will ever submit to rules of conduct in any field" (cited in Coffin 1966: 93–95).

As the United States moved away from Moscow, relations with Western Europe became tighter. The countries of Western Europe also grew closer to each other. Britain is a good example, since it had previously been reluctant to draw too closely to the Continent. By the end of 1947, however, Foreign Minister Ernest Bevin had firmly decided in favor of cooperation with Western Europe against the Soviets. In a January 1948 speech to the House of Commons, Bevin reviewed Soviet actions in the Balkans, Hungary, Poland, Germany, Iran, and Turkey (cited in Spaak 1971: 144; see also Hogan 1987: 112–14): "surely all these developments which I have been describing point to the conclusion that the free nations of Western Europe must now draw closely together." In March 1948, Britain, France, and the Benelux countries signed the Brussels Treaty, under which each promised to aid the others if attacked.

In summary, the vestiges of wartime cooperation mean that the United States had more allies than adversaries after the war. The Cold War made both the alliance and adversary relationships more intense but did not change the basic fact that the United States had more allies than adversaries. While the United States lost the Soviet Union as an ally, both West Germany and Japan developed ties with the United States that blossomed into formal alliances. As a result, I expect malevolent hegemony.

Cooperation may counteract this malevolence, and under malevolent hegemony such cooperation is especially likely among followers. A tight alliance also makes deeper cooperation more likely for all countries, including the United States. With the start of the Cold War, deeper cooperation and multilateralism became more likely.

Economic Plans and Policies, 1944–46

In the first two years of the postwar period, the United States gave every sign of repeating the mistakes of the 1920s. American tariffs remained highly protective, and a Republican Congress was elected in 1946 on a platform of still greater protectionism. As a result of such policies, the United States had an export surplus of $6.5 billion in 1946. Such protectionism is a common feature of malevolent hegemony.

Europe's huge deficit with the United States in 1946 was financed with United Nations Relief and Rehabilitation Administration (UNRRA) aid and by a $2 billion depletion of foreign dollar and gold reserves. (European exports to the United States totaled only $1 billion a year.) This gold outflow was so large that wartime flows, used to finance Lend-Lease and American troops overseas in 1941–44, were completely annulled by 1947 (Milward 1984: 45).

Such imbalances forced the Europeans to limit dollar imports. Because of a widespread dollar shortage, many Europeans were forced to discriminate against goods from dollar-zone currencies. The dollar shortage also had a detrimental effect on international liquidity, much as similar trends had in the 1920s.

As long as the United States is part of an overlarge coalition, we expect such malevolent leadership. Indeed, malevolence remained the dominant characteristic of American policy toward the Soviet Union and Eastern Europe after the Cold War. Goods from nations that do not cooperate economically with the United States by granting mutual MFN still enter the country under the 1930 Smoot-Hawley tariff code. This fact highlights in stark terms the way that international cooperation can overcome hegemonic malevolence.

Many argue that the protectionist policies of 1944–46 led to an economic crisis in 1946–47. Shortages of capital equipment, manpower, coal and steel; low production and high inflation; and the harsh winter of 1946–47 in Britain and several other countries combined to make the crisis worse. Reflecting views common at the time, Assistant Secretary of State for Economic Affairs William Clayton believed that

Europe is steadily deteriorating. The political position reflects the economic. One political crisis after another merely denotes the existence of grave economic distress. Millions of people in the cities are slowly starving. (cited in Milward 1984: 2)

Germany was in an especially deep crisis. Clay complained of unnecessary occupation expenses, recommending economic unification of Germany and increased trade within Western Europe, higher levels of industrial production, and the end of reparation transfers (Clay 1950).

In contrast, Alan Milward (1984) has staked out a revisionist interpretation of these years. He argues that conditions had improved over 1946 and that there was no general economic crisis other than acute payments imbalances in a few countries. Though some of his points are well taken, Milward exaggerates the health of the European economy in 1947 by selecting biased data, described with loaded words such as "very few indicators of . . . crisis," and "no more than technical difficulties" (see especially Kindleberger 1987: 245–65). Milward also minimizes the real obstacles of the payments problem and dollar shortage; David Wightman (1985) notes that this allegedly technical difficulty threatened both European recovery and political stability. Moreover, whatever the "facts," almost all decision makers believed that there was a crisis (Diebold 1988: 434–35).

If the crisis was exaggerated at the time, many of the very real problems nonetheless reflected American malevolence. High American tariffs and massive gold and dollar movements into the United States could not have failed to affect European recovery. Only explicit cooperation, which I consider in the next section, could overcome this tendency.

Bargaining in 1944–46

Economic cooperation is one possible response to malevolent hegemony. Chapter 7 suggests that cooperation among nonhegemonic states is especially likely, though I cannot rule out the leader's participation. I also expect cooperation to take place regardless of alliance ties.

Trade cooperation between the United States and the other major powers was often elusive in 1945–46, notwithstanding the framework created by the International Trade Organization (ITO). Foremost on the list of American concerns was the British system of imperial preference, which the United States opposed much more strenuously than tariffs per se; in the opinion of Undersecretary of State Sumner Wells in May 1943, "the whole history of British Empire Preferences is a history of economic aggression" (cited in Russell 1947: 11).

To combat this "aggression," the United States drove a hard bargain with the British in the Anglo-American Financial Agreement of December 1945 (see Block 1977; Kindleberger 1987; Pollard 1985). This obligated the British to end the sterling-area dollar pool after one year and to end import quotas on American goods. Britain was to restore sterling convertibility by May 1947 and to scale down the large sterling balances other countries had accumulated during the war. (Large balances would create a strong preference for the purchase of British goods over American.) The British also pledged not to increase imperial preference, and they ultimately reduced about 30 percent of the preferences. In exchange, they received a low-interest loan of $3.75 billion, elimination of the $20 billion Lend-Lease account, and could buy more than $6 billion worth of surplus and "pipeline" equipment at only one-tenth its value (see Block 1977: 63–69). Still, the results of this agreement were disappointing, and the United Kingdom was soon forced to suspend sterling convertibility.

The Truman administration followed up the British loan with $650 million in EximBank loans to France in exchange for tariff concessions. The Truman administration also sought to extend the Soviets approximately $1 billion in EximBank loans, and internal Treasury Department documents proposed reconstruction loans of as much as $10 billion as an incentive to participate in the postwar monetary system (Gaddis 1982: 23). However, the Soviets ultimately rejected such a deal as the Cold War deepened.

The countries of Western Europe also moved toward bilateralism with each other and with third parties. European countries were particularly interested in signing bilateral trade treaties with developing countries to guarantee supplies of much-needed raw materials (Block 1977: 80–81). Britain's agreements with Commonwealth countries, many of which provided critical raw materials, were also important. Through such agreements, Europeans tried to maintain at least minimal levels of trade even without requiring the American market to do so.

Bilateral payments arrangements with other European countries were another important part of trade cooperation. Such agreements allowed a certain range of bilateral deficits or surpluses to facilitate trade. However, they were subject to sudden interruptions if a country reached its debt limit against the other, forcing it to cut off all further imports from that source (Milward 1984: 221). The alternative would be to pay for goods with gold or dollars, both in very short supply.

The theory suggests that all these bilateral agreements make multilateralism more likely in the future. Anyone who defected on one bilateral agreement would retain the benefits of others, reducing the sanction each state had against others. Linking bargains multilaterally would raise this sanction and facilitate deeper bargains.

Necessary Multilateralism and the Failure of Bilateralism

As is well known, the American response to this situation was the unprecedented ERP, better known as the Marshall Plan. George Marshall's offer to the Europeans, made in a commencement speech at Harvard, set only one condition for aid to Western Europe: that the participating countries coordinate their aid requests instead of asking the United States to allocate aid on a country-by-country and project-by-project basis. This condition suggests that the Marshall Plan was necessarily multilateral in the sense of chapter 9, because it implied that the United States would reject an otherwise equivalent plan of European recovery relying on bilateral bargains with other states. This section will demonstrate the claim that the Marshall Plan was necessarily multilateral and that an equivalent set of bilaterals would not have been acceptable.

Theory aside, Marshall's condition presents an interesting substantive puzzle. A series of bilateral agreements was a plausible alternative for Marshall, since bilateralism had been the approach of 1945–46. It is also odd that Congress would not accept a series of sixteen aid programs but would accept an otherwise equivalent aid package to sixteen countries. Moreover, the multilateral framework had little substantive impact on the Marshall Plan. One leading historian of the period, Milward (1984), argues that multilateralism made almost no difference, since the sixteen separate programs were simply stapled together into one. Yet the theory in chapter 9 shows that even if sixteen separate programs were merely stapled into one, the United States might still rationally prefer the stapled bargain to the unstapled bargain. The packaging is important primarily as part of an enforcement strategy, and this enforcement makes the multilateral package possible. The approach here explains what Milward cannot: that the ERP could be substantively equivalent to sixteen separate bilateral programs, and yet the United States could rationally insist on the multilateral framework for enforcement reasons.

Marshall's demand makes sense in terms of the bargaining theory if an aid package that did not meet Marshall's condition would not have been a stable bargain for the United States. Given chapter 9's definition of necessary multilateralism, this requires that at least one bilateral bargain was not feasible. The argument does not require that all previous bilateral agreements were failures, because the proof required only that at least one of these agreements was not stable. Even so, we would have more confidence in the argument if several important bilateral bargains were not feasible.

For reasons of space, I limit consideration to bilateral agreements between the United States and Great Britain and between the United States and France and to agreements over German reconstruction in a bilateral perspective instead of a multilateral one.[4] Showing that these bilaterals would not be feasible requires arguing from counterfactuals, but they are generally reasonable. Repeat of the British loan was clearly impossible; the first loan had passed Congress by only one vote, the United States no longer supported the "key currency" idea on which the loan was based, and in any case the British had suspended sterling convertibility very soon after Marshall's speech (Kindleberger 1987: 101). The United States now preferred Europe-wide payment-deficit financing as part of general reconstruction.

The British loan also demonstrated that bilateral arrangements were inadequate for the problems of reconstruction (Nau 1990: 92). For example, Britain paid for its imports in pounds that suppliers converted to dollars, whereas it received inconvertible currencies for many of its exports. This situation put additional pressure on the pound, making it desirable to have everyone move to currency convertibility simultaneously.

A repeat of the French loan would also have been impossible. It was clear by 1947 that financing French payments bilaterally would indirectly support the Monnet Plan, which had unacceptable consequences for German heavy industry because it would raise American occupation costs. French industrial policy would have to be placed in a multilateral context if it were to obtain American support, as the later development of the Schuman Plan and the European Coal and Steel Community shows (Milward 1984).

Any bilateral reconstruction of Germany also looked increasingly unattractive to American planners. Direct aid to Germany was likely to finance reparations to France and the Soviet Union rather than reconstruction. From the standpoint of the occupation army, direct aid to European countries obviated the need for German reparations, allowing an export-oriented increase in German production. This increased production would reduce the expenses of feeding and otherwise supplying the population.

In other words, bilateral cooperation with Britain, France, and Germany

---

4. The role of American occupation authorities in Germany complicates this. The occupation authorities often came to represent German interests in Washington in some surprising ways, generally because of an interest in reducing occupation expenses.

was unattractive to the United States. It is difficult to say that such cooperation would have been impossible, since the terms of these agreements also changed alongside the switch from bilateralism to multilateralism. Still, these general difficulties with bilateralism across the major countries of Western Europe make it more likely that for at least one country, bilateral cooperation of equivalent size would have been impossible. If an agreement such as the ERP were to occur, it would need to be multilateral.

The Bargaining Model and the Marshall Plan

After the failure of these bilateral arrangements, American policymakers who wished to construct a stable and cooperative postwar economic system had two choices. First, they could decrease the size of economic cooperation. Under the circumstances, this would mean an aid program sufficiently harmless not to provoke the ire of those in the United States opposed to overseas involvement. This would be an odd choice in an increasingly polarized world where closer security ties between the United States and Western Europe made larger bargains more likely.

Alternatively, internationalists could expand the scope of the bargain, increasing the number of countries participating in it. Truman (1956: 111) presents a concise summary of these issues in his memoirs, conveniently appropriating the State Department's analysis as his own: "By 1947 . . . after two years of substantial, though piecemeal, emergency assistance, it was apparent that an even larger and more comprehensive program was needed to achieve the rebuilding of the economy of Europe."

This bargain would be multilateral. By reducing the relative role of the United States within that bargain, such a change might also succeed in making a bargain stable for the United States. It might even be true that the American share became sufficiently small, so that large bargains were more likely to be stable for the United States. If contrasted with a series of bilateral bargains, the increasing rewards of cooperation would also make multilateral cooperation more likely.

The internationalists chose this second option, not surprisingly. Both the United States and Western Europe apparently preferred extensive cooperation to American isolationism, if any enforcement problems could be solved. Having decided on greater U.S. involvement overseas, the internationalists then put together a series of working papers and proposals leading to the Marshall Plan. George Kennan and his Policy Planning Staff argued that American cooperation with Europe should take the form of a multilateral aid program

(PPS memo to Marshall, May 23, 1947, cited in Kennan 1967: 337; see also Kindleberger 1987; Mee 1984: 89–90; Hogan 1987: 40–45):

> The program which this country is asked to support must be a joint one, agreed to by several European nations. While it may be linked to individual national programs, such as the Monnet Plan in France, it must, for psychological and political, as well as economic, reasons, be an internationally agreed program. The request for our support must come as a joint request from a group of friendly nations, not as a series of isolated and individual appeals.

Marshall agreed with his staff's recommendation. His ERP set only one condition for aid to Western Europe: that the participating countries must coordinate their aid requests instead of asking the United States to allocate aid on a country-by-country and project-by-project basis. Marshall's condition was written into the law establishing the ERP, and its definition of *participating country* included the clause "provided it adheres to, and for so long as it remains an adherent to, a joint program for European recovery designed to accomplish this Act" (U.S. Senate 1948).

A first glance at the history shows that Marshall's condition was met exactly. Foreign Ministers Ernest Bevin and Georges Bidault convened the 1947 Paris Conference, which created a Committee of European Economic Cooperation (CEEC) to oversee the ERP. The CEEC's technical committees and executive committee then began work on a common program. Acting on a September report from the CEEC, the U.S. Congress passed the Economic Cooperation Act, authorizing the first year's expenditure of $5.3 billion, to be administered by a separate department, the European Cooperation Agency (ECA). The CEEC became a permanent organization in April 1948, the Organization for European Economic Cooperation (OEEC, now the OECD).

As a condition of ERP aid, each recipient signed a bilateral enabling agreement with the United States. These were typically boilerplate treaties, and the centerpiece of each bound the recipient by the multilateral agreement of the OEEC. These ostensibly bilateral agreements merely formalized the multilateral agreement (see U.S. House 1948: 249–50). The executive intended that the agreement be multilateral in reality as well as in form. Further evidence is provided by the fact that the standard bilateral agreement was rather insensitive to the problems of many countries, especially the smaller ones (see especially Lundestad 1980: chap. 5).

This multilateralism was a necessary part of the Marshall Plan. This argument does not rule out other factors; many scholars believe that security concerns, for example, were an important reason for the ERP. The theory here makes a slightly different claim by distinguishing the probability of cooperation from the size of a bargain. The Cold War probably did not make cooperation more likely.[5] Cooperation was already occurring, though some important bilaterals were at risk of not being renewed. However, the Cold War undoubtedly made cooperation bigger, covering more goods and nontrade issues than the parties would have otherwise. These foreign-policy concerns also played an important role in obtaining the consent of previously isolationist Republicans such as Senator Arthur Vandenberg (Hudson 1977; Tompkins 1970).

Despite the subtle difference from relative-gains theory, this is hardly a novel claim. It may even be a neo-Realist article of faith. John Mearsheimer (1992: 216–17) summarizes the argument well:

the cold war was largely responsible for the unusually high levels of economic integration and political cooperation over the past forty-five years. . . . Britain, Germany and France no longer worried about each other because all faced a greater menace from the Soviets. In fact, each Western democracy had a vested interest in seeing its alliance partners grow more powerful economically and militarily, since each additional increment of power helped deter a Soviet attack.

Reasonable as that sounds, the empirical record is ambiguous on this point. The Soviets were invited to participate in the Marshall Plan, and communist governments were only excluded from ERP assistance after the Soviet Union, Czechoslovakia, and Poland had already rejected aid. Still, one should not read too much into the open invitation to the Soviets, since the Americans expected a Soviet rejection that they could exploit for propaganda (Hogan 1987: 52). Tellingly, American officials chose not to organize Marshall aid through the United Nations' Economic Commission for Europe, a multilateral forum in which the Soviets had a voice; instead, U.S. leaders formed a new organization for the purpose (and a new agency at home, the ECA).

For different reasons, the United States also decided against other multilateral forums, a decision that historians see as a change in policy away from globalism toward multilateral regionalism. The United States had initially fun-

---

5. Recall that chapter 7 argued that alliances may make cooperation either more or less likely, and we thus should not expect any overall relationship. This would be consistent with a claim that a specific alliance made a particular agreement more likely, although this would not be a falsifiable claim.

neled a significant amount of aid through the UNRRA, where American funds made up three-fourths of the first two tranches. The UNRRA distributed aid largely on a nondiscriminatory basis, with about half of it going to Soviet-occupied territories. However, the United States had only one vote in the UNRRA council, which had seventeen members. As a result, the administration believed that its money was not being used as it wished. In 1946–47, it began using bilateral approaches for aid to Austria, Greece, Hungary, Italy, Poland, Trieste, and China. After 1947, aid to noncommunist recipients became multilateral through the ERP and CEEC/OEEC.

Such choices among multilateral institutions lie outside the theory. The argument here rests more narrowly on the choice between some multilateral institution and the hitherto dominant bilateral forms of cooperation.

Conjectures and Enforcement Strategies

If the Marshall Plan was necessarily multilateral, I can explain it if the United States enforced it in way consistent with the assumptions in chapter 9. This section will argue that the United States evaluated proposed multilateral bargains against individually feasible bilateral bargains, comparing a package deal against the need to negotiate bilateral agreements with country after country. Enforcement of an existing multilateral bargain worked differently, with something like hegemonic enforcement.

Consider first multilateral proposals, which Washington typically compared to a series of individually feasible bilateral bargains. The State Department, for instance, was tired of asking Congress for program after program (Kindleberger 1987: 111–12). Georgia Senator Walter George, probably the most important Democrat on the Foreign Relations Committee, favored the ERP's multilateralism in part because:

> it is the only door through which we can enter into European affairs at all except running the risk of having them slide right back into a simple undertaking between country X over there and ourselves, very much as we are bogged up with Greece at the moment. (U.S. Senate, 1948: 175)

William Diebold (1988: 433) states that the executive also concluded "that its only chance of getting a large amount of money was for an aid program for 'Europe' and not a series of individual countries." Given the standard of individual feasibility, increasing the rewards of cooperation makes cooperation more likely. The primary attraction of multilateralism is its greater rewards compared to individual bilaterals.

Once the ERP was in place, the United States ceased comparing it to a series of bilateral bargains. Instead, it enforced cooperation hegemonically, which depended on a willingness to punish cheaters in a particular way—by pulling out of the multilateral bargain altogether.

Simply by packaging the aid programs, the United States used a global enforcement strategy, with the Congress being the potential sanctioner. By voting down ERP appropriations in toto, Congress could cut off all aid in response to whatever violations it deemed worthy of punishment. Indeed, major foreign-policy figures in the majority party of Congress thought in terms of an enforcement strategy based on European behavior in the aggregate. When Senator Robert Taft advocated experimental authorization of Marshall aid for a single year, Vandenberg responded that if the Europeans were still cooperating in a year, he hoped that Taft would vote to renew aid; Taft said that he might (Pogue 1987: 250–51). Taft clearly would oppose renewal if the Europeans were not cooperating. Vandenberg did not say what he would do if the Europeans were not cooperating, but I think that the inference is clear that he might vote against. In this way, the entire aid package was contingent on cooperation as the Americans defined it.

The executive branch also thought in terms of such an enforcement strategy. ECA officials played an important advisory role in the drafting of European requests and in advocating congressional approval of ERP assistance. This role gave the State Department an excellent opportunity to threaten Europeans with rejection of ERP aid should their plans be insufficiently cooperative.

Was the United States willing to punish all Europeans simultaneously for any unacceptable plan? Evidence from the planning stage suggests that it was. The State Department's guidelines to Clayton and Jefferson Caffery at the 1947 Paris Conference insisted that the Europeans propose a truly multilateral program. After seeing the CEEC's preliminary work, State repeated its concerns: reports were "disappointing," the aid request included duplications, the request was too large, and the program needed a regional approach rather than a mere adding up of aid requests (Gimbel 1976: 256–62; Mee 1984: 178–85). When the Europeans at the CEEC tried to reduce the program by applying a fixed percentage cut to each country's aid requests, Undersecretary of State Robert Lovett rejected this draft as well (see Mee 1984: 178–203; Milward 1984: 180–89).

In short, the American executive was willing to reject the whole package as an enforcement mechanism. This was true even if a single country could be identified as the primary violator. One illuminating example is the planning for the 1949–50 allocations. Throughout, the Americans' working assumption was that aid would be allocated in proportion to the recipients' hard-currency-payments deficits (Milward 1988: 95); unfortunately, knowing this decision rule distorted the recipients' incentives. Britain was the worst offender, exaggerating its import needs to increase its hard-currency deficits in the draft plan, Britain's estimated current-account deficit was so large that its aid request comprised 40 percent of the total. In response, the United States rejected the OEEC draft plan in full rather than excluding only the British. In other words, the United States did use the drastic metastrategy implied by symmetric conjectures.[6]

The importance of multilateral enforcement is also evident because proposed switches to bilateral enforcement did not resonate. Philip D. Reed, chairman of the board of General Electric and formerly chief of the U.S. Mission for Economic Affairs in London, advocated bilateralism in his testimony before the House Foreign Affairs Committee:

> I think we have got to make our agreements bilateral agreements so that we can in the case of each individual country deal with them at the end of the 15 months or a year individually, and hold them responsible for their performance under that agreement.
>
> If you have a great multilateral deal, I do not think you could hold anybody responsible really, except the whole group, and that does not make a great deal of sense. (U.S. House 1948: 607)

In other words, Reed did not believe that hegemonic enforcement relied on reasonable conjectures. Ohio Representative John M. Vorys responded critically to Reed's bilateralism:

> Our experience in [bilateral] settlements under lend-lease makes me hope that [multilateralism] will have a different type of result in the long run. I do not see where we get by having so many different agreements and by having each of 16 countries seeking a little different or a little better terms than the other country gets. (U.S. House 1948: 607)

---

6. The dispute was eventually resolved in a manner acceptable to both sides by making shares a technical problem to be solved by a committee of eminent experts. The shares recommended in the resulting Snoy-Marjolin Report (1949) became fixed for subsequent years (see Hogan 1987: 244–45; Milward 1984: 204–7).

In other words, multilateralism was preferable to individually feasible bilateral deals. Vorys was in the majority, which believed that holding the whole group responsible did indeed make a great deal of sense.

While the primary sanction was withdrawal from the entire multilateral package, country-specific sanctioning devices also played a small role. This is the kind of coercive leadership found in many existing hegemonic theories. The primary such tool was the American ability to withhold approval of each country's use of its counterpart funds. The United States held up expenditures in Italy in 1949 to force the government to relax its deflationary policies and to develop a national investment budget; for similar reasons, the United States chose to release French funds on a monthly basis in 1949, as budgetary and tax reforms progressed (Hogan 1987: 206–7).

Though they could be used to enforce cooperation, the counterpart funds were normally used more subtly, as a bargaining lever rather than as an enforcement mechanism. The American ambassador to Italy, James Clement Dunn, thought it unwise to "kill the child" by shutting off aid to uncooperative nations but saw the counterpart funds as an important lever over the Europeans: "He who controls the so-called lire fund will control the monetary and fiscal, and in fact the entire economic policy of Italy" (cited in Hogan 1987: 152). Despite his exaggerated view of the leverage the funds provided, it is interesting that he explicitly rejected a metastrategy of bilateral Grim Trigger— that is, a total aid cutoff. His more subtle strategy of influencing Italian investment-allocative decisions goes far beyond the simplifications of the model. There were similar uses of the counterpart funds elsewhere. For example, counterpart funds were used to allow American corporations to repatriate profits from European operations if the companies so desired (Milward 1984: 120).

In sum, the evidence suggests that the United States intended an enforcement strategy based on the multilateral bargain as a whole, knowing that doing so implied a cutoff of funds to all recipients if necessary. In addition to this metastrategy, the United States made minor use of country-specific delays as a bargaining tool. The enforcement strategy is consistent with the kind of conjectures we would expect from the analysis in chapter 9.

Finally, this section has looked at the Marshall Plan solely from the American perspective. We should recall that multilateral cooperation is more likely for the hegemon but less likely for followers under individually feasible bargains. It is suggestive that the United States pushed multilateralism, while others tried to work around it. Great Britain, in particular, was hesitant to join a multilateral bargain because of the unique role of sterling, its global responsibilities to the Commonwealth, and its position as a co-occupier of Germany. The smaller states, in contrast, generally supported large bargains both multilateral and bilateral.

It is also worth noting that chapter 9 argued that hegemonic enforcement of multilateral cooperation requires the forbearance of third parties. As that argument would predict, we see no European enforcement of postwar bargains against other Europeans. While this makes it look as if the Europeans were colluding in trying to evade American goals (Milward 1992), we would expect exactly this pattern from the analysis of hegemonic enforcement. Europeans' indifference to the "cheating" of other Europeans is not a sign of European opposition to American goals but is simply a characteristic of a particular kind of multilateral equilibrium, hegemonic enforcement.

Alternative Explanations of Marshall's Multilateralism

Though the evidence is consistent with the theory, skeptics might ask whether enforcement concerns are the best explanation for Marshall's multilateral condition. One alternative explanation sees Marshall's condition as a bargaining ploy in the game between the United States and Western Europe (see Kennan 1967). Each European country wanted as much aid as possible and was happy to sign off on everyone else's aid requests; the United States wanted to avoid duplication and reduce the total aid package. The United States hoped that multilateralism would change European incentives since the OEEC framework would force the Europeans to inspect one another's aid requests in the course of putting together a common plan.[7]

If this was the motive for the OEEC, it failed (Mee 1984; Milward 1984). The Europeans did not scrutinize one another's requests. American planners were soon forced to design an alternative decision rule, first allocating aid in proportion to the recipients' hard-currency-payments deficits and then using a fixed-proportion rule (Milward 1988: 95). Moreover, once this failure became apparent, the United States did not seek to break the multilateral bargain into bilateral agreements. This failure is especially surprising in light of theoretical

---

7. There were two reasons to believe this might work. The first was informational asymmetries, since the Europeans probably knew more about one another than the United States knew about them. Thus, the Europeans could serve as a better check on one another than could any American agency in Washington. Second, a multilateral organization should create a better incentive framework because aid funds would appear scarce to the organization once the United States announced a budget; within a bilateral framework, aid funds appear abundant to each country since any increase in its aid has implications only for third parties. Keohane (1984: 145) has a related power-based interpretation of the Marshall Plan.

arguments that bilateral agreements maximize the power of large states over others (see esp. Hirschman 1945/1980). Therefore, this issue cannot explain multilateralism; more precisely, solving the bargaining problem over allocations was not a necessary condition for a multilateral bargain.

Another alternative explanation sees postwar multilateralism as resting on the nature of American domestic politics. For example, many argue that the policy reflected a coalition around the politics of productivity or a projection of the New Deal regulatory state into international affairs (Block 1977; Burley 1993; Goldstein 1993; Hogan 1987; Maier 1977; Ruggie 1983, 1993). While domestic preferences and coalitions obviously may affect foreign policy, such an argument has trouble explaining variation in postwar policy over time.[8] In particular, it is hard to see how relatively constant domestic coalitions might explain variation from the bilaterals of 1946 and 1947 to the multilateralism thereafter.

The European Payments Union

The Marshall Plan was not the only important form of multilateral cooperation between the United States and its European allies after the start of the Cold War. In monetary affairs, the European Payments Union (EPU) played an important role after its creation in 1950. It replaced the existing system of bilateral payments agreements. Participating countries offset credits and debits on current-account transactions through an automatic multilateral system, making European currencies fully convertible for trade. Each country would be in net surplus or deficit only to the group as a whole, settling these imbalances through new credits from, or gold and dollar payments to, the EPU. Each received an initial quota to cover the maximum surplus or debit allowed through the union, and the United States set aside $350 million to get the system running in July 1950 (Hogan 1987: 295–96, 323; Milward 1984). The EPU also financed trade between Europe and the sterling area when the pound was subject to strict exchange controls (Block 1977: 122–29). In these ways, the EPU supported trade liberalization and created liquidity that could finance trade within Europe.

The United States insisted that this clearing system be multilateral. Persistent debtors, led by the United Kingdom, often favored a more bilateral system

---

8. Alternative explanations should also account for the variation with the interwar period. The United States was willing to discuss war debts and reparations only bilaterally, not multilaterally, in the 1920s. It ultimately negotiated bilateral settlements with thirteen countries from 1923 to 1926 (Kindleberger 1973: 41).

since it allowed them to discriminate against persistent creditors (Milward 1984). The United States refused to consider any such bilateral alternative. Even those American officials who opposed the EPU were likely to argue for greater multilateralism. The Treasury Department, for instance, generally complained that the union would violate the nondiscriminatory multilateralism of the IMF and the GATT.

Multilateralism triumphed in the negotiations with Europe when ECA administrator Paul Hoffman warned that a "suitable payments union" was the sine qua non of additional aid (cited in Hogan 1987: 303). In other words, Hoffman would be willing to use a total aid cutoff as a sanctioning device to enforce multilateral cooperation in the EPU. However, other factors outside the theory were also at work in the EPU case. There were important technical advantages to a regional clearing system, which was characterized by economies of scale. There were also distributional effects: the Netherlands had surpluses with Germany and the United Kingdom but deficits with every other country and would only join a multilateral system if it included Germany and the United Kingdom; Italy, which had large sterling balances, found the distributional consequences of any EPU troublesome without British membership (Milward 1984: 306–13). Still, the attractiveness of multilateral enforcement also lay behind the EPU.

Increasingly tight alliances made such a large bargain more likely to be stable. The State Department strongly supported the EPU for foreign-policy reasons: "We felt that EPU combined with the trade liberalization program was a step towards the U.S. objective of west European unification" (cited in Milward 1992: 350). Economic agencies opposed it on economic grounds, which suggests that political motives were indeed central. For instance, Frank A. Southard, Jr., then associate director of research at the Federal Reserve Board, believed that the EPU would divert Western European exports to Western Europe and away from the dollar area, preventing the accumulation of dollar reserves and thus postponing global currency convertibility (Milward 1984: 322).

This attitude represented a stark contrast from the first postwar years. The dollar shortage and the resulting liquidity problems had been around since the end of the war. Yet, as Henry Nau (1990: 89) rightly notes, "although the dollar was the only usable international currency after the war, the United States in 1944–1945 had no strong political reasons to supply the dollars." When these political reasons appeared in the form of containment and the Cold War, the United States found a multilateral way to fix the dollar shortage.

Military-Economic Linkages and Scandinavian Cooperation

The focus of this chapter so far has been on American policy. However, there was variation in the reaction of others to American leadership, both from one country to another and within a single country over time. This section will look at some of these in a most-similar comparative case approach.

If a state rejects a bargain, what might make its future cooperation more likely? Chapter 7 provides some subtle answers to this question. Though tighter security relations may have no direct effect on the likelihood of cooperation, making military cooperation a larger share of a bargain among allies would, for a sufficiently small state, make larger bargains more likely to be stable. Testing such a proposition requires finding a small nation that rejected significant economic cooperation at first but that underwent a rapid increase in military participation in Western Europe. We expect this state to find it attractive to increase the size of an economic bargain.

Though this may be an unlikely constellation of independent variables, Norway fits the bill. It had a cordial security relationship with both Britain and the United States after the war but wanted to avoid hostility with the Soviet Union if possible. As it saw small states like Czechoslovakia fall under the Soviet yoke, it came to support NATO as a defense against Finlandization. Norway and Turkey were the only NATO members who actually bordered the USSR, and as such they tended to make larger contributions to common defense.[9] In this way, military cooperation became a larger part of the postwar bargain for Norway than for most others. Sweden, an otherwise similar country that did not join NATO, and Denmark, a more consistently pro-Western country in this period, provide convenient contrasts.

The socialist governments of both Norway and Sweden had sought to pursue a bridge-building policy between the Soviet Union and the major Western powers, perhaps within the framework of Nordic security arrangements (see Brofoss 1977; Lundestad 1980; Pharo 1976; Sundelius and Wiklund 1979). Neither played any important role in the system of postwar bilateral cooperation, in part because of an interest in national planning (Bjerve 1959; Lundberg 1961; Montgomery 1962). As a result, American planners came to see both as stumbling blocks to a strong European economic organization (Lundestad 1980: 105–6).

However, all the Scandinavian states cooperated with the United States

---

9. See Murdoch and Sandler 1982; Sandler and Forbes 1980 for empirical confirmation of this claim within a quasi-public alliance-spending model.

and Western Europe in a number of smaller ways. Norway received a $50 million credit from the EximBank in 1946, though it used only a small portion of it. Denmark also used only a portion of the credits the United States offered, while Sweden did not have any need for credits prior to 1948 (Lundestad 1980: 56–57, 102–3). These countries also signed various trade agreements with the United Kingdom and other countries, with Anglo-Danish relations probably the most filled with conflict (see Olsen 1962).

While Scandinavian foreign policy did not preclude cooperation, these countries intentionally sought to keep cooperation small because they desired good relations with both East and West. For example, Sweden attended the 1947 Paris Conference only on the condition that the ERP not bypass the United Nations, interfere with Swedish trade in Eastern Europe, or compromise Sweden's neutrality (Hogan 1987: 60). Norway sent only economic experts to the conference to signal its reluctance to give the Marshall Plan any political significance. As one then minister noted, "If economic considerations had prevailed, we would initially have asked for a much larger amount [of aid]" (Brofoss 1977: 241) This position exactly corresponds to the argument here—that security relationships affect the size of cooperation, not its likelihood.

Norway changed its mind in 1948 in response to a worsening security environment after the Czech coup and Soviet pressure against Finland (Pharo 1976: 153). Despite some domestic controversy over the issue, Norway was a founding member of NATO and came to make contributions to joint defense that were large compared to other small countries. As a result, it also became willing to agree to deeper forms of economic cooperation, and it ultimately ceased being a brake on institutions such as the ERP or EPU.

Denmark underwent a much less dramatic shift in foreign policy, since it had been significantly more pro-Western than Norway throughout. Denmark also made much smaller contributions to NATO than Norway, in part because Denmark could free ride on occupation forces in Germany that protected it from the most likely Soviet approach. The start of the Cold War did not lead to any significant shift in Danish economic cooperation, which remained centered on relations with the United Kingdom and Germany, its largest markets.

We do not see deepening economic cooperation with Sweden; as a neutral, it was not making large military contributions to linked bargains. Again, the theory would predict that the absence of an alliance would not make economic cooperation with Sweden any less likely than cooperation with Norway or Denmark. Sweden continued to cooperate with Western countries, though either cooperation or noncooperation would be consistent with the theory's ambiguous predictions in such cases.

Instead of looking at the ambiguous predictions about the probability of cooperation, the hypotheses concerning the size of the bargain provide a better test of the theory. While Sweden was a recipient of Marshall Plan aid, its neutrality often meant that it received smaller concessions from the United States than did other countries. For example, the State Department told the Erlander government not to apply for $75 million in credits from EximBank in early 1948, because Sweden would not receive them. Swedish neutrality was an important reason for the American position (Lundestad 1980: 102–3). Again, security ties affect not the probability of cooperation but the size of the bargain reached.

Security relations affected the substance of Swedish-American cooperation in other ways as well. For example, the United States' increasingly strong embargo on strategic goods forced an especially important concession from Sweden because of its significant trade with the East. The Swedes ultimately agreed not to export any ERP goods to Eastern Europe and agreed to receive copies of the 1-A list of proscribed items "for their own use" in trade negotiations with Eastern Europe (Lundestad 1980: 139). In such cases, the United States asked for substantial intangible concessions in areas of national sovereignty and foreign policy.

Finland was not a Marshall Plan recipient because the Soviets did not want it to be. However, the United States was sympathetic to the needs of Finland's geographic position and sought economic cooperation in a number of small ways. Finland received export licenses, for example, as long as it remained democratic (Heikkilä 1983). Finland's foreign-policy position did not preclude cooperation but reduced the size of the bargains reached.

The cross-national and intertemporal variation in Scandinavian foreign policy has allowed me to test some of the more subtle propositions of the model. As I have found elsewhere, variation in alliances affects not the probability of cooperation but the size of any bargain reached. In addition, for a state making sufficiently small contributions to linked bargains, increasing the role of military cooperation makes larger bargains more likely. Evidence consistent with these propositions adds to the plausibility of the bargaining model as a whole.

Cooperation after the Marshall Plan

The end of the Marshall Plan in 1952 meant the temporary end of deep multilateral cooperation between the United States and Western Europe. With the cease-fire in Korea and the death of Stalin, East-West military tensions eased.

By lowering alliance tightness, these changes meant that very large bargains such as the ERP were no longer likely to be stable. One indication of how these reduced tensions affected alliance cooperation was a significant reduction in the number of goods whose export was restricted through NATO's Consultative Committee (COCOM) (see Long 1989; Mastanduno 1988).

Meanwhile, the global regimes that play an important role today were moribund. Andrew Shonfield (1976: 24) notes that the GATT "had been fairly quiescent during most of the 1950s." The United States had essentially shelved the IMF as inadequate to the task of postwar monetary relations, substituting Marshall funds and the EPU. By 1953, the IMF had total capital of only $3.3 billion; the ERP had spent $13.5 billion in four years. As another indication of weakness, the United Kingdom had a tranche of only $340 million available for it to borrow from the IMF, while it had run a deficit of nearly $1.5 billion through the EPU in the 1951–52 fiscal year alone (Milward 1992: 351, 361, 365).

Both the United States and Western Europe searched for new forms of cooperation in the mid–1950s (see Milward 1992; Shonfield 1976: chap. 1; Strange 1976 for overviews). Six continental countries settled on the European Economic Community (EEC) for reasons outside the theory here. A second group led by the United Kingdom responded by forming the European Free Trade Area (EFTA).

This follower-led cooperation makes sense in terms of chapter 7's theory. Again, when a leader is surrounded by allies, cooperation is likely among followers. In a world in which states negotiate agreements one at a time, in the language of chapter 9 they consider these individually feasible bargains under symmetric conjectures. Under such conjectures, the followers' cooperation means that the leader is more likely to join multilateral cooperation.

This situation provides the background for two new forms of multilateral cooperation in the late 1950s and 1960s, the Dillon and Kennedy rounds of the GATT and monetary cooperation among the major powers in the Group of Seven (G-7). The multilateral cooperation of the 1960s was not a result of any grand American design for the postwar order but a response to follower-led cooperation and to the underlying malevolence of American leadership. However, even more than in chapter 8, extensive cooperation calls into question any simple distinction between malevolent and benevolent hegemony.

Mainstream hegemonic theory interprets cooperation in the 1960s as a result of declining American power (see esp. Keohane 1984: chap. 9). However, this theory has problems explaining changes in this period, because variation in American relative power cannot explain variation in outcomes (Nau 1990).

Looking at the ways in which American participation in multilateral cooperation responded to cooperation among followers provides a new way to understand some of the changes in the decades after World War II.

Multilateralism and the General Agreements on Trade and Tariffs

To see how follower-led cooperation induced greater multilateralism, I begin with the trade regime. The conventional wisdom is that the GATT is an important pillar of the postwar multilateral political economy (e.g., Goldstein 1993; Ruggie 1993). It is easy to forget today that the GATT (now WTO) was an afterthought, taking provisional effect until the International Trade Organization (ITO) was established. Moreover, the GATT only gradually came to perform some of the tasks originally assigned the ITO. The large multilateral trade negotiations that we now associate with the GATT/WTO system were not characteristic of its first decade; early rounds at Annecy (1949), Torquay (1951), and Geneva (1956) were of little importance and consisted mostly of bilateral negotiations. Though apparently a multilateral institution, part of the GATT's success was its ability to encompass either multilateral or bilateral tariff negotiations.

Important multilateral tariff reductions began with the Dillon round (1960–61). The United States initiated the round as a response to the creation of two European trading areas from which it had been excluded, the EEC and the EFTA. As the EEC developed a common external tariff, some American exports would inevitably lose ground to European competitors producing behind the tariff wall. Accordingly, the United States sent Undersecretary of State C. Douglas Dillon to Europe to drum up support for multilateral negotiations that might prevent any greater tariff barriers when the common external tariff took effect (Curzon and Curzon 1976: 168).

The United States received encouragement from the pro-multilateral lobby in the EEC, led by Germany and the Benelux countries. Because the EEC would use a weighted average of existing tariffs for its new common tariff, these low-tariff countries would see increases in their own barriers to imports. As a result, they favored tariff reductions through the GATT that could counteract these increases.

The result was a round of multilateral tariff reductions and tariff bindings by which nations agreed not to increase tariffs in the future. Soon thereafter President John F. Kennedy launched the round that came to bear his name. This was the high-water mark of multilateral tariff reductions, using linear cuts that reduced all tariffs by a certain proportion (see Bhagwati 1990; Curzon and Curzon 1976; Finlayson and Zacher 1983). Subsequent rounds, such as the Tokyo and Uruguay rounds, would be dominated by negotiations over nontariff barriers or dispute resolution (Krasner 1979).

The International Monetary Fund

Like trade policy, international monetary policy also underwent important changes in the late 1950s and 1960s. Central to these changes was a shift toward greater multilateralism. Whereas multilateralism in trade was a response to nonhegemonic cooperation in regional trading blocs, multilateral monetary cooperation stemmed more from the workings of malevolent hegemony. In particular, the way that the Bretton Woods system worked in the 1950s proved to be destabilizing for the system as a whole and to give the leader unique advantages that gave the United States power to negotiate favorable forms of cooperation by which other states took on a disproportionate share of the costs of monetary adjustment.

The IMF established a gold-dollar system in which the United States backed the dollar with gold while other countries fixed their currencies against the dollar (Cohen 1977; Gowa 1983; Shonfield 1976; Strange 1976). While it provided exchange-rate stability for all participants, the United States gained several additional advantages (Gowa 1983: 43–44). For example, foreign willingness to hold dollars as reserves made the United States immune to the monetary discipline that other countries faced when their external deficits exceeded their reserves.[10] If other countries tried to discipline the United States by converting surplus dollars to gold, the United States could simply suspend convertibility of the dollar. France under Charles de Gaulle objected most strenuously to this feature of the system, as Andrew Shonfield (1976: 55) summarizes:

If the Americans could unload dollars in unlimited quantities on the rest of the world in settlement of any debts which they incurred, and the dollar was not convertible into gold, then this meant that the United States was uniquely free from the constraints on national policy imposed on all other nations by the state of their balance of payments.

---

10. The reserve role also meant that the dollar was overvalued because of the foreign demand for dollar holdings. This overvaluation let Americans purchase foreign industries more cheaply, though it also harmed American exports.

Since the United States did not face a monetary constraint, it did not need to face the costs of exchange-rate adjustment. Instead, others paid those costs. In terms of the model, the United States could reduce its contributions to monetary adjustment, knowing that other states would adjust instead.

At the same time, the model does not capture some of the dynamic effects of this cost shifting. In particular, persistent American deficits revealed systematic problems in the working of the international monetary system by the late 1950s. The most important of these is the Triffin Paradox (1961): having a dollar standard required American external deficits to supply international liquidity, yet these deficits undermined international confidence in the dollar.

Problems with the American deficit repeatedly led to international monetary cooperation in the 1960s. The United States and the major European countries created a multilateral gold pool in 1961 to supply gold to the London market when the price increased (Strange 1976: 65–79). The Group of Ten (minus France) created special drawing rights (SDRs) in the IMF in March 1968 at the insistence of the United States (Nau 1990: 148–50; Odell 1982; Strange 1976). These SDRs were a nonnational currency and source of international liquidity. These agreements sought to accommodate American deficits while continuing to supply international liquidity—without forcing the United States to devalue the dollar or pay other costs of monetary adjustment.

Malevolent leadership gave the United States a favorable reversion point, which affected cooperation. Shonfield (1976: 36–39) argues that the underlying U.S. ability to alter the monetary system unilaterally let the Americans decide the form of monetary cooperation in the 1960s. Europeans had to go along with agreements they would not normally favor, such as the Two-Tier Gold Agreement of March 1968. By this agreement, the Europeans (except the French) agreed not to demand gold for dollars or purchase additional gold from the private market; this promise left the undervalued dollar as the primary source of reserves.

These various agreements did not solve the underlying problems of the Bretton Woods system, though they did postpone the crisis until the early 1970s (see Gowa 1983; Odell 1982). These problems, which rely on the dynamics of the system and on changing foreign confidence in the dollar, lie well outside the model. While a decent first cut, the model points towards a need for more research on the politics of international leadership and cooperation in monetary affairs.[11]

---

11. For an interesting start, see Eichengreen 1985, 1987.

Conclusion

This chapter has claimed that postwar security patterns led initially to malevolent hegemony and small to moderate levels of economic cooperation. The start of the Cold War increased military cooperation between the United States and Western Europe, making deeper economic cooperation more likely. Multilateralization helped facilitate these larger bargains, which are usually problematic for large nations such as the United States. Several variables, including the existing network of bilateral cooperation, combined to make this multilateral cooperation a likely solution. Existing cooperation, as well as underlying hegemonic malevolence, also played an important role in the greater multilateralism of the 1960s.

I have argued that the Cold War made cooperation deeper without affecting the probability of cooperation per se. A brief comparison of the Scandinavian countries provided evidence for this claim by controlling for much of the nonsecurity variation. The Scandinavian comparison also let me examine variation in states' contributions to linked bargains.

Like the contentions of orthodox historians, the argument assumes that security concerns are exogenous and do not depend directly on economic interests, as revisionists have argued (see Block 1977; Kolko and Kolko 1972; William Appleman Williams 1959/1972). Unlike the historians, I have used deduction to derive testable propositions about exactly how security concerns affect international cooperation. Still, the claim that the Cold War led to larger bargains would probably not be objectionable to most historians, though the claim that this larger bargain made multilateralism more likely is novel.

By arguing that security concerns were primary, this account glosses over some other possibilities. The conventional wisdom among historians is that the crisis of 1946–47 explains the change from deflationary to expansionist policies (see also Keohane 1984: 141–50). However, we should be skeptical of any argument that policy failure is sufficient to explain policy change, because there are certainly many dysfunctional yet persistent policies. Even if policy failure contributes to policy innovation, such an account cannot really explain the predatory policy of 1944–46. American experience in the interwar period meant that most policymakers wanted to avoid the kind of malevolence that characterized policy in the 1920s. Michael Hogan (1987), who emphasizes the continuity with the 1920s and 1930s, is forced to blame the failure of 1946–47 on overly optimistic assumptions. That failure, if such it was, was easily anticipated by all those who had lived through the 1920s. Malevolent and largely noncooperative deflation, followed by expansionist cooperation, is consistent with the kind of theoretical distinctions made throughout this book and offers at least as plausible an account of these events.

That success aside, there is obviously much that the theory here cannot explain. The bargaining theory may be consistent with the evidence, but it does not make predictions at any level of detail. For instance, Hogan (1987) argues that the stress on public-private cooperation in the American New Deal coalition exerted a decisive impact on the nature of European cooperation. Even if correct, this contention is not inconsistent with the bargaining theory, but it also does not follow from the theory. However, by taking several steps back from the morass of historical detail, we can use the hypotheses from the theory to help structure an account of the negotiation.

This chapter has also provided an opportunity for some synthesis of the various models presented in this book. The first half of this chapter used results from chapters 5 and 7 to explain the pattern of American policy and cooperation between 1944 and 1949. By pulling together threads from the arguments of several different theoretical chapters, this argument shows how the various theoretical claims of this book can fit together in a synthetic theory of hegemonic leadership. The second half of the chapter examined a more narrow question, using chapter 9 to explore the multilateral features of postwar cooperation. The Marshall Plan, which explicitly required multilateralism, is an especially important test of the theory. The increasing multilateralization that occurred in the 1960s provided the foundation for the extensive multilateral cooperation among industrial democracies that characterize the world today.

Part 4
Conclusions

CHAPTER 11

The Future of
International Leadership

This book began with the question of whether leadership of the international system matters, and if so, how. A series of formal models and empirical tests has showed that leadership is indeed important for the international political economy. However, it matters in ways that are quite different from what the conventional wisdom tells us. Because the theory here enjoys substantial empirical support, it is an attractive alternative to existing theory.

One way that this theory differs from the conventional wisdom is that its propositions depend critically on whether we define hegemony in quantitative or qualitative terms. Quantitative forms of hegemony, such as the hegemon's share of global resources or resource concentration in the system, are irrelevant in the single-play version of a public-goods game. However, relative size does affect the outcome of a repeated-play bargaining game in that large states prefer smaller bargains, smaller states larger bargains. Qualitative hegemony, which I model as Stackelberg leadership, plays an important role in both types of models.

In light of these findings, we should think of hegemony predominantly in qualitative terms. The leader enjoys a position in the international political economy that makes it structurally different than other states, a position I have modeled as moving first. Therefore, the hegemon is not simply the largest state in the system. Instead, it is a state whose salience makes it qualitatively different from other states.

Malevolence and Benevolence

This book also asked whether international leadership is malevolent or benevolent. Malevolent hegemony theory argues that the most powerful states in a system act to establish a system in their own interest. For example, states with market power should choose optimum tariffs (Conybeare 1987; Johnson 1953–54); financially powerful states should exploit seigneurage in the international monetary system. Powerful states should also endeavor to create regimes that strengthen and perpetuate their dominance (Gilpin 1981). Benevolent-hegemony theory, in contrast, argues that a sufficiently large leader will have an incentive to provide public goods unilaterally. A hegemon will also take a leading role in international economic cooperation and in the construction of international regimes (Keohane 1984).

Part 2 showed that Stackelberg leadership is normally malevolent. The leader reduces its share of public goods, forcing others to pay more. Adding security relations to this simple model had surprising effects, however. On the one hand, a leader with many allies forces others to bear the cost of public-goods provision. On the other hand, a leader with many military rivals is benevolent, exercising military restraint and increasing its contributions to public goods.

Empirical demonstration of malevolence or benevolence is difficult because both rely on counterfactual claims of what the leader would do if it were not a leader or what the system would look like if there were no leader at all. However, I have repeatedly drawn inferences about benevolence/malevolence from indirect evidence. The models here point us toward a simple rule of thumb: when a leader's policies move in the same direction as the policies of the rest of the world, then leadership is benevolent; when they move in opposite directions, leadership is malevolent. The intuition behind this rule of thumb is clear when we consider how the rest of the world reacts when the leader chooses openness. Followers who respond in kind are better off, while those who respond with protection are worse off. What matters, then, is the direction of the one country's response to another.

The public-goods assumption is just one way to analyze the problem of malevolence. Indeed, various chapters of this book find reasons for positive or negative correlations between states' choices that have little to do with public goods, and appendix A shows that some of these are robust in a completely different kind of model. A hegemon might act benevolently when it lacks allies to avoid sparking an arms race and spiral of declining openness. This logic appeared not only in the public-goods game but in a simpler guns-and-butter game with private goods. A network of cooperative agreements implies that each state's openness is positively related to its trading partners' openness. This

kind of positive correlation appears in most models of international cooperation and is not peculiar to public-goods theory.[1]

While the question of malevolence and benevolence has played an analytically helpful role in this book, the analysis of cooperation in part 3 showed
how this schema is incomplete. Cooperation makes both states better off, and
their policies move in the same direction, yet cooperation may occur as a
response to either malevolent or benevolent hegemony. At a minimum, then,
we need to distinguish cooperation from the question of malevolence. Moreover, as I argued in chapters 7 and 9, malevolence can be a cause of cooperation
in general and multilateral cooperation in particular.

Table 20, which expands table 10 in the light of part 3, makes these distinctions explicit, with reference to some of the historical periods discussed in
this book. Mainstream theory thinks of hegemonic leadership as both benevolent and cooperative at all times. In the theory here, leadership is both benevolent and cooperative only when a hegemon cooperates with others in addition
to acting benevolently in noncooperative situations.[2] Such leadership is somewhat uncommon, but it is not terribly hard to find examples. The Cobden-
Chevalier Treaty of 1860, like the other smaller trade treaties concluded
between 1821 and 1866, fits this category well.

However, benevolent hegemony is usually tacit, lacking much international cooperation. Though such cases are anomalous for mainstream theory,
chapter 7 predicts that a benevolent leader is unlikely to cooperate. This pattern characterizes British leadership in 1821–54. While Britain did cooperate

TABLE 20.   Hegemony and Cooperation

	Hegemony	
	Benevolent	Malevolent
Cooperation	Leadership	"The followers shall lead"
	Cobden-Chevalier, 1860	Western Europe, 1870–1914
Little	Tacit hegemony	(Systemic) power
Cooperation	United Kingdom, 1821–54	United States, 1919–39

---

1. The only case in which cooperation leads to negatively correlated choices is when, in a
repeated-play game of Chicken, two states agree to alternate plays of C and D. However, this is only
one of several equilibria in this game.

2. Since I cannot simultaneously observe both the outcomes without cooperation and the
outcomes with cooperation, evidence for these claims must be indirect.

with others in this period, especially in a series of shipping-reciprocity treaties, significant bargains were rare. Followers also had little incentive to cooperate with each other, aside from the *Zollverein*.

Followers are more likely to cooperate whenever the hegemon acts malevolently. Chapter 8 showed that this pattern best describes British leadership in the second half of the nineteenth century. The network of MFN treaties created by Austria-Hungary, France, and Italy dominated this period. Even the dominions were more likely to cooperate with each other than the mother country was. In this period, then, the followers' cooperation was the dominant characteristic of the international political economy. The economic results were so good in between 1870 and 1913 that one is tempted to conclude that malevolent hegemony is the best possible outcome if it stimulates international cooperation.

Because the theory of cooperation is probabilistic, other kinds of outcomes are also possible. For example, even a malevolent leader may cooperate with followers, as the United States did after 1945. In these cases the best test of the model is either the size or form of a bargain. Large bargains are more likely among tight allies, as became true of European-American cooperation after the start of the Cold War. Such bargains are also more likely to take a multilateral form, as chapter 9 showed.

A hegemon may also act malevolently without leading to significant international cooperation. The best example is American leadership in the interwar period. While there was some international economic cooperation that I did not discuss in chapter 4, these bargains tended to be regional in scope and small in size (see Pahre 1990: chap. 8). The United States cooperated little with others before the Reciprocal Trade Agreements Act of 1934, and even then most treaties were signed with the smaller countries of Latin America. Such cases most nearly approximate the simple exercise of power that is at the center of malevolent-hegemony theory as well as many Marxist theories of hegemony.

Because malevolent hegemony makes cooperation more likely and benevolent hegemony reduces the incentive to cooperate, most periods will fall along the southwest-northeast diagonal in table 20. Even so, the table oversimplifies these historical cases, and it remains difficult to classify some periods. One good example of the problem is the American role after World War II. This period does not fit the categories in table 20 very neatly because the United States treated Western Europe and Eastern Europe differently. The full force of American malevolence hit the Soviet Union and its allies, while cooperation in the West unleashed a period of unprecedented economic growth among developed market economies. This example highlights, once again, that malevolence seems desirable only when it induces states to cooperate.

The theory also addresses the dynamics of cooperation in only an incomplete way. Several results suggest that cooperation by some states makes cooperation by others more likely; in other words, cooperation is subject to contagion, or spread effects. Third-party cooperation also makes the leader's participation in multilateral cooperation more likely. Though these effects did not influence British cooperation in the nineteenth century, they were common after World War II because tight alliances further increased the rewards of cooperation.

However, such claims assume a kind of myopia that is unusual in rational-choice theories. In particular, the models do not assume that states foresee these contagion effects. While this myopia may make for interesting results that seem to capture the role of some sequence and historical context, a richer theoretical understanding of these contagion effects must await future research.

Modeling Assumptions and Theory a la Carte

This book's argument rests on a cluster of related models, applied to a disparate set of historical periods. Using a simple model of public goods as a starting point, subsequent theories add assumptions about Stackelberg leadership, alliances, repeated play, the size and share of bargains, issue linkage, and multilateralism. Each variation of the basic theory was useful for a different period.

This structure of the theory allows empirical research to use only a simple version of the basic model "a la carte" for particular applications. Where security concerns are unimportant or among friendly states, the simple models of chapters 2, 3, and the first part of 7 suffice. If there is a small shadow of the future, bargaining should be relatively unimportant, and we do not need the complications of chapters 7 and 9. If we are not interested in the choice between multilateral and bilateral forums, then chapter 9 is superfluous.

Some applications might require adding assumptions to one of the basic models. For example, bargaining within the European Union takes place subject to certain norms and institutions that limit the cost-sharing formulas that bargains will use. Taking these rules into account is one way to extend the public-goods model here (see Pahre 1995). Other applications may find it useful to relax the assumption of public goods and model club goods such as discriminatory regional regimes.

This strategy of letting a scholar choose one of a cluster of models is not as epistemologically suspect as it may first appear. Consider a standard physics textbook, which will have separate chapters on subjects such as falling objects, orbiting planets, friction and air resistance, quantum mechanics, and the like. The models of different chapters have only a loose connection to one another and sometimes have no real connection at all. A physicist will choose the "right" model for describing a ball rolling down a hill instead of applying, say, quantum mechanics to every problem. This is a perfectly reasonable state of affairs and does not make physics internally inconsistent, unfalsifiable, tautological, or otherwise suspect.[3] This state of affairs is a natural consequence of using models to simplify a complex world.

Analogously, each theoretical chapter here represents a stand-alone model that may be useful for future research even if other models are ultimately rejected. For example, the assumption of security externalities underlying the model in chapter 5 has come under strong attack in recent years, mostly on theoretical rather than empirical grounds (see esp. Powell 1991, 1993). Whatever one's assessment of that assumption, it does not affect the pure public-goods model of chapters 2 and 3, the bargaining model in the first half of chapter 7, or the analysis of multilateralism in chapter 9. Similarly, rejecting the public-goods assumption that is critical to part 2 would have only a minor effect on chapter 7, which could be reanalyzed as bargains over either club goods or externalities. The conjectures and enforcement strategies that drive the results on multilateralism in chapter 9 are also independent of the public-goods assumption. However, these conjectures were nonstandard, and more orthodox theorists could easily reject that chapter without affecting other chapters' arguments.

Besides being a convenient simplification, using several variations of a basic model helps us assess how robust any single result is. Some formal results depend on a particular set of assumptions, while many other results are robust across models and assumptions. For example, the sizable formal literature on war, which uses a variety of game forms and assumptions about interests, always finds that incomplete information is a necessary condition for war (see esp. Bueno de Mesquita and Lalman 1992). For this reason, we can be confident in this claim, which is also found among some nonformal theories (Blainey 1973). In contrast, different formal models of bluffing during the crises leading up to war are quite sensitive to assumptions about the size of threats and the equilibrium refinement concept used (see Pahre and Papayoanou 1997).

In this book, one simple claim holds across all the models: when the lead-

---

3. For a dissenting view, see Cartwright 1983.

ers' policies are positively correlated with the followers' policies, leadership is benevolent; when these policies are negatively correlated, leadership is malevolent. This result holds in the simple public-goods model, with or without security externalities, and encompasses the mutually beneficial nature of international cooperation in repeated play models. The result also holds in appendix A, where I use a model that does not assume public goods. There is every reason to believe that this logic would hold in other models as well. In optimal tariff theory, for example, a large state chooses a tariff that harms the smaller state, which always chooses free trade. Their strategies are negatively correlated. When two small states both choose low tariffs or two large states both choose higher tariffs that they then negotiate downward, their policies are positively correlated (see Conybeare 1987 for these examples). These outcomes are likely to be satisfactory for both states.

Regardless of how well these results extend to different kinds of models, public goods remain an important problem for the international political economy. While it is easy for scholars to dismiss the public-goods assumption as a distortion of the problem of international free trade, doing so is probably not a good decision. There are many problems of externalities in the international political economy and even some nearly public goods. As the findings in chapter 6 suggest, the assumption of a pure public good overstates the problem, yet it captures something worth including in our theories. Theories of the international political economy should continue to include international public goods as an important subject of study.

Theory and History

As this discussion of theory a la carte should make clear, a formal model is nothing more than a metaphor for behavior. The first stage in applying a model (or any other metaphor) to reality is to draw out a mapping between the parts of the model and some referents in the real world (Pahre 1996a; Snidal 1986).

The metaphor is useful if it does more than describe reality and generates falsifiable propositions about behavior. A model should also point us toward things that we otherwise would not have seen. For instance, the public-goods assumption told me to look for negative correlations between two states' choices that stem from the externalities of each state's behavior on the other. The quantitative evidence confirms that the publicness assumption exaggerated the size of this negative effect. But the effect is there nevertheless, and I would not have seen it without the model telling me to look.

Hypothesis testing aside, the theory also brings out historical evidence that has been overlooked by most others. Huskisson's reforms in the 1820s have not played a prominent role in the conventional wisdom on hegemony. Cooperation in the *Zollverein* or the French MFN network has been treated as an ugly fact to be played down by hegemonic theorists, a striking anomaly by the theory's critics. However, the model points directly at this cooperation, suggesting that I also look at cooperation among the British dominions in the same period.

Besides a shifting of substantive focus, formal theory can add insight and explanation to many historical case studies. It is puzzling for the historiography that George Marshall insisted on a multilateral ERP, since it did not affect the substance of the Marshall Plan. Some have seen this multilateralism as unnecessary (Milward 1984), others as emblematic of a postwar ideology of multilateralism (e.g., Ruggie 1993). Reality may be more explicable, if prosaic, in the sense that multilateralism merely established a particular enforcement strategy that happened to be important for one state in a particular instance.

Theory sometimes also points out conceptual distinctions that historians have not made but that would be congenial to historical narrative. The distinction in chapter 7 between the size of a bargain and the shares of each state is in no way peculiar to public-goods problems. Using this conceptual framework may be a useful way to think about how a state responds to unacceptable offers (see Pahre 1995 for an example).

Another use of a modeling metaphor is its ability to point out lawlike generalizations that may be useful for narrative.[4] For example, historians are inclined to attribute many economic treaties to general foreign-policy motives. However, the distinction here between the probability of cooperation and the size of a bargain suggests that a more nuanced claim is appropriate. The reasons for cooperation are many and varied, as any historian would appreciate, but alliances do not make cooperation any more or less likely. At the same time, security concerns do increase the size of cooperation, for reasons that should be consistent with historiographical intuition.

By applying formal theory to a series of historical case studies, this book also poses a challenge to many critics of formal theory in the social sciences. James Caporaso (1992: 628), for example, criticizes rational-choice theory for its inattention to sequence, context, and narrative. Yet chapter 9 pointed me to exactly these concerns. Going further, David Green and Ian Shapiro (1994) have argued that formal theory is difficult or impossible to test against the real

---

4. Works on the theory of history usually advocate greater attention to such lawlike generalizations and less use of ad hoc reasoning among historians. See Bloch 1954; Braudel 1962; Carr 1961; Fischer 1970.

world and that when it has been tested it has been found to be false.[5] I hope this book demonstrates that there is nothing inherent in the method that makes it incapable of empirical testing or historical narrative.

The Contemporary Period

Finally, we may ask how this theory fits the contemporary world. The first question is whether the United States is a hegemon today. There has been significant debate on this question, though it seems to have quieted down after the end of the Cold War (see Gilpin 1981; Kennedy 1987; Keohane 1984; Russett 1985; Strange 1982).

One can imagine the concern under a quantitative definition of hegemony, where the American share of global resources is critical and could fall below some imaginable threshold (as in Lake 1983, 1984, 1988). A qualitative definition leaves less ambiguity, for the United States certainly remains a Stackelberg leader today. Kenneth Waltz (1979: 179) argues forcefully, "However one measures, the United States is the leading country." In nearly every measure of resources, from GNP to armed services, the United States overshadows all others after the Cold War. The United States makes up something on the order of one-fourth to one-third of global production. It is the world's largest trading nation. It has the largest navy and air force, which give it an unequaled ability to project power around the globe; the collapse of the Russo-Soviet military machine has made these advantages more obvious. The United States is an essential player in monetary affairs, and the dollar is still the major reserve currency. For all these reasons, others await American decisions before making their own.

A related question for many in the mainstream literature is whether the United States should choose to continue to lead the international system. Henry R. Nau (1990: chap. 1) maintains that the United States can choose between leadership and decline; Richard Rosecrance (1986) argues that the United States can choose between a trading strategy and a military-political strategy.[6] The logical structure of these analyses is similar to Charles Kindleberger's (1973) assertion that the United States chose not to lead the international monetary system in the 1920s and 1930s.

---

5. Green and Shapiro neglect a sizable formal literature in international relations (e.g., Bueno de Mesquita 1981; Bueno de Mesquita and Lalman 1992; Niou, Ordeshook, and Rose 1989), for almost all of their argument relies on the study of American domestic politics and institutions.

6. There is an analogous literature for would-be leaders. For example, Scalera and Kahn 1976 argue that Japan may choose between active leadership or a continued passive role.

This policy-choice perspective implies that the U.S. government should have preferences for international goods that are different than the preferences it currently has. There may well be force to such arguments, but it is notoriously difficult to figure out where preferences come from, much less how to change them. Moreover, even if these scholars can help change American preferences, we would still want to know how other countries will react and what the net effect of these changes will be. The models in this book are geared toward these kinds of questions. They suggest that a choice to lead may cause others to free ride unless such leadership rests on international cooperation.

The theory also fills in essential background for policy decisions. First, the theory tells us to look at the security relations between the leader and other states. The world currently lacks strong security rivalries among major powers. Chinese disputes with India, Russia, and the United States may well be the most significant outstanding areas of great-power hostility, but these conflicts of interest pale in comparison with past rivalries. There are, of course, many smaller countries engaged in enduring rivalries with great powers, from the United Kingdom and Argentina to the United States and Iraq. There are regional conflicts in the former Yugoslavia, the Middle East, South Asia, and elsewhere. Still, the appropriate model for understanding this world will assume either that we can ignore security concerns (as in chapter 3) or that the leader has many more friends than rivals (as in chapter 5).

Either assumption produces the same result: we should expect malevolent leadership in the absence of cooperation. Of course such cooperation is ubiquitous, and institutionalized. The most impressive cooperation is among non-hegemonic states, the members of the European Union. It is impossible to tell as of this writing, but other regions, such as Mercosur, may also see substantial economic cooperation among follower states. Other regional cooperation, such as NAFTA and perhaps APEC, will involve the United States. All this is a perfectly natural response to malevolent hegemony.

Lurking underneath this cooperation lie some signs of possible malevolence. Because the dollar serves as an international reserve currency, for example, the United States gains seigneurage. Awareness of this potential malevolence has reached the level of mass-market news and analysis. *Newsweek* (December 30,1996–January 6, 1997, 42) argued that

In the late 1990s, however Americans think of themselves, the rest of the world sees an aggressive bully. Washington has forced open foreign markets, demanding specific market shares for U.S. goods, while threatening sanctions against those who do business with Cuba or Libya. It has kept the dollar undervalued, pricing competitors out of business. It has thrown its weight around, sending troops or missiles to Iraq, central Africa, Haiti, the Taiwan Strait. It first insulted and then fired a secretary-general of the United Nations, while continuing to be behind in its U.N. dues.

Some of this is old-fashioned power-seeking behavior, while some is more tightly linked to the focus of this book.

As the theory would expect, U.S. policy in the 1970s and 1980s has forced a number of costs onto others. Japan, for example, has had to make increasingly large contributions to international public goods (Rosecrance and Taw 1990). Japan accepted a fall in the U.S. dollar from 260 to 90 yen without engaging in competitive devaluation. The costs have occasionally been very large; for example, the decline in exports in 1988 reduced the Japanese growth rate by nearly two percentage points. Moreover, Japanese foreign direct investment into the United States, which effectively recycles American trade surpluses, has suffered huge paper losses because of the dollar's general decline since the 1970s.

Still, such large cost shifting is the exception. International cooperation, whether in trade or monetary affairs or even in coordinated macro and fiscal policies, remains the norm. In this, the 1980s and 1990s are much like trade policy in between 1870 and 1914.

As this suggests, one final use of theory is its ability to guide our choice of historical analogies. Traditional hegemonic theory has seen analogies between the 1930s and the 1970s as periods of hegemonic decline or absence (e.g., Bergsten 1972; "The World Economy" 1991; Kindleberger 1973: 307–8; 1981).[7] David Lake (1988: 228–37) draws a more idiosyncratic analogy between the 1980s and 1912–30 as periods of two near-hegemons.

The analysis in this book points to a different period, 1870–1914, as an analogy for the present. In the 1980s and 1990s, as in 1870–1914, we see a leader with few military rivals. While this situation normally leads to malevolent hegemony, both periods are characterized by significant international cooperation that more than counteracts this malevolence. In both cases, cooperation among nonhegemonic states is very important, such as the Austrian and French networks of MFN treaties between 1860 and 1914 or the European Union today. Today, as in the previous century, we should be more concerned about the future of international cooperation than about the policies of the

---

7. Theorists who look at how changing patterns of international trade affect domestic politics often draw an analogy between the 1970s or 1980s and the 1930s. (For a novel use of this analogy, see Milner 1988.)

hegemon per se. The leader is more actively engaged today than in the 1890s, thanks to the extensive use of multilateral regimes that can induce the United States to contribute. We must look for the continuation of these regimes rather than to the leadership of a potentially malevolent hegemon for mutually beneficial policies in the coming years.

Appendixes

A Political Support
Model of Trade

This appendix explores the robustness of the public-goods model in the text by examining a completely different kind of model. This model of trade policy is a simplified version of so-called endogenous tariff theory models (Magee, Brock, and Young 1989 inter alia), in which trade policy-making is endogenous to a theory of domestic politics. Because it yields many results identical to those of the public-goods model, this trade-policy model suggests that the results in the text are robust to different kinds of models. In the belief that this kind of robustness will interest primarily those readers familiar with formal theory, the presentation here is more sparse than in the main text.

Like the public-goods model in the main text, this model is state centered. Unlike that model, the appendix explicitly includes domestic politics as a constraint on state decision making, albeit in a reduced-form way. While the model does not explicitly capture demand functions, factor endowments, or production technologies, its simpler functional representations point toward fuller models of political economy in future research.

Unlike the model in the main text, I exclude security affairs here. The reasons for this decision are discussed at the end of the appendix. However, the robustness of the basic public-goods model suggests that future models of trade and security relations may well obtain results similar to those in the text.

Single Country Model

Consider a reduced-form model of the economy, with export prices p_1, import prices p_2, and relative prices $p \equiv p_2/p_1$. Setting aside both the demand side (consumer preferences) and supply side (production functions), income is simply a function of these prices: exporters' incomes $Y_1(p)$ and import-competers' incomes $Y_2(p)$, with $\partial Y_1/\partial p < 0$ and $\partial Y_2/\partial p > 0$ by the definition of exporters and import-competers. National income is $Y = Y_1 + Y_2$, which is at a maximum when $\partial Y_1/\partial p + \partial Y_2/\partial p = 0$. This represents free trade for a price-taker.

Politics is also reduced form, with actors giving political support as an increasing function of their incomes. Thus, the political leader maximizes political support in the form $M(Y_1, Y_2)$, with $\partial M/\partial Y_1 > 0$, $\partial M/\partial Y_2 > 0$, subject to diminishing returns $\partial^2 M/\partial Y_1^2 < 0$, $\partial^2 M/\partial Y_2^2 < 0$. The support-maximizing equilibrium is $(\partial M/\partial Y_1)(\partial Y_1/\partial p) + (\partial M/\partial Y_2)(\partial Y_2/\partial p) = 0$, which differs from the income-maximization equilibrium when $\partial M/\partial Y_1 \neq \partial M/\partial Y_2$.

To look at trade policy, I need to distinguish domestic prices in the two sectors (p_{d1}, p_{d2}) from the world prices (p_{w1}, p_{w2}). These define domestic and international price levels $p_d \equiv p_{d2}/p_{d1}$ and $p_w \equiv p_{w2}/p_{w1}$. For our purposes, any trade policy can be converted into its tariff equivalent. An ad valorem tariff (t) on imports raises domestic prices above world prices, with $p_d = p_w(1 + t)$.

Now producer incomes are $Y_1(p_d)$ and $Y_2(p_d)$, with $\partial Y_1/\partial p_d < 0$ and $\partial Y_2/\partial p_d > 0$. Political support is still a function of producer incomes, with $M = [Y_1(p_d), Y_2(p_d)]$. The political support equilibrium is at $(\partial M/\partial Y_1)(\partial Y_1/\partial p_d) + (\partial M/\partial Y_2)(\partial Y_2/\partial p_d) = 0$.

Two-Country Model

With two countries, I must distinguish incomes in country A, $Y_{1A}(p_{dA}, t_B)$ and $Y_{2A}(p_{dA})$, from those in B, $Y_{1B}(p_{dB}, t_A)$ and $Y_{2B}(p_{dB})$. Here, the foreign tariff affects exporters in the home country, perhaps because of market imperfections or optimal-tariff concerns. As a result, each country's trade policy has political externalities for the other country, though this model entirely avoids an approach in which externalities are related to public goods.

The politicians in both countries continue to maximize their political support functions, $M_A = M_A [Y_{1A}(p_{dA}, t_B); Y_{2A}(p_{dA})]$ and $M_B = M_B [Y_{1B}(p_{dB}, t_A); Y_{2B}(p_{dB})]$. The political support equilibrium now occurs where $(\partial M_A/\partial Y_{1A})(\partial Y_{1A}/\partial p_{dA}) + (\partial M_A/\partial Y_{2A})(\partial Y_{2A}/\partial p_{dA}) = 0$ and $(\partial M_B/\partial Y_{1B})(\partial Y_{1B}/\partial p_{dB}) + (\partial M_B/\partial Y_{2B})(\partial Y_{2B}/\partial p_{dB}) = 0$.

To find how A's tariff depends on changes in B's tariff, I use the implicit function rule:

$$\frac{\partial M_A}{\partial Y_{1A}} \frac{\partial^2 Y_{1A}}{\partial p_{dA} \partial t_B} + \frac{\partial Y_{1A}}{\partial p_{dA}} \frac{\partial^2 M_A}{\partial Y^2_{1A}} \frac{\partial Y_{1A}}{\partial t_B} + \frac{\partial Y_{2A}}{\partial p_{dA}} \frac{\partial^2 M_A}{\partial Y_{1A} \partial Y_{2A}} \frac{\partial Y_{1A}}{\partial t_B} \qquad (A.1)$$

$$= - $$

$$p_w \left[\frac{\partial M_A}{\partial Y_{1A}} \frac{\partial^2 Y_{1A}}{\partial p^2_{dA}} + \left(\frac{\partial Y_{1A}}{\partial p_{dA}} \right)^2 \frac{\partial^2 M_A}{\partial Y^2_{1A}} + 2 \frac{\partial Y_{1A}}{\partial p_{dA}} \frac{\partial^2 M_A}{\partial Y_{1A} \partial Y_{2A}} \frac{\partial Y_{2A}}{\partial p_{dA}} + \frac{\partial M_A}{\partial Y_{2A}} \frac{\partial^2 M_A}{\partial p^2_{dA}} + \left(\frac{\partial Y_{2A}}{\partial p_{dA}} \right)^2 \frac{\partial^2 M_A}{\partial Y^2_{2A}} \right]$$

With additional assumptions over some cross-partials in this term, it is unambiguously negative. I make the standard assumption that $\partial^2 M_A/\partial Y_{1A}\partial Y_{2A} = \partial^2 M_A/\partial Y_{2A}\partial Y_{1A} > 0$, that $\partial^2 Y_{1A}/\partial p_{dA}^2$, $\partial^2 Y_{2A}/\partial p_{dA}^2 < 0$ (price changes have a diminishing marginal effect on incomes), and that $\partial^2 Y_{1A}/\partial p_{dA}\partial t_B = \partial^2 Y_{1A}/\partial t_B \partial p_{dA} < 0$. This last assumption is the most problematic and implies that as p_{dA} increases, domestic goods become more expensive for exporters, reducing the effects of foreign tariffs on exporters' real incomes.

Even without these assumptions, the derivative will often be negative. That is, the assumptions are sufficient but not necessary to yield the following hypothesis:

Hypothesis 1. Increasing protection in one country reduces protection in the other country, and vice versa (i.e., trade policies will be negatively correlated).

This is the same as in the public-goods model, where each country's contributions to public goods are negatively related to the other country's contributions. The two results rest on a similar logic. Because a government benefits from foreign trade liberalization and foreign contributions to public goods, it will reduce its own liberalization (contributions) when foreigners increase theirs.

Stackelberg Leadership

Because of the negative relationship between home and foreign tariffs, Stackelberg leadership has the same effects here as in the public goods model. The leader maximizes the function $M_A = M_A [Y_{1A}(p_{dA}, t_B^*); Y_{2A}(p_{dA})]$ where $t_B^* = F(t_A)$ and $dt_B^*/dt_A < 0$ by hypothesis 1. With $\partial p_{dA}/\partial t_A = p_w$, A chooses t_A such that $(\partial M_A/\partial Y_{1A})(\partial Y_{1A}/\partial p_{dA})(p_w + dt_B^*/dt_A) + (\partial M_A/\partial Y_{2A})(\partial Y_{2A}/\partial p_{dA}) = 0$. In the Cournot-Nash equilibrium, in contrast, A chose t_A such that $(\partial M_A/\partial Y_{1A})(\partial Y_{1A}/\partial p_{dA})p_w + (\partial M_A/\partial Y_{2A})(\partial Y_{2A}/\partial p_{dA}) = 0$. Because $dt_B^*/dt_A < 0$, the new condition requires that A redistribute more income to Y_{1A} in the

Stackelberg equilibrium than in the Cournot-Nash equilibrium. This change raises $(\partial M_A/\partial Y_{1A})(\partial Y_{1A}/\partial p_{dA})$ and lowers $(\partial M_A/\partial Y_{2A})(\partial Y_{2A}/\partial p_{dA})$ through an increase in t_A.

The follower responds by lowering the tariff compared with Cournot-Nash, because $dt_B^*/dt_A < 0$. In summary:

Hypothesis 2. The leader imposes a higher tariff in the Stackelberg equilibrium than it does in the Cournot-Nash, while the follower imposes a lower tariff in the Stackelberg equilibrium than in the Cournot-Nash.

This parallels the main result in chapter 3, that a hegemon reduces its contributions to public goods, forcing the follower to contribute more. Again, it follows from the externalities logic of the trade-policy model, which it shares with the public-goods model in the main text. Because the leader's policy is negatively correlated with the follower's policy, the leader chooses less of what both states value (low tariffs) to get more of what only the leader values (income in its import-competing sector).

Reciprocal Tariff Liberalization

Because of the externalities that each country's tariffs impose on the exporters of the other, there are mutual gains to A and B from reducing tariffs jointly. Politician A can maintain her equilibrium level of political support despite a lower negotiated t_A if $dM_A|_{dpw=0} = (\partial M_A/\partial Y_{1A})(\partial Y_{1A}/\partial p_{dA})dp_{dA} + (\partial M_A/\partial Y_{1A})$ $(\partial Y_{1A}/\partial t_A)dt_B + (\partial M_A/\partial Y_{2A})(\partial Y_{2A}/\partial p_{dA})dp_{dA}$. Both A and B can lower their tariffs while maintaining at least this level of support for A under the following condition:

$$\left. \frac{dt_A}{dt_B} \right|_{M_A = M_{A'}, dp_w = 0} = \frac{-\dfrac{\partial M_A}{\partial Y_{1A}} \dfrac{\partial Y_{1A}}{\partial t_B}}{p_w \left(\dfrac{\partial M_A}{\partial Y_{1A}} \dfrac{\partial Y_{1A}}{\partial p_{dA}} + \dfrac{\partial M_A}{\partial Y_{2A}} \dfrac{\partial Y_{2A}}{\partial p_{dA}} \right)} \tag{A.2}$$

Reciprocal liberalization requires that $dt_A/dt_B > 0$, which is true iff $(\partial M_A/\partial Y_{1A})(\partial Y_{1A}/\partial t_A) + (\partial M_A/\partial Y_{2A})(\partial Y_{2A}/\partial t_A) > 0$. This condition holds when $t_A < t^*_A$—that is, when A and B agree to reduce tariffs below their equilibrium level. In short, two countries can always sign a reciprocity treaty reducing tariffs but not one increasing tariffs because, for a sufficiently high discount rate, the loss of future discounted benefits from noncooperation exceed the discounted gains from jointly reducing tariffs (by any amount).

This implies in turn

Hypothesis 3. When two countries sign a trade agreement, their tariffs will be positively correlated. (Thus, hypothesis 1 does not apply.)

This parallels the positive relationship between two countries' contributions to public goods in the model of cooperation in chapters 7 and 9.

Though I will not do it here, I could express the reciprocal tariff cuts as shares of one another or as shares of some aggregate tariff reduction, that is, as $dt_A = \alpha h$ and $dt_B = (1 - \alpha)h$. This translates the tariff model here into the "size and shares" framework of chapter 7. Because these tariff cuts are not pure public goods, the results may differ slightly from the results in that chapter.

Once they have signed a tariff agreement, politicians must decide whether to adhere to it. In each round of a repeated-play game, they may defect from the agreement or continue to cooperate. With discount factors δ_A, δ_B, A's payoff from continued adherence to a bargain with tariffs $\{t_A, t_B\}$ is $(1 - \delta_A)^{-1}M_A$ $[Y_{1A}(p_{dA}(t_A), t_B); Y_{2A}(p_{dA}(t_A))]$. If A defects from the bargain today, returning to the single play tariff t^*_A,[1] B will return to its single-play tariff t^*_B in subsequent rounds, yielding the payoff $\delta_A M_A [Y_{1A}(p_{dA}(t^*_A), t_B); Y_{2A}(p_{dA}(t_A))] + (1 - \delta_A)^{-1}\delta_A M_A [Y_{1A} (p_{dA} (t^*_A), t^*_B); Y_{2A} (p_{dA} (t^*_A))]$.

It is easy to show that A will continue to cooperate iff

$$\delta_A \geq \frac{M_A[Y_{1A}(p_{dA}(t^*_A),t_B);Y_{2A}(p_{dA}(t^*_A))] - M_A[Y_{1A}(p_{dA}(t_A),t_B);Y_{2A}(p_{dA}(t_A))]}{M_A[Y_{1A}(p_{dA}(t^*_A),t_B);Y_{2A}(p_{dA}(t^*_A))] - M_A[Y_{1A}(p_{dA}(t^*_A),t^*_B);Y_{2A}(p_{dA}(t^*_A))]} \quad (A.3)$$

To find out how the preagreement tariff levels affect the probability of a tariff treaty, I take the partial derivative of the right-hand side with respect to t^*_A. The denominator is always greater than zero, so the sign of the derivative depends on the sign of $\{M_A [t^*_A, t_B] - M_A[t^*_A, t^*_B]\}$ $(\delta M_A/\delta Y_{1A})$ $(\delta Y_{1A}/\delta p_{dA})(\delta p_{dA}/dt^*_A) + \{M_A[t^*_A, t_B] - M_A[t_A, t_B]\}$ $(\delta M_A/\delta Y_{2A})(\delta Y_{2A}/\delta p_{dA})$ $(\delta p_{dA}/dt^*_A)$. This term is positive if $M_A[t^*_A, t_B][(\delta M_A/\delta Y_{1A})(\delta Y_{1A}/\delta p_{dA})) +$

---

1. An alternative assumption would be that A defects by choosing the tariff $t^{**}_A > t^*_A$ that maximizes M_A when B's tariff is $t_B < t^*_B$, reverting to t^*_A when B retaliates with t^*_B. This assumption complicates the notation and the subsequent algebra but does not change the analysis with respect to changes in t^*_A.

$(\delta M_A/\delta Y_{2A})(\delta Y_{2A}/\delta p_{dA})]$ > $M_A[t_A, \; t_B](\delta M_A/\delta Y_{2A})(\delta Y_{2A}/\delta p_{dA})$ + $M_A[t^*_A, \; t^*_B](\delta M_A/\delta Y_{1A})(\delta Y_{1A}/\delta p_{dA})$.

In the trade-treaty equilibrium, a given price increase will yield a greater marginal increase in political support from import-competers than its marginal loss from exporters, so $|(\delta M_A/\delta Y_{1A})(\delta Y_{1A}/\delta p_{dA})|$ < $(\delta M_A/\delta Y_{2A})$ $(\delta Y_{2A}/\delta p_{dA})$. Because $(\delta M_A/\delta Y_{1A})(\delta Y_{1A}/\delta p_{dA})$ < 0 < $(\delta M_A/\delta Y_{2A})(\delta Y_{2A}/\delta p_{dA})$, the previous term is greater than zero, and the numerator of the derivative is positive. This means that increases in the single-play tariff t^*_A increase the right-hand side of the stability condition, making cooperation less likely:

Hypothesis 4. Trade cooperation is less likely to be stable for high-tariff countries than for low-tariff countries.

A similar analysis shows how foreign tariffs affects the home likelihood of cooperation. Assuming for simplicity that the cooperative tariff t_B is independent of the single-play tariff t^*_B,[2] then it is easy to show that

Hypothesis 5. Trade cooperation is more likely to be stable when foreign tariffs begin high than when foreign tariffs begin low.

Proof follows easily from equation A3.

In conjunction with hypothesis 1, hypotheses 4 and 5 imply that the leader will be less likely to sign a trade agreement than the followers. The leader is a high-tariff country and faces low-tariff followers in comparison with each country's Cournot-Nash levels. Again, this parallels the result in chapter 7 that a Stackelberg leader is less likely to cooperate, while its followers are more likely to cooperate. In both models, the changed reversion point of the Stackelberg equilibrium plays an important role in affecting the likelihood of cooperation.

Conclusion

This appendix has shown that the main results on reaction functions and Stackelberg leadership are robust to a completely different kind of model. This makes it likely that the public-goods model in the main text provides a useful simplification of the general externalities problem across many issue areas.

Though a useful guide, the model in this appendix is admittedly incom-

---

2. Relaxing this assumption, the sign of the derivative depends on the sign of $[(\partial Y_{1A}/\partial t_B)(\partial t_B/\partial t_B^*) - \partial Y_{1A}/\partial t_B^*]$.

plete. This focus on incomes ignores demand and production functions, among other things. Security goods raise the problem of such functions in a stark way, making it hard to easily extend this model. Some of these questions are: Is government a producer or a purchaser of security goods? Is the government the sole demander of military production, and if so, can it pay monopsonistic prices for military goods? Can the military conscript labor or capital or otherwise pay producers less than the market rate of return? Does the income of military producers matter politically in addition to the military goods produced? Experimenting with different answers to these questions persuaded me that there was no straightforward way to bring security production into the trade-policy game.

Though actually having a model would be best, the trade-off logic behind many of the results in chapter 5 should be robust to various specifications of military production. Of course, this appendix does not prove that the main results follow in all kinds of models, since only a full-blown model of, for example, security affairs and monetary policy can prove that. However, the model here does show that public goods may be a useful way to think about many different issue areas simultaneously at a high level of abstraction.

Data Sources

The starting point for import and GNP data was Brian Mitchell's *European Historical Statistics* (1975). What I label *GNP* throughout the text is in fact GNP for France, Italy, and the United Kingdom, NNP for Germany, and GDP for Norway and Sweden. For additional British data, I consulted Imlah 1958.

The measure of concentration in the text is the Hirschman-Herfindahl index, $\Sigma(B_i/\Sigma B_i)^2$. If resources are evenly divided among n states, this index takes the value $1/n$ and thus equals one if all resources are concentrated in a single state.

Data on military spending and military alliances came from the Correlates of War (COW) project. I sometimes coded diplomatic relationships differently, such as the Entente Cordiale in chapter 6. See the text for the details of such cases.

Trade treaty data came from the Trade Agreements Database (TAD) project. Any treaty, exchange of letters, or other understanding was coded as a trade agreement if the states made mutual tariff concessions or granted each other mutual MFN status. An agreement was coded as a shipping treaty if the states made mutual concessions on shipping regulations or granted each other mutual MFN status or national treatment in such regulations.

The list of countries used in TAD is more expansive than in other lists, such as COW, since I included as a country any entity that had tariff autonomy. Examples include Liechtenstein, Monaco, preindependence Norway, and various German and Italian states prior to unification. These have a significant effect only for the Prussian treaty counts before 1870; see figure 5.

A trade agreement was counted as being in effect in a given year if it was in effect for at least six months of that year. It was also counted as being in effect if the parties agreed to honor a former treaty provisionally while negotiating a new one. The sources did not list the expiration dates for many treaties, which were counted as being in effect for the same length as comparable treaties signed by those states at roughly the same time. Some of the decline in treaties in the database after 1900 is probably more apparent than real, reflecting treaties that were honored without appearing as such in the official treaty series; the secondary literature on Britain and France is often helpful in catching such cases.

The list of trade agreements discussed in this book were compiled from Augier 1906; Böhnke 1888; Boiteau 1863/1970; Cobden Club 1875; Henderson 1939; Hertslet 1875– ; Martens 1878; Ministerio degli Affari Esteri 1865–99; Neumann and de Plason 1877–1912; Nogaro and Marcel 1931; Recueil 1878– ; Triepel 1909– ; and Judith Blow Williams 1972. Further information about TAD is available on the Worldwide Web at http://www-personal.umich.edu/~pahre/tad.html.

References

Aggarwal, Vinod K. 1985. *Liberal Protectionism: The International Politics of Organized Free Trade.* Berkeley: University of California Press.

Aldcroft, Derek H. 1977. *From Versailles to Wall Street, 1919–1929.* Berkeley: University of California Press.

Allison, Graham, and Gregory F. Treverton, eds. 1992. *Rethinking America's Security: Beyond Cold War to New World Order.* New York: Norton for the Council on Foreign Relations.

Alt, James E., Randall L. Calvert, and Brian D. Humes. 1988. "Reputation and Hegemonic Stability: A Game-Theoretic Analysis." *American Political Science Review* 82 (June): 445–66.

Anderson, Gary M., and Robert D. Tollison. 1985. "Ideology, Interest Groups, and the Repeal of the Corn Laws." *Zeitschrift für die Gesamte Staatswissenschaft* 141 (June): 197–212.

Arkes, Hadley. 1972. *Bureaucracy, the Marshall Plan, and the National Interest.* Princeton: Princeton University Press.

Ashley, Percy. 1926. *Modern Tariff History: Germany–United States–France.* New York: E. P. Dutton.

Augier, Charles. 1906. *La France et les traités de commerce.* Paris: Librairie Chevalier et Rivière.

Avery, William P., and David P. Rapkin, eds. 1982. *America in a Changing World Political Economy.* New York: Longman.

Axelrod, Robert. 1984. *The Evolution of Cooperation.* New York: Basic Books.

Axelrod, Robert. 1986. "An Evolutionary Approach to Norms." *American Political Science Review* 80 (December): 1095–1112.

Axelrod, Robert, and Douglas Dion. 1988. "The Further Evolution of Cooperation." *Science* 242 (9 December): 1385–98.

Axelrod, Robert, and Robert O. Keohane. 1986. "Achieving Cooperation under Anarchy: Strategies and Institutions." In *Cooperation under Anarchy,* ed. Oye, 226–54.

Aydelotte, William O. 1966. "Parties and Issues in Early Victorian England." *Journal of British Studies* 5 (May): 95–114.

Aydelotte, William O. 1967. "The Country Gentleman and the Repeal of the Corn Laws." *English Historical Review* 82 (January): 47–60.

Aydelotte, William O. 1977. "Constituency Influence on the British House of Commons, 1841–1847." In *The History of Parliamentary Behavior,* ed. William O. Aydelotte, 225–46. Princeton: Princeton University Press.

Baldwin, David. 1985. *Economic Statecraft.* Princeton: Princeton University Press.

Baldwin, Robert E., and Gerald M. Lage. 1971. "A Multilateral Model of Trade-Balancing Tariff Concessions." *Review of Economics and Statistics* 53 (August): 237–44.

Beloff, Max. 1970. *Imperial Sunset,* vol. 1, *Britain's Liberal Empire, 1897–1921.* New York: Alfred A. Knopf.

Bergsten, C. Fred. 1972. "The New Economics and U.S. Foreign Policy." *Foreign Affairs* 50 (January): 199–222.

Bergstrom, Theodore, Lawrence Blume, and Hal Varian. 1986. "On the Private Provision of Public Goods." *Journal of Public Economics* 29 (February): 25–49.

Bhagwati, Jagdish. 1990. "Departures from Multilateralism: Regionalism and Aggressive Unilateralism." *Economic Journal* 100 (December): 1304–17.

Bjerve, Petter Jakob. 1959. *Planning in Norway, 1947–1956.* Amsterdam: North Holland.

Blainey, Geoffrey. 1973. *The Causes of War.* London: Macmillan.

Bloch, Marc. 1954. *The Historian's Craft.* Manchester, Eng.: Manchester University Press.

Block, Fred L. 1977. *The Origins of International Economic Disorder: A Study of United States International Monetary Policy from World War II to the Present.* Berkeley: University of California Press.

Böhnke, A. 1888. *Recueil des traités et conventions conclus par la Russie avec les puissances étrangères.* St. Petersburg, Russia: Ministère des Voies des Communications.

Boiteau, Paul. 1863/1970. *Les traités de commerce: Texte de tous les traités en vigeur, notamment des traités conclus avec l'Angleterre, la Belgique, la Prusse (Zollverein), et Italie.* New York: Burt Franklin.

Bourne, Kenneth. 1970. *The Foreign Policy of Victorian England 1830–1902.* Oxford: Clarendon.

Brady, Alexander. 1928. *William Huskisson and Liberal Reform: An Essay on the Changes in Economic Policy in the Twenties of the Nineteenth Century.* London: Oxford University Press.

Braudel, Fernand. 1962. "Histoire et sociologie." In *Traité de sociologie,* ed. G. Gurvitch, 1:83–98. Paris: Presses Universitaires de France.

Braudel, Fernand. 1979. *Civilization and Capitalism.* New York: Harper and Row.

Brawley, Mark R. 1993. *Liberal Leadership: Great Powers and Their Challengers in Peace and War.* Ithaca: Cornell University Press.

Brebner, John Bartlett. 1945. *North Atlantic Triangle: The Interplay of Canada, the United States, and Great Britain.* New York: Columbia University Press.

Breton, Albert, and Raymond Breton. 1969. "An Economic Theory of Social Movements." *American Economic Review* 59 (May): 198–205.

Bridge, Roy. 1979. "Allied Diplomacy in Peacetime: The Failure of the Congress 'System,' 1815–1823." In *Europe's Balance of Power, 1815–1848*, ed. Alan Sked, 34–53. London: Macmillan.

Briggs, Asa. 1959. *The Making of Modern England, 1783–1867: The Age of Improvement.* New York: Harper and Row.

Brock, William R. 1941. *Lord Liverpool and Liberal Toryism, 1820 to 1827.* London: Cass.

Brofoss, Erik. 1977. "The Marshall Plan and Norway's Hesitation." *Scandinavian Journal of History* 2: 241–42.

Brown, Lucy. 1958. *The Board of Trade and the Free-Trade Movement, 1830–1842.* Oxford: Clarendon.

Browning, George. 1834. *The Domestic and Financial Condition of Great Britain; Preceded by a Brief Sketch of Her Foreign Policy; and of the Statistics and Politics of France, Russia, Austria, and Prussia.* London: Longman, Rees, Orme, Brown, Green, and Longman.

Bruce, Neil. 1990. "Defence Spending in Allied and Adversarial Relationships." *Defence Economics* 1 (May): 179–95.

Bueno de Mesquita, Bruce. 1981. *The War Trap.* New Haven: Yale University Press.

Bueno de Mesquita, Bruce. 1990. "Multilateral Negotiations: A Spatial Analysis of the Arab-Israeli Dispute." *International Organization* 44 (summer): 317–40.

Bueno de Mesquita, Bruce, and David Lalman. 1992. *War and Reason: Domestic and International Imperatives.* New Haven: Yale University Press.

Bullen, Roger. 1974. *Palmerston, Guizot, and the Collapse of the Entente Cordiale.* London: University of London, Athlone Press.

Bureau, Dominique, and Paul Champsaur. 1992. "Fiscal Federalism and European Economic Integration." *American Economic Review* 82 (May): 88–92.

Burley, Anne-Marie. 1993. "Regulating the World: Multilateralism, International Law, and the Projection of the New Deal Regulatory State." In *Multilateralism Matters*, ed. John Gerard Ruggie, 125–56.

Calleo, David P. 1987. *Beyond American Hegemony: The Failure of the Western Alliance.* New York: Basic Books.

Calleo, David P., and Benjamin M. Rowland. 1973. *America and the World Political Economy.* Bloomington: Indiana University Press.

Calvert, Randall L. 1989. "Reciprocity among Self-Interested Actors: Uncertainty, Asymmetry, and Distribution." In *Models of Strategic Choice in Politics,* ed. Peter C. Ordeshook, 269–93. Ann Arbor: University of Michigan Press.

Campbell, John Creighton. 1993. "Japan and the United States: Games That Work." In *Japan's Foreign Policy after the Cold War: Coping with Change,* ed. Gerald Curtis, 43–61. Armonk, N.Y.: M. E. Sharpe.

Caporaso, James A. 1992. "International Relations Theory and Multilateralism: The

Search for Foundations." *International Organization* 46 (summer): 598–632. Reprinted in *Multilateralism Matters,* ed. Ruggie, 51–90.

Carr, E. H. 1939/1962. *The Twenty Years' Crisis.* London: St. Martin's.

Carr, E. H. 1961. *What is History?* New York: St. Martin's.

Cartwright, Nancy. 1983. *How the Laws of Physics Lie.* New York: Oxford University Press.

Caspary, William R. 1967. "Richardson's Model of Arms Races: Description, Critique, and an Alternative Model." *International Studies Quarterly* 11 (March): 63–88.

Cecil, David. 1954. *Melbourne.* Indianapolis: Bobbs-Merrill.

Chamberlin, John. 1974. "Provision of Collective Goods as a Function of Group Size." *American Political Science Review* 68 (June): 701–16.

Chamberlin, John. 1978. "A Collective Goods Model of Pluralist Political Systems." *Public Choice* 33:97–113.

Chase-Dunn, Christopher K. 1981. "Interstate System and Capitalist World-Economy: One Logic or Two?" *International Studies Quarterly* 25 (March): 19–42.

Chase-Dunn, Christopher K. 1982. "International Economic Policy in a Declining Core State." In *America in a Changing World Political Economy,* ed. Avery and Rapkin, 77–96.

Clarke, Stephen V. O. 1967. *Central Bank Cooperation, 1924–1931.* New York: Federal Reserve Bank of New York.

Clay, Lucius D. 1950. *Decision in Germany.* Garden City, N.Y.: Doubleday.

Cobden Club. 1875. *Free Trade and the European Treaties of Commerce (with an Intro-duction).* London: Cassell.

Coffin, Tristram. 1966. *Senator Fulbright: Portrait of a Public Philosopher.* New York: Dutton.

Cohen, Benjamin J. 1977. *Organizing the World's Money: The Political Economy of Inter-national Monetary Relations.* New York: Basic Books.

Conacher, J. B. 1972. *The Peelites and the Party System, 1846–52.* Newton Abbot, Eng.: David and Charles.

Conybeare, John A. C. 1983. "Tariff Protection in Developed and Developing Coun-tries: A Cross-Sectional and Longitudinal Analysis." *International Organization* 37 (summer): 441–67.

Conybeare, John A. C. 1984. "Public Goods, Prisoners' Dilemmas, and the Interna-tional Political Economy." *International Studies Quarterly* 28 (March): 5–22.

Conybeare, John A. C. 1987. *Trade Wars: The Theory and Practice of International Com-mercial Rivalry.* New York: Columbia University Press.

Cornes, Richard, and Todd Sandler. 1986. *The Theory of Externalities, Public Goods, and Club Goods.* Cambridge: Cambridge University Press.

Cowhey, Peter F., and Edward Long. 1983. "Testing Theories of Regime Change: Hege-monic Decline or Surplus Capacity?" *International Organization* 37 (spring): 157–83.

Cox, Robert W. 1977. "Labor and Hegemony." *International Organization* 31 (summer): 385–424.

Cox, Robert W. 1986. "Social Forces, States, and World Orders: Beyond International Relations Theory." In *Neorealism and Its Critics,* ed. Keohane, 204–54.

Craig, Gordon. 1978. *Modern Germany, 1866–1945.* New York: Oxford University Press.

Crosby, Travis L. 1976. *Sir Robert Peel's Administration, 1841–1846.* Newton Abbot, Eng.: David and Charles.

Curzon, Gerard, and Victoria Curzon. 1976. "The Management of Trade Relations in the GATT." In *International Economic Relations of the Western World, 1959–1971,* ed. Andrew Shonfield, Gerard Curzon, Victoria Curzon, T. K. Warley, and George Ray, 1:143–286. London: Oxford University Press for the Royal Institute of International Affairs.

Deardorff, Alan V. 1984. "Testing Trade Theories and Predicting Trade Flows." In *Handbook of International Economics,* ed. R. W. Jones and P. B. Kenen, 467–517. New York: Elsevier Science.

Deutsch, Karl W., and J. David Singer. 1964. "Multipolar Power Systems and International Stability." *World Politics* 16 (April): 390–406.

Diebold, William, Jr. 1988. "The Marshall Plan in Retrospect: A Review of Recent Scholarship." *Journal of International Affairs* 41 (summer): 421–35.

Dixit, Avinash. 1979. "A Model of Duopoly Suggesting a Theory of Entry Barriers." *Bell Journal of Economics* 10 (spring): 20–32.

Dixit, Avinash. 1980. "The Role of Investment in Entry Deterrence." *Economic Journal* 90 (March): 95–106.

Dixit, Avinash, and Victor Norman. 1980. *Theory of International Trade: A Dual, General Equilibrium Approach.* Cambridge: Cambridge University Press.

Dixon, Peter. 1976. *Canning: Politician and Statesman.* London: Weidenfeld and Nicolson.

Drage, Geoffrey. 1911. *The Imperial Organization of Trade.* London: Smith, Elder.

Dreyer, F. A. 1965. "The Whigs and the Political Crisis of 1845." *English Historical Review* 80 (July): 514–37.

Dunham, Arthur Louis. 1930. *The Anglo-French Treaty of Commerce of 1860 and the Progress of the Industrial Revolution in France.* Ann Arbor: University of Michigan Press.

East, Maurice. 1973. "Size and Foreign Policy Behavior: A Test of Two Models." *World Politics* 25 (July): 556–76.

Eichengreen, Barry. 1985. "International Policy Coordination in Historical Perspective: A View from the Interwar Years." In *International Economic Policy Coordination,* ed. Willem H. Buiter and Richard C. Marston, 139–83. New York: Cambridge University Press.

Eichengreen, Barry. 1987. "Conducting the International Orchestra: Bank of England

Leadership under the Classical Gold Standard." *Journal of International Money and Finance* 6 (March): 5–29.

Falkus, M. E. 1971. "United States Economic Policy and the 'Dollar Gap' of the 1920's." *Economic History Review* 24 (November): 599–623.

Fay, C. R. 1932. *The Corn Law and Social England.* Cambridge: Cambridge University Press.

Fearon, James. 1992. "Counterfactuals and Hypothesis Testing in Political Science." *World Politics* 43 (January): 169–95.

Fearon, Peter. 1987. *War, Prosperity, and Depression: The U.S. Economy 1917–1945.* Lawrence: University Press of Kansas.

Feis, Herbert. 1950. *The Diplomacy of the Dollar: First Era, 1919–1932.* Baltimore: Johns Hopkins University Press.

Fetter, Frank Whitson. 1980. *The Economist in Parliament, 1780–1860.* Durham: Duke University Press.

Finlayson, Jock A., and Mark W. Zacher. 1983. "The GATT and the Regulation of Trade Barriers: Regime Dynamics and Functions." In *International Regimes,* ed. Krasner, 273–314.

Fischer, David Hackett. 1970. *Historians' Fallacies: Toward a Logic of Historical Thought.* New York: Harper.

Frieden, Jeffry. 1987. *Banking on the World: The Politics of American International Finance.* New York: Harper and Row.

Frieden, Jeffry. 1988. "Sectoral Conflict and U.S. Foreign Economic Policy, 1914–1940." In *The State and American Foreign Economic Policy,* ed. Ikenberry, Lake, and Mastanduno, 59–90.

Frohlich, Norman, and Joe A. Oppenheimer. 1970. "I Get by with a Little Help from My Friends." *World Politics* 23 (October): 104–20.

Frohlich, Norman, and Joe A. Oppenheimer. 1974. "The Carrot and the Stick: Optimal Program Mixes for Entrepreneurial Political Leaders." *Public Choice* 19 (fall): 43–61.

Frohlich, Norman, Joe A. Oppenheimer, and Oran R. Young. 1971. *Political Leadership and Collective Goods.* Princeton: Princeton University Press.

Fudenberg, Drew, and Eric Maskin. 1986. "The Folk Theorem in Repeated Games with Discounting or with Incomplete Information." *Econometrica* 54 (May): 533–54.

Gaddis, John Lewis. 1982. *Strategies of Containment: A Critical Appraisal of Postwar American National Security Policy.* New York: Oxford University Press.

Gallagher, John, and Ronald Robinson. 1953. "The Imperialism of Free Trade." *Economic History Review,* 2d ser., 6 (August): 1–15.

Gash, Norman. 1951. "Peel and the Party System 1830–50." *Transactions of the Royal Historical Society,* 5th ser., 1:47–69.

Gash, Norman. 1972. *Sir Robert Peel: The Life of Sir Robert Peel after 1830.* London: Longman.

Gathorne-Hardy, G. M. 1950. *A Short History of International Affairs, 1920–1939.* 4th ed. London: Oxford University Press under the auspices of the Royal Institute of International Affairs.

Gill, Stephen. 1986. "Hegemony, Consensus, and Trilateralism." *Review of International Studies* 12 (July): 205–21.

Gilpin, Robert. 1972. "The Politics of Transnational Economic Relations." In *Transnational Relations and World Politics*, ed. Keohane and Nye, 48–69.

Gilpin, Robert. 1975. *U.S. Power and the Multinational Corporation.* New York: Basic Books.

Gilpin, Robert. 1981. *War and Change in World Politics.* Cambridge: Cambridge University Press.

Gimbel, John. 1976. *The Origins of the Marshall Plan.* Stanford: Stanford University Press.

Goldstein, Judith. 1993. "Creating the GATT Rules: Politics, Institutions, and American Policy." In *Multilateralism Matters,* ed. Ruggie, 201–32.

Gordon, Barry. 1976. *Political Economy in Parliament, 1819–1823.* London: Macmillan.

Gordon, Barry. 1979. *Economic Doctrine and Tory Liberalism, 1824–1830.* London: Macmillan.

Gourevitch, Peter. 1986. *Politics in Hard Times: Comparative Responses to International Economic Crises.* Ithaca: Cornell University Press.

Gowa, Joanne. 1983. *Closing the Gold Window: Domestic Politics and the End of Bretton Woods.* Ithaca: Cornell University Press.

Gowa, Joanne. 1989a. "Bipolarity, Multipolarity, and Free Trade." *American Political Science Review* 83 (December): 1245–56.

Gowa, Joanne. 1989b. "Rational Hegemons, Excludable Goods, and Small Groups: An Epitaph for Hegemonic Stability Theory?" *World Politics* 41 (April): 307–24.

Gowa, Joanne. 1994. *Allies, Adversaries, and International Trade.* Princeton: Princeton University Press.

Gowa, Joanne, and Edward D. Mansfield. 1993. "Power Politics and International Trade." *American Political Science Review* 87 (June): 408–20.

Green, David P., and Ian Shapiro. 1994. *Pathologies of Rational Choice Theory: A Critique of Applications in Political Science.* New Haven: Yale University Press.

Greenwood, Gordon. 1955. "National Development and Social Experimentation, 1901–1914." In *Australia: A Social and Political History,* ed. Gordon Greenwood, 196–257. Sydney: Angus and Robertson.

Greif, Avner, Paul Milgrom, and Barry Weingast. 1990. *The Merchant Gild as a Nexus of Contracts.* Hoover Institution Working Paper in Political Science #P-90-9. Palo Alto: Stanford University.

Grieco, Joseph M. 1988. "Realist Theory and the Problem of International Cooperation: Analysis with an Amended Prisoner's Dilemma Model." *Journal of Politics* 50 (August): 600–624.

Grieco, Joseph M. 1990. *Cooperation among Nations: Europe, America, and Non-Tariff Barriers to Trade.* Ithaca: Cornell University Press.

Grossman, Herschel I. 1990. "The Political Economy of War Debt and Inflation." In *Monetary Policy for a Changing Financial Environment*, ed. William S. Haraf and Philip Cagan, 166–81. Washington, D.C.: AEI Press.

Grossman, Herschel I., and Taejoon Han. 1993. "A Theory of War Finance." *Defence Economics* 4 (February): 33–44.

Grossman, Herschel I., and John B. Van Huyck. 1988. "Sovereign Debt as a Contingent Claim: Excusable Default, Repudiation, and Reputation." *American Economic Review* 78 (December): 1088–97.

Guttman, J. M. 1978. "Understanding Collective Action: Matching Behavior." *American Economic Review Papers and Proceedings* 68:251–55.

Guttman, J. M. 1987. "A Non-Cournot Model of Voluntary Collective Action." *Economica* 54 (February): 1–19.

Haggard, Stephan, and Beth Simmons. 1987. "Theories of International Regimes." *International Organization* 41 (summer): 491–517.

Haight, Frank Arnold. 1941. *A History of French Commercial Policies*. New York: Macmillan.

Heikkilä, Hannu. 1983. "The United States and the Question of Export Licenses to Finland, 1947–1948." *Scandinavian Journal of History* 8:247–59.

Henderson, W. O. 1939. *The Zollverein*. Cambridge: Cambridge University Press.

Hertslet, Sir Edward. 1875–. *Treaties and Tariffs Regulating the Trade between Great Britain and Foreign Nations*. London: Butterworth's.

Hilton, Boyd. 1977. *Corn, Cash, Commerce: The Economic Policies of the Tory Governments, 1815–1830*. Oxford: Oxford University Press.

Hirsch, Fred, Michael Doyle, and Edward Morse. 1977. *Alternatives to Monetary Disorder*. New York: McGraw-Hill.

Hirschman, Albert O. 1945/1980. *National Power and the Structure of Foreign Trade*. Berkeley: University of California Press.

Hirshleifer, Jack. 1988. "The Analytics of Continuing Conflict." *Synthese* 76 (November): 201–33.

Hirshleifer, Jack. 1989. "Conflict and Rent-Seeking Success Functions: Ratio vs. Difference Models of Relative Success." *Public Choice* 63 (November): 101–12.

Hirshleifer, Jack, and Juan Carlos Martinez Coll. 1988. "What Strategies Can Support the Evolutionary Emergence of Cooperation?" *Journal of Conflict Resolution* 32 (June): 367–98.

Hobsbawm, Eric. 1969. *Industry and Empire: An Economic History of Britain since 1750*. London: Weidenfeld and Nicolson.

Hogan, Michael J. 1987. *The Marshall Plan: America, Britain, and the Reconstruction of Western Europe, 1947–1952*. Cambridge: Cambridge University Press.

Hudson, Daryl J. 1977. "Vandenberg Reconsidered: Senate Resolution 239 and American Foreign Policy." *Diplomatic History* 1 (winter): 46–63.

Ikenberry, G. John, David A. Lake, and Michael Mastanduno, eds. 1988. *The State and American Foreign Economic Policy*. Ithaca: Cornell University Press.

Imlah, Albert H. 1958. *Economic Elements in the Pax Britannica: Studies in British Foreign Trade in the Nineteenth Century.* Cambridge: Harvard University Press.

Irwin, Douglas A. 1988. "Welfare Effects of British Free Trade: Debate and Evidence from the 1840s." *Journal of Political Economy* 96 (December): 1142–64.

Irwin, Douglas A. 1989. "Political Economy and Peel's Repeal of the Corn Laws." *Economics and Politics* 1 (spring): 41–59.

James, Scott C., and David A. Lake. 1989. "The Second Face of Hegemony: Britain's Repeal of the Corn Laws and the American Walker Tariff of 1846." *International Organization* 43 (winter): 1–30.

Jervis, Robert. 1978. "Cooperation under the Security Dilemma." *World Politics* 30 (January): 167–214.

Jervis, Robert. 1986. "From Balance to Concert: A Study of International Security Cooperation." In *Cooperation under Anarchy*, ed. Oye, 58–79.

Johnson, Harry G. 1953–54. "Optimum Tariffs and Retaliation." *Review of Economic Studies* 21:142–53.

Kaplan, Morton. 1957. *System and Process in International Politics.* New York: Wiley.

Katzenstein, Peter J., ed. 1978. *Between Power and Plenty: Foreign Economic Policies of Advanced Industrial States.* Madison: University of Wisconsin Press.

Katzenstein, Peter J. 1986. *Small States in World Markets: Industrial Policy in Europe.* Ithaca: Cornell University Press.

Kennan, George F. 1967. *Memoirs, 1925–1950.* New York: Pantheon.

Kennedy, Paul. 1976. *The Rise and Fall of British Naval Mastery.* London: Allen Lane.

Kennedy, Paul. 1980. *The Rise of the Anglo-German Antagonism, 1860–1914.* London: Allen and Unwin.

Kennedy, Paul. 1987. *The Rise and Fall of the Great Powers.* New York: Vintage Books.

Kennedy, Paul. 1991. "American Grand Strategy, Today and Tomorrow: Learning from the European Experience." In *Grand Strategies in War and Peace*, ed. Paul Kennedy, 167–84. New Haven: Yale University Press.

Keohane, Robert O. 1979. "U.S. Foreign Economic Policy toward Other Advanced Capitalist States: The Struggle to Make Others Adjust." In *Eagle Entangled*, ed. Kenneth Oye et al., 91–122.

Keohane, Robert O. 1980. "The Theory of Hegemonic Stability and Changes in International Economic Regimes, 1967–1977." In *Change in the International System*, ed. Ole Holsti, Randolph M. Siverson, and Alexander L. George, 131–63. Boulder, Colo.: Westview Press.

Keohane, Robert O. 1982a. "The Demand for International Regimes." In *International Regimes*, ed. Stephen D. Krasner, 141–71.

Keohane, Robert O. 1982b. "Hegemonic Leadership and U.S. Foreign Economic Policy in the 'Long Decade' of the 1950s." In *America in a Changing World Political Economy*, ed. Avery and Rapkin, 49–76.

Keohane, Robert O. 1984. *After Hegemony: Discord in the World Political Economy.* Princeton: Princeton University Press.

Keohane, Robert O., ed. 1986a. *Neorealism and Its Critics.* New York: Columbia University Press.

Keohane, Robert O. 1986b. "Theory of World Politics: Structural Realism and Beyond." In *Neorealism and Its Critics,* ed. Keohane, 158–203.

Keohane, Robert O. 1990. "Multilateralism: An Agenda for Research." *International Journal* 45 (autumn): 731–64.

Keohane, Robert O., and Joseph S. Nye, eds. 1972. *Transnational Relations and World Politics.* Cambridge: Harvard University Press.

Kindleberger, Charles P. 1973. *The World in Depression, 1929–1939.* Chicago: University of Chicago Press.

Kindleberger, Charles P. 1975. "The Rise of Free Trade in Western Europe, 1820–1875." *Journal of Economic History* 35 (March): 20–55.

Kindleberger, Charles P. 1976. "Systems of International Economic Organization." In *Money and the Changing World Order,* ed. David P. Calleo, 15–39. New York: New York University Press for the Lehman Institute.

Kindleberger, Charles P. 1981. "Dominance and Leadership in the International Economy." *International Studies Quarterly* 25 (June): 242–54.

Kindleberger, Charles P. 1987. *Marshall Plan Days.* Boston: Allen and Unwin.

Kissinger, Henry A. 1957. *A World Restored.* Boston: Houghton Mifflin.

Kitson Clark, G. S. R. 1951. "The Electorate and the Repeal of the Corn Laws." *Transactions of the Royal Historical Society,* 5th ser., 1: 109–26.

Kolko, Joyce, and Gabriel Kolko. 1972. *The Limits of Power: The World and United States Foreign Policy, 1945–1954.* New York: Harper and Row.

Krasner, Stephen D. 1976. "State Power and the Structure of International Trade." *World Politics* 28 (April): 317–413.

Krasner, Stephen D., ed. 1983. *International Regimes.* Ithaca: Cornell University Press.

Krauthammer, Charles. 1992. "The Unipolar Moment." In *Rethinking America's Security,* ed. Allison and Treverton, 295–306.

Kreps, David, Paul Milgrom, John Roberts, and Robert Wilson. 1982. "Rational Cooperation in the Finitely Repeated Prisoners' Dilemma." *Journal of Economic Theory* 27 (August): 245–52.

Kreps, David M. 1990. *A Course in Microeconomic Theory.* Princeton: Princeton University Press.

LaFeber, Walter. 1980. *America, Russia, and the Cold War, 1945–1966.* New York: Wiley.

Laitin, David D. 1982. "Capitalism and Hegemony: Yorubaland and the International Economy." *International Organization* 36 (autumn): 687–713.

Lakatos, Imre. 1970. "Falsification and the Methodology of Scientific Research Programmes." In *Criticism and the Growth of Knowledge,* ed. Imre Lakatos and Alan Musgrave, 91–196. Cambridge: Cambridge University Press.

Lake, David A. 1983. "International Economic Structures and American Foreign Economic Policy, 1887–1934." *World Politics* 35 (July): 517–43.

Lake, David A. 1984. "Beneath the Commerce of Nations: A Theory of International Economic Structures." *International Studies Quarterly* 28 (June): 143–70.

Lake, David A. 1988. *Power, Protection, and Free Trade: International Sources of U.S. Commercial Strategy, 1887–1939.* Ithaca: Cornell University Press.

Lake, David A. 1993. "Leadership, Hegemony, and the International Economy: Naked Emperor or Tattered Monarch with Potential?" *International Studies Quarterly* 37 (December): 459–89.

Lary, Hal B. 1943. *The United States in the World Economy: The International Transactions of the United States during the Interwar Period.* U.S. Department of Commerce, Bureau of Foreign and Domestic Commerce, International Economics and Statistics Unit, Economics Series no. 23. Washington, D.C.: U.S. Government Printing Office.

Laver, Michael. 1980. "Political Solutions to the Collective Action Problem." *Political Studies* 28 (June): 195–209.

Lawson, Fred H. 1983. "Hegemony and the Structure of International Trade Reassessed: A View from Arabia." *International Organization* 37 (spring): 317–37.

League of Nations, Economic, Financial, and Transit Department. 1944. *International Currency Experience: Lessons of the Inter-War Period.* Princeton: Princeton University Press for the League of Nations.

Linnemann, Hans. 1966. *An Econometric Study of International Trade Flows.* Amsterdam: North Holland.

Lipson, Charles. 1983. "The Transformation of Trade: The Sources and Effects of Regime Change." In *International Regimes,* ed. Krasner, 233–71.

Lipson, Charles. 1984. "International Cooperation in Economic and Security Affairs." *World Politics* 37 (October): 1–23.

Lipson, Charles. 1986. "Bankers' Dilemmas: Private Cooperation in Rescheduling Sovereign Debts." In *Cooperation under Anarchy,* ed. Oye, 200–225.

Lohmann, Susanne D. 1997. "Issue-Linkage, Player-Linkage, and Domestic-International Linkage." *Journal of Conflict Resolution* 41 (February): 38–67.

Long, William O. 1989. *U.S. Export Control Policy: Executive Autonomy vs. Congressional Reform.* New York: Columbia University Press.

Longford, Elizabeth. 1972. *Wellington: Pillar of State.* New York: Harper and Row.

Lundberg, Erik. 1961. "Stability Problems in the Scandinavian Countries during the Postwar Period." *American Economic Review* 51 (May): 378–89.

Lundestad, Geir. 1980. *America, Scandinavia, and the Cold War, 1945–1949.* New York: Columbia University Press.

Lundestad, Geir. 1986. "Empire by Invitation? The United States and Western Europe, 1945–1952." *Journal of Peace Research* 23 (September): 263–77.

Luterbacher, Urs. 1975. "Arms Race Models: Where Do We Stand?" *European Journal of Political Research* 3 (September): 199–217.

Macmillan Committee on Finance and Industry. 1931. *Report.* Abridged version reprinted in *The Gold Standard in Theory and History*, ed. Barry Eichengreen, 185–225. New York: Methuen, 1985.

Magee, Stephen P., William A. Brock, and Leslie Young. 1989. *Black Hole Tariffs and Endogenous Policy Theory*. Cambridge: Cambridge University Press.

Maier, Charles S. 1977. "The Politics of Productivity." Reprinted in *In Search of Stability: Explorations in Historical Political Economy*. Cambridge: Cambridge University Press, 1987.

Mansfield, Edward D. 1992. "The Concentration of Capabilities and International Trade." *International Organization* 46 (summer): 731–63.

Mansfield, Edward D. 1994. *Power, Trade, and War*. Princeton: Princeton University Press.

Margolis, Julius. 1955. "A Comment on the Pure Theory of Public Expenditures." *Review of Economics and Statistics* 37 (November): 347–59.

Marshall, George C. 1947. "Address at the Commencement Exercises of Harvard University, Cambridge, Massachusetts, June 5, 1947." Reprinted in Mee, *The Marshall Plan*, 271–73.

Martens, F. 1878. *Recueil des traités et conventions conclus par la Russie avec les puissances étrangères*. St. Petersburg, Russia: Chez A. Devrient.

Martin, Lisa L. 1992. *Coercive Cooperation: Explaining Multilateral Economic Sanctions*. Princeton: Princeton University Press.

Martin, Lisa L. 1993. "The Rational State Choice of Multilateralism." In *Multilateralism Matters*, ed. Ruggie, 91–121.

Mastanduno, Michael. 1988. "Trade as a Strategic Weapon: American and Alliance Export Control Policy in the Early Postwar Period." In *The State and American Foreign Economic Policy*, ed. Ikenberry, Lake, and Mastanduno, 121–50.

McCloskey, Donald N. 1980. "Magnanimous Albion: Free Trade and British National Income, 1841–1881." *Explorations in Economic History* 17 (July): 303–20.

McGinnis, Michael. 1986. "Issue Linkage and the Evolution of Cooperation." *Journal of Conflict Resolution* 30 (March): 141–70.

McKeown, Timothy J. 1983. "Hegemonic Stability Theory and Nineteenth Century Tariff Levels in Europe." *International Organization* 37 (winter): 73–92.

McKeown, Timothy J. 1989. "The Politics of Corn Law Repeal and Theories of Commercial Policy." *British Journal of Political Science* 19 (July): 353–80.

McKeown, Timothy J. 1991. "A Liberal Trade Order? The Long-Run Pattern of Imports to the Advanced Capitalist States." *International Studies Quarterly* 35 (June): 151–72.

McLean, Iain. 1992. "Rational Choice and the Victorian Voter." *Political Studies* 40 (September): 496–515.

McNeil, William C. 1986. *American Money and the Weimar Republic: Economics and Politics on the Eve of the Great Depression*. New York: Columbia University Press.

Mearsheimer, John J. 1992. "Disorder Restored." In *Rethinking America's Security*, ed. Allison and Treverton, 213–38.

Mee, Charles L., Jr. 1984. *The Marshall Plan: The Launching of the Pax Americana*. New York: Simon and Schuster.

Meyer, Richard Hemmig. 1970. *Bankers' Diplomacy: Monetary Stabilization in the Twenties*. New York: Columbia University Press.

Milner, Helen V. 1988. *Resisting Protectionism: Global Industries and the Politics of International Trade*. Princeton: Princeton University Press.

Milward, Alan S. 1979. *War, Economy and Society, 1939–1945*. Berkeley: University of California Press.

Milward, Alan S. 1984. *The Reconstruction of Western Europe, 1945–1951*. Berkeley: University of California Press.

Milward, Alan S. 1992. *The European Rescue of the Nation-State*. Berkeley: University of California Press.

Ministerio degli Affari Esteri. 1865–99. *Trattati e convenzioni fra il regno d'Italia ed i governi esteri*. Roma: Tipografia Bencini.

Mitchell, Brian R. 1975. *European Historical Statistics, 1750–1970*. Abridged ed. New York: Columbia University Press.

Modelski, George. 1978. "The Long Cycle of Global Politics and the Nation-State." *Comparative Studies in Society and History* 20 (April): 214–38.

Modelski, George. 1982. "Long Cycles and the Strategy of U.S. International Economic Policy." In *America in a Changing World Political Economy*, ed. Avery and Rapkin, 97–118.

Modelski, George. 1987. *Long Cycles in World Politics*. Seattle: University of Washington Press.

Montgomery, Arthur. 1962. "The Swedish Economy in the 1950s." *Scandinavian Economic History Review* 10:220–32.

Morgenthau, Hans J. 1978/1985. *Politics among Nations: The Struggle for Power and Peace*. New York: Knopf.

Morrow, James D. 1991. "Alliances and Asymmetry: An Alternative to the Capability Aggregation Model of Alliances." *American Journal of Political Science* 35 (November): 904–33.

Morrow, James D., Randolph M. Siverson, and Tressa Tabares. 1996. "Terms of Trade: The Political Determinants of Major-Power International Trade, 1907–1965." Unpublished manuscript.

Murdoch, J. C., and Todd Sandler. 1982. "A Theoretical and Empirical Analysis of NATO." *Journal of Conflict Resolution* 26 (June): 237–63.

Nau, Henry R. 1990. *The Myth of America's Decline: Leading the World Economy into the 1990s*. New York: Oxford University Press.

Neumann, Léopold, and Adolphe de Plason. 1877–1912. *Recueil des traités et conventions conclus par l'Autriche avec les puissances étrangères, depuis 1763 jusqu'a nos jours*. Vienna: Imprimerie I. et R. de la Court et de l'Etat.

Niou, Emerson M. S., Peter C. Ordeshook, and Gregory F. Rose. 1989. *The Balance of*

Power: Stability in International Systems. Cambridge: University of Cambridge Press.

Nogaro, Bertrand, and Moye Marcel. 1931. *La régime douanier de la France.* Paris: Librairie de Recueil Sirey.

Nogués, Julio. 1990. "The Choice between Unilateral and Multilateral Trade Liberalization Strategy." *World Economy* 13 (March): 15–26.

North, Douglass C., and Barry R. Weingast. 1989. "Constitutions and Commitment: The Evolution of Institutions Governing Public Choice in Seventeenth-Century England." *Journal of Economic History* 49 (December): 803–33.

Nye, John Vincent. 1990. *Revisionist Tariff History and the Theory of Hegemonic Stability.* Political Economy Working Paper. St. Louis, Mo.: Washington University.

Odell, John S. 1982. *U.S. International Monetary Policy: Markets, Power, and Ideas as Sources of Change.* Princeton: Princeton University Press.

Olsen, Erling. 1962. *Danmarks økonomiske historie siden 1750.* Copenhagen: G. E. C. Gads Forlag.

Olson, Mancur. 1965/1971. *The Logic of Collective Action.* Cambridge: Harvard University Press.

Olson, Mancur, and Richard Zeckhauser. 1966. "An Economic Theory of Alliances." *Review of Economics and Statistics* 48 (August): 266–79.

Organski, A. F. K. 1968. *World Politics.* 2d ed. New York: Knopf.

Oudiz, Gilles, and Jeffrey Sachs. 1984. "Macroeconomic Policy Coordination among the Industrial Economies." *Brookings Papers on Economic Activity* 1:1–75.

Oye, Kenneth A., ed. 1986a. *Cooperation under Anarchy.* Princeton: Princeton University Press.

Oye, Kenneth A. 1986b. "Explaining Cooperation under Anarchy: Hypotheses and Strategies." In *Cooperation under Anarchy,* ed. Oye, 1–24.

Oye, Kenneth A. 1986c. "The Sterling-Dollar-Franc Triangle: Monetary Diplomacy 1929–1937." In *Cooperation under Anarchy,* ed. Oye, 173–99.

Oye, Kenneth A., Donald Rothschild, and Robert J. Lieber, eds. 1979. *Eagle Entangled: U.S. Foreign Policy in a Complex World.* New York: Longman.

Pahre, Robert. 1990. "Hegemonic Strategies: Leadership in the International Political Economy, 1815–1975." Ph.D. diss, University of California, Los Angeles.

Pahre, Robert. 1994. "Multilateral Cooperation in an Iterated Prisoners' Dilemma." *Journal of Conflict Resolution* 38 (June): 326–52.

Pahre, Robert. 1995. "Wider and Deeper: The Links between Expansion and Integration in the European Communities." In *Towards a New Europe: Stops and Starts in Regional Integration,* ed. Gerald Schneider, Patricia A. Weitsman, and Thomas Bernauer, 111–36. Boulder, Colo.: Praeger/Greenwood.

Pahre, Robert. 1996a. "British Hegemony and the Repeal of the Corn Laws." In *The Rise of Free Trade,* vol. 4, *Free Trade Reappraised: The New Secondary Literature,* ed. Schonhardt-Bailey, 570–96.

Pahre, Robert. 1996b. "Mathematical Discourse and Crossdisciplinary Communities: The Case of Political Economy." *Social Epistemology* 10 (January–March): 55–73.

Pahre, Robert. 1997. "Endogenous Domestic Institutions in Two-Level Games and Parliamentary Oversight in the European Union." *Journal of Conflict Resolution* 41 (February): 147–74.

Pahre, Robert, and Paul A. Papayoanou. 1997. "Using Game Theory to Link International and Domestic Politics." *Journal of Conflict Resolution* 41 (February): 4–11.

Palmer, Glenn. 1990. "Corralling the Free Rider: Deterrence and the Western Alliance." *International Studies Quarterly* 34 (June): 147–64.

Patterson, G. D. 1968. *The Tariff in the Australian Colonies, 1856–1900.* Melbourne: Cheshire.

Pharo, Helge O. 1976. "Bridgebuilding and Reconstruction: Norway Faces the Marshall Plan." *Scandinavian Journal of History* 1:125–53.

Platt, D. C. M. 1968. *Finance, Trade, and Politics in British Foreign Policy, 1815–1914.* Oxford: Clarendon.

Pogue, Forrest C. 1987. *George C. Marshall: Statesman, 1945–1959.* New York: Penguin.

Polachek, Solomon W. 1980. "Conflict and Trade." *Journal of Conflict Resolution* 24 (February): 55–78.

Polanyi, Karl. 1944. *The Great Transformation.* Boston: Beacon.

Pollard, Robert A. 1985. *Economic Security and the Origins of the Cold War, 1945–1950.* New York: Columbia University Press.

Pollins, Brian M. 1989. "Does Trade Still Follow the Flag?" *American Political Science Review* 83 (June): 465–80.

Powell, Robert. 1991. "Absolute and Relative Gains in International Relations Theory." *American Political Science Review* 85 (December): 1303–20.

Powell, Robert. 1993. "Guns, Butter, and Anarchy." *American Political Science Review* 87 (March): 115–32.

Pöyhönen, Pentti. 1963. "A Tentative Model for the Volume of Trade between Countries." *Weltwirtschaftliches Archiv* 90:93–99.

Putnam, Robert D., and Nicholas Bayne. 1987. *Hanging Together: Cooperation and Conflict in the Seven-Power Summits.* Rev. ed. London: Sage.

Rapkin, David P., and William P. Avery. 1982. "U.S. International Economic Policy in a Period of Hegemonic Decline." In *America in a Changing World Political Economy,* ed. Avery and Rapkin, 3–26.

Rapkin, David P., and William H. Thompson, with Jon A. Christopherson. 1979. "Bipolarity and Bipolarization in the Cold War: Conceptualization, Measurement, and Validation." *Journal of Conflict Resolution* 23 (June): 261–95.

Rasler, Karen A., and William R. Thompson. 1989. *War and State Making: The Shaping of the Global Powers.* Boston: Unwin Hyman.

Ratcliffe, Barry M. 1978. "The Tariff Reform Campaign in France, 1831–1836." *Journal of European Economic History* 7 (spring): 61–138.

Rattinger, Hans. 1976. "Econometrics and Arms Races: A Critical Review and Some Extensions." *European Journal of Political Research* 4 (December): 421–39.

Recueil des traités et conventions conclus par la royaume des Pays-Bas avec les puissances étrangères, depuis 1813 jusqu'a nos jours. 1858–. The Hague: Belinfante Frères.

Richardson, J. David. 1988. "International Coordination of Trade Policy." In *International Economic Cooperation,* ed. Martin Feldstein, 167–204. Chicago: University of Chicago Press.

Richardson, Lewis Fry. 1960. *Arms and Insecurity: A Mathematical Study of the Causes and Origins of War.* Pittsburgh: Boxwood.

Rogowski, Ronald. *Commerce and Coalitions: How Trade Affects Domestic Political Alignments.* Princeton: Princeton University Press.

Romberg, Alan D. 1992. "U.S.-Japan Relations in a Changing Strategic Environment." In *Rethinking America's Security,* ed. Allison and Treverton, 362–74.

Rosecrance, Richard. 1986. *The Rise of the Trading State.* New York: Basic Books.

Rosecrance, Richard, and Jennifer Taw. 1990. "Japan and the Theory of International Leadership." *World Politics* 42 (January): 184–209.

Rubinstein, A. 1982. "Perfect Equilibria in a Bargaining Model." *Econometrica* 50 (January): 97–109.

Ruggie, John Gerard. 1972. "Collective Goods and Future International Collaboration." *American Political Science Review* 66 (September): 874–93.

Ruggie, John Gerard. 1983. "International Negotiations, Transactions, and Change: Embedded Liberalism in the Postwar Economic Order." In *International Regimes,* ed. Krasner, 195–231.

Ruggie, John Gerard. 1992. "Multilateralism: The Anatomy of an Institution." *International Organization* 46 (summer): 561–98.

Ruggie, John Gerard, ed. 1993. *Multilateralism Matters: The Theory and Praxis of an Institutional Form.* New York: Columbia University Press.

Russell, Ronald S. 1947. *Imperial Preference: Its Development and Effects.* London: Empire Economic Union.

Russett, Bruce. 1985. "The Mysterious Case of Vanishing Hegemony; or, Is Mark Twain Really Dead?" *International Organization* 39 (spring): 207–31.

Salisbury, Robert. 1969. "An Exchange Theory of Interest Groups." *Midwest Journal of Politics* 13 (February): 1–32.

Samuelson, Paul A. 1954. "The Pure Theory of Public Expenditures." *Review of Economics and Statistics* 36 (November): 387–89.

Samuelson, Paul A. 1955. "Diagrammatic Exposition of a Theory of Public Expenditures." *Review of Economics and Statistics* 37 (November): 350–56.

Samuelson, Paul A. 1958. "Aspects of Public Expenditure Theories." *Review of Economics and Statistics* 40 (November): 332–38.

Sandler, Todd. 1977. "Impurity of Defense: An Application to the Economics of Alliances." *Kyklos* 30: 443–60.

Sandler, Todd. 1992. *Collective Action: Theory and Applications.* Ann Arbor: University of Michigan Press.

Sandler, Todd, and J. F. Forbes. 1980. "Burden Sharing, Strategy, and the Design of NATO." *Economic Inquiry* 18 (July): 425–44.

Scalera, Garrett, and Herman Kahn. 1976. "Japan's Role in the World." In *Japan, America, and the Future World Order,* ed. Morton A. Kaplan and Kinhide Mushakoji, 199–224. New York: Free Press for the Center for Policy Study at the University of Chicago.

Schelling, Thomas C. 1960. *The Strategy of Conflict.* Cambridge: Harvard University Press.

Schonhardt-Bailey, Cheryl. 1991a. "Lessons in Lobbying for Free Trade in Nineteenth-Century Britain: To Concentrate or Not." *American Political Science Review* 85 (March): 37–58.

Schonhardt-Bailey, Cheryl. 1991b. "Specific Factors, Capital Markets, Portfolio Diversification, and Free Trade: Domestic Determinants of the Repeal of the Corn Laws." *World Politics* 43 (July): 545–69.

Schonhardt-Bailey, Cheryl. 1994. "Linking Constituency Interests to Legislative Voting Behaviour: The Role of District Economic and Electoral Composition in the Repeal of the Corn Laws." In *Computing Parliamentary History: George III to Victoria,* ed. John A. Phillips, 86–118. Edinburgh: Edinburgh University Press.

Schonhardt-Bailey, Cheryl, ed. 1996. *The Rise of Free Trade.* 4 vols. London: Routledge.

Schuyler, Robert Livingston. 1945. *The Fall of the Old Colonial System: A Study in British Free Trade, 1770–1870.* New York: Oxford University Press.

Sebenius, James K. 1983. "Negotiation Arithmetic: Adding and Subtracting Issues and Parties." *International Organization* 37 (spring): 281–316.

Semmel, Bernard. 1970. *The Rise of Free Trade Imperialism: Classical Political Economy and the Empire of Free Trade and Imperialism, 1750–1850.* Cambridge: Cambridge University Press.

Shaw, A. G. L. 1955/1983. *The Story of Australia.* 5th rev. ed. London: Faber and Faber.

Shonfield, Andrew. 1965. *Modern Capitalism: The Changing Balance of Public and Private Power.* London: Oxford University Press.

Shonfield, Andrew. 1976. "International Relations of the Western World: An Overall View." In *International Economic Relations of the Western World, 1959–1971,* ed. Andrew Shonfield, Gerard Curzon, Victoria Curzon, T. K. Warley, and George Ray, 1:1–142. London: Oxford University Press for the Royal Institute of International Affairs.

Simmons, Beth A. 1994. *Who Adjusts? Domestic Sources of Foreign Economic Policy during the Interwar Years.* Princeton: Princeton University Press.

Singer, J. David. 1961. "The Level-of-Analysis Problem in International Relations." *World Politics* 14 (October): 77–92.

Singer, J. David, and Melvin Small. 1970. "Alliance Aggregation and the Onset of War,

1815–1945." In *Alliances: Latent War Communities in the Contemporary World,* ed. Francis A. Beer, 12–67. New York: Holt, Rinehart, and Winston.

Sked, Alan, ed. 1979. *Europe's Balance of Power, 1815–1848.* London: Macmillan.

Smith, Michael Stephen. 1980. *Tariff Reform in France, 1860–1900: The Politics of Economic Interest.* Ithaca: Cornell University Press.

Snidal, Duncan. 1979. "Public Goods, Property Rights, and Political Organization." *International Studies Quarterly* 23 (December): 532–66.

Snidal, Duncan. 1985a. "Coordination versus Prisoner's Dilemma: Implications for International Cooperation and Regimes." *American Political Science Review* 79 (December): 923–42.

Snidal, Duncan. 1985b. "The Limits of Hegemonic Stability Theory." *International Organization* 39 (autumn): 579–614.

Snidal, Duncan. 1986. "The Game *Theory* of International Politics." In *Cooperation under Anarchy,* ed. Oye, 25–57.

Snidal, Duncan. 1991a. "International Cooperation among Relative Gains Maximizers." *International Studies Quarterly* 35 (December): 387–402.

Snidal, Duncan. 1991b. "Relative Gains and the Pattern of International Cooperation." *American Political Science Review* 85 (September): 701–26.

Spaak, Paul-Henri. 1971. *The Continuing Battle: Memoirs of a European, 1936–1966.* Trans. Henry Fox. Boston: Little, Brown.

Spence, A. M. 1977. "Entry, Capacity, Investment, and Oligopolistic Pricing." *Bell Journal of Economics* 8 (autumn): 534–44.

Spence, A. M. 1979. "Investment Strategy and Growth in a New Market." *Bell Journal of Economics* 10 (spring): 1–19.

Stein, Arthur A. 1980. "The Politics of Linkage." *World Politics* 33 (October): 62–81.

Stein, Arthur A. 1983. "Coordination and Collaboration: Regimes in an Anarchic World." In *International Regimes,* ed. Krasner, 115–40.

Stein, Arthur A. 1984. "The Hegemon's Dilemma: Great Britain, the United States, and the International Economic Order." *International Organization* 38 (spring): 355–86.

Steiner, Zara S. 1977. *Britain and the Origins of the First World War.* New York: St. Martin's.

Stewart, Robert. 1969. "The Ten Hours and Sugar Crises of 1844: Government and the House of Commons in the Age of Reform." *Historical Journal* 12 (March): 35–57.

Stigler, George J. 1974. "Free Riders and Collective Action." *Bell Journal of Economic and Management Science* 5 (autumn): 359–65.

Strange, Susan. 1976. *International Monetary Relations: International Economic Relations of the Western World, 1959–1971.* Vol. 2. London: Oxford University Press.

Strange, Susan. 1982. "Still an Extraordinary Power: America's Role in a Global Monetary System." In *The Political Economy of International and Domestic Monetary Relations,* ed. Raymond E. Lombra and William E. Witte, 73–93. Ames: Iowa State University Press.

Sugden, Robert. 1985. "Consistent Conjectures and Voluntary Contributions to Public Goods: Why the Conventional Theory Doesn't Work." *Journal of Public Economics* 27 (June): 117–24.

Sundelius, Bengt, and Claes Wiklund. 1979. "The Nordic Community: The Ugly Duckling of Regional Cooperation." *Journal of Commun Market Studies* 18.

Sykes, Alan. 1979. *Tariff Reform in British Politics, 1903–1913.* Oxford: Clarendon.

Sylvan, David J. "The Newest Mercantilism." *International Organization* 35 (spring): 375–93.

Taylor, A. J. P. 1954. *The Struggle for Mastery in Europe, 1848–1918.* Oxford: Clarendon.

Taylor, Michael. 1976. *Anarchy and Cooperation.* London: Wiley.

Taylor, Michael. 1987. *The Possibility of Cooperation.* (Rev. ed of *Anarchy and Cooperation.*) Cambridge: Cambridge University Press.

Temin, Peter. 1976. *Did Monetary Forces Cause the Great Depression?* New York: Norton.

Temperley, Harold. 1925. *The Foreign Policy of Canning, 1822–1827: England, the Neo-Holy Alliance, and the New World.* London: Bell.

Thomas, Robert P., and Donald N. McCloskey. 1981. "Overseas Trade and Empire, 1700–1860." In *The Economic History of Britain since 1700,* ed. Roderick C. Floud and Donald N. McCloskey, 1:87–102. Cambridge: Cambridge University Press.

Tinbergen, Jan. 1962. *Shaping the World Economy: Suggestions for an International Economic Policy.* New York: Twentieth Century Fund.

Tirole, Jean. 1988. *The Theory of Industrial Organization.* Cambridge: MIT Press.

Tollison, Robert D., and Thomas D. Willett. 1979. "An Economic Theory of Mutually Advantageous Issue Linkages in International Organization." *International Organization* 33 (autumn): 425–559.

Tompkins, C. David. 1970. *Senator Arthur H. Vandenberg: The Evolution of a Modern Republican, 1884–1945.* East Lansing: Michigan State University Press.

Trebilcock, Clive. 1981. *The Industrialization of the Continental Powers, 1780–1914.* London: Longman.

Triepel, Heinrich. 1909–. *Nouveau Recueil général de traités et autres actes relatifs aux rapports de droit international de martens.* Leipzig: Librarie Dietrich.

Trevelyan, G. M. 1926. *History of England.* London: Longmans, Green and Co.

Triffin, Robert. 1961. *Gold and the Dollar Crisis.* New Haven: Yale University Press.

Truman, Harry S. 1956. *Memoirs,* vol. 2, *Years of Trial and Hope.* Garden City, N.Y.: Doubleday.

Tsebelis, George. 1990. *Nested Games: Rational Choice in Comparative Politics.* Berkeley: University of California Press.

U.S. House. 1948. *United States Foreign Policy for a Postwar Recovery Program: Hearings before the House Foreign Affairs Committee.* 80th Cong., 2d sess., January 15, 27.

U.S. Senate. 1948. *Hearings before the Committee on Foreign Relations.* 80th Cong., 2d sess., February 10–12.

U.S. Tariff Commission. 1920. *Reciprocity with Canada: A Study of the Arrangement of 1911.* Washington, D.C.: U.S. Government Printing Office.

Van Evera, Stephan. 1986. "Why Cooperation Failed in 1914." In *Cooperation under Anarchy,* ed. Oye, 80–117.

Veitch, John M. 1986. "Repudiations and Confiscations by the Medieval State." *Journal of Economic History* 46 (March): 31–36.

Viner, Jacob. 1948. "Power versus Plenty as Objectives of Foreign Policy in the Seventeenth and Eighteenth Centuries." *World Politics* 1 (October): 1–24.

von Stackelberg, H. 1934. *Marktform und Gleichgewicht.* Vienna: Julius Springer.

von Stackelberg, H. 1952. *The Theory of the Market Economy (Grundlagen der Theoretischen Volkswirtschaftslehre* [1943]). Trans. Alan T. Peacock. New York: Oxford University Press.

Wallerstein, Immanuel. 1974. *The Modern World-System: Capitalist Agriculture and the Origins of the European World-Economy in the Sixteenth Century.* New York: Academic Press.

Wallerstein, Immanuel. 1979. *The Capitalist World Economy.* Cambridge: Cambridge University Press.

Wallerstein, Immanuel. 1989. *The Modern World System III: The Second Era of Great Expansion of the Capitalist World-Economy, 1730–1840s.* San Diego: Academic Press.

Waltz, Kenneth. 1959. *Man, the State, and War.* New York: Columbia University Press.

Waltz, Kenneth. 1979. *Theory of International Politics.* Reading, Mass.: Addison Wesley.

Warr, Peter G. 1983. "The Private Provision of a Public Good Is Independent of the Distribution of Income." *Economics Letters* 13:207–11.

Weber, Steve. 1992. "Shaping the Postwar Balance of Power: Multilateralism in NATO." *International Organization* 46 (summer): 633–80.

Webster, C. K. 1925. *The Foreign Policy of Castlereagh, 1815–1822: Britain and the European Alliance.* London: Bell.

Weitowitz, Rolf. 1978. *Deutsche Politik und Handelspolitik unter Reichskanzler Leo von Caprivi, 1890–1894.* Düsseldorf: Droste Verlag.

Wightman, David. 1985. Review of *The Reconstruction of Western Europe, 1945–1951,* by Alan S. Milward. *Journal of Economic Literature* 23 (September): 1229–30.

Williams, Judith Blow. 1972. *British Commercial Policy and Trade Expansion, 1750–1850.* Oxford: Clarendon.

Williams, William Appleman. 1959/1972. *The Tragedy of American Diplomacy.* 2d rev. ed. New York: Dell.

"The World Economy: Echoes of the 1930s." 1991. *The Economist* 318 (5 January): 15–16+.

Yarbrough, Beth V., and Robert M. Yarbrough. 1985. "Free Trade, Hegemony, and the Theory of Agency." *Kyklos* 38: 348–64.

Yarbrough, Beth V. and Robert M. Yarbrough. 1986. "Reciprocity, Bilateralism, and

Economic 'Hostages': Self-Enforcing Agreements in International Trade." *International Studies Quarterly* 30 (March): 7–21.

Yarbrough, Beth V., and Robert M. Yarbrough. 1987. "Cooperation in the Liberalization of International Trade: After Hegemony, What?" *International Organization* 41 (winter): 1–26.

Zinnes, Dina, and John V. Gillespie. 1973. "Analysis of Arms Race Models: USA vs. USSR and NATO vs. WTO." In *Modeling and Simulation* vol. 4, ed. William C. Vogt and Marlin H. Mickle, Pittsburgh: Instrument Society of America. 149–54.

Index